FIRST AMENDMENT
Cases and Materials

2000 SUPPLEMENT

By

WILLIAM W. VAN ALSTYNE
William R. & Thomas S. Perkins Professor of Law
Duke University School of Law

Westbury, New York
FOUNDATION PRESS
2000

TEXT IS PRINTED ON 10% POST CONSUMER RECYCLED PAPER

TABLE OF CONTENTS

Numbers on the left indicate where the new materials fit into the casebook.
Cases set out at length are in **bold face** and *italic*.

TABLE OF CONTENTS

TABLE OF CONTENTS

TABLE OF CONTENTS

CHAPTER 7. "*** OR PROHIBITING THE FREE EXERCISE THEREOF"

———

CHAPTER 8.   DEFINING "RELIGION"

TABLE OF CASES

Principal cases are in italic and bold.
References are to page numbers.

TABLE OF CASES

TABLE OF CASES

TABLE OF CASES

This Supplement includes recent major movements in the legislation and Supreme Court decisions affecting the first amendment since August 1996.

Chapter 2
THE FIRST AMENDMENT IN FORMATIVE TRANSITION AND THE CENTRALITY OF UNTRAMMELED SOCIAL ADVOCACY IN THE UNITED STATES

Casebook, p. 33
Additional Recent Works

Abel, Richard, Speaking Respect, Respecting Speech (1998).

Bollinger, Lee, The Tolerant Society: Freedom of Speech and Extremist Speech in America (1986).

Butler, Judith, Excitable Speech: A Politics of the Performative (1997).

Corner, Richard C., The Kingfish and the Constitution: Huey Long, the First Amendment, and the Emergence of Modern Press Freedom in America (1996).

Ferber, Daniel, The First Amendment (1998).

Fish, Stanley, The Trouble with Principle (1999).

Fiss, Owen, Liberalism Divided: Freedom of Speech and the Many Uses of State Power (1996).

Golding, Martin, Free Speech on Campus (2000).

Gurstein, Rochelle, The Repeal of Reticence: A History of America's Cultural and Legal Struggles over Free Speech, Obscenity, Sexual Liberation, and Modern Art (1996).

Gutman, Amy and Thompson, Dennis, Democracy and Disagreement (1996).

Hamilton, James T., Channeling Violence: The Economic Market for Violent Television Programming (1998).

Kors, A.C., and Silvergate, H.A., The Shadow University: The Betrayal of Liberty on America's Campuses (1998).

Lowenthal, David, No Liberty for License: The Forgotten Logic of the First Amendment (1997).

MacKinnon, Catherine and Dworkin, Andrea (eds.), In Harm's Way: The Pornography
Civil Rights Hearings (1998).

Menand, Louis (ed.), The Future of Academic Freedom (1996).

O'Neil, Robert M., Free Speech in the College Community (1997).

Post, Robert C., ed., Censorship and Silencing: Practices of Cultural Regulation (1998).

Rabban, David, Free Speech in Its Forgotten Years (1997).

Rawls, John, Political Liberalism (1993).

Shiffrin, Steven H., Dissent, Injustice, and the Meanings of America (1999).

Smolla, Rodney, Free Speech in an Open Society (1992).

Strossen, Nadine, Defending Pornography: Free Speech, Sex and the Fight for Women's Rights (1995).

Van Alstyne (ed.), Freedom and Tenure in the Academy (1993).

Vanderham, Paul, James Joyce and Censorship: The Trials of Ulysses (1998).

Weinstein, James, Hate Speech, Pornography, and the Radical Attack on Free Speech Doctrine (1999).

————

Casebook, p. 40
Add as a footnote reference to the last sentence of the last paragraph:

For consideration of still other views strongly advanced during this time, respecting the protection the First Amendment should be deemed to provide for freedom of socially-agitative speech, see David Rabban, Free Speech in its Forgotten Years (1997).

————

Casebook, p. 160
Add as a footnote to the last sentence of the first paragraph

For a fuller description of *Grosjean*, see the recent book by Richard C. Corner, The Kingfish and the Constitution: Huey Long, The First Amendment, and the Emergence of Modern Press Freedom in America (1996).

————

Casebook, p. 212
Add to footnote 96, end of fifth paragraph

See also Rice v. Paladin Enterprises, 128 F.3d 233 (4th Cir. 1997), *cert. denied*, 118 S. Ct. 151 (1998) (commercial publisher of a book ("Hit Man"), in which the author detailed methods of how to succeed as a hired killer, held liable to relatives in wrongful death action and for civil damages for "aiding and abetting" murder of victim slain by killer who, attracted by book title and publisher's representations, followed instructions provided in the book, where publisher stipulated "it not only knew [the book's] instructions might be used by murderers, but...intended to provide assistance to murderers and would-be murderers;" dicta approving the viability of such tort claims without such a stipulation).

Add as new reference to last sentence of footnote 96, sixth paragraph

See also Sandra Davidson, *Blood Money: When Media Expose Others to Risk of Bodily Harm*, 19 Hastings Comm./Ent. L.J. 225 (1997); David Anderson, *Torts, Speech and Contracts*, 75 Texas L.Rev. 1499, 1504-1513 (1997).

————

Casebook, p. 213
Add to footnote 97

For a variation in the trademark infringement and trademark dilution context, see *Mattel Inc. v. MCA Records*, 28 F. Supp. 2d 1120 (C.D. Cal. 1998) (release of song entitled "Barbie Girl" with the singers referring to Barbie as a "blond bimbo girl" who loves to party and whose "life is plastic").

Casebook, p. 251
Add to footnote 111 in NOTES following *Hustler Magazine v. Falwell*

See also Debora Shuger, *Civility and Censorship in Early Modern England*, in Censorship and Silencing: Practices of Cultural Regulation (Post, ed., 1998) (useful discussion of efforts in Tudor and Stuart England to suppress "satire").

Casebook, p. 278
Add to NOTES ON *MITCHELL* AND *R.A.V.*

For a review of recent, widely varying statutes loosely lumped together as "hate crime laws," see Terry Maroney, *The Struggle Against Hate Crimes: Movement at a Crossroads*, 73 N.Y.U. L. Rev. 564, 589-95 (1998). They continue to reflect some of the same problematic qualities previously reviewed in the **NOTES**. Characteristically, they make a special offense, or attach an automatic sentence enhancement to a pre-existing offense, when the defendant commits some act against the person or property of another "because of," or "on account of," some characteristic (or perceived characteristic) of that person, e.g., his or her race, religion, gender, or disability. Typically, the label of these laws suggests the statute proceeds from an intention to deter crimes based on "animus" or "bias" or "prejudice." The list (of "biases" or of "prejudices") is partial. For example, some include "age," while others do not; some include "political affiliation," while others do not; some include "sexual orientation," while others do not (and, oppositely, some include "sexual orientation" but not "sex"). Nor is it always clear what will be deemed to fit within the idea of a "bias" or "prejudice," or what constitutes "prejudice" as distinct from a socially-approved "healthy" sense of repugnance, not covered by the act (e.g., of persons whose "sexual orientation" is an orientation of attraction to children, or animals?).

Moreover, the actual link of these statutes as requiring actions taken from "animus" or "bias" or "prejudice" or "hatred" is frequently unclear, exactly as in the *Mitchell* case itself. Indeed, it may be nonexistent. For example, § 3A1.1 of the U.S. Sentencing Commission Guidelines Manual now authorizes a three-level sentence increase if the "finder of fact at trial . . . determines beyond a reasonable doubt that the defendant *intentionally selected any victim* or any property . . . *because of* the actual or perceived race, color, religion, national origin, ethnicity, gender, disability, or sexual orientation of that person." (Notice on the face of the guidelines, it is the basis for selecting the "victim" that evidently matters, not why, i.e., evidently, there need be no animus involved — no "hatred" or hostility of any kind.)[126]

---

126. For example, a well-informed African American man may principally select white victims as preferred "victims" for ordinary street crimes (e.g., muggings), if he knows from experience what studies also confirm: that, in what is but a very brief encounter, such persons may later not be as readily able to recall any special identifying features of their assailants, at least not as well as another black person might be able to do. Is this a "hate" crime?

Chapter 3

THE FIRST AMENDMENT IN SPECIFIC ENVIRONMENTS

Casebook, p. 345
Add as additional reference in footnote 26

Robert C. Post, *Subsidized Speech*, 106 Yale L.J. 151 (1996).

E. The Government's Management of Public Property: First Amendment Rights of Access and Use

Casebook, p. 420
Add as new paragraph to Note

As noted in the casebook (nn. 43-44), in *Rutan v. Republican Party of Illinois*, the Supreme Court held that the first amendment protection of public employees from being fired because of some unacceptable public position they expressed on some public issue, or because of some support, financial or otherwise, they gave to the "wrong" political party, extended not just to protection from retaliatory firing, but also to protection from other adverse actions (e.g., punitive transfer, failure to promote, or mere refusal to hire). Notwithstanding, the issue remained unsettled whether independent contractors would be treated differently, somehow distinguished from employees or prospective employees, and therefore "left out in the cold." As noted in note 44, the courts of appeals were divided on this question. In *O'Hare Truck Service, Inc. v. City of Northlake*, 47 F.3d 883 (7th Cir. 1995), the Seventh Circuit declined to apply either the *Pickering* doctrine (on free speech, public issues, and public employment) or the *Elrod* doctrine (on the spoils system — party fealty — and public employment) to independent contractors. In *Umbehr v. McClure*, 44 F.3d 876, 883 (10th Cir. 1995), the Tenth Circuit took the opposite position, declaring that "an independent contractor is protected under the first amendment from retaliatory governmental action, just as an employee would be." In 1996, the Supreme Court reviewed both *O'Hare* and *Umbehr*. On June 28, 1996, by a vote of seven-to-two (Scalia and Thomas, JJ., dissenting), the Court affirmed the Tenth Circuit position in *Umbehr* and reversed the Seventh Circuit position in *O'Hare*. See *Board of County Commissioners v. Umbehr*, 518 U.S. 668 (1996), and *O'Hare Truck Service, Inc. v. City of Northlake*, 518 U.S. 712 (1996).

Casebook, p. 471
Add following *Madsen v. Women's Health Center*

1. See also *Schenck v. Pro-Choice Network of Western New York*, 519 U.S. 357 (1997) (*sustaining* injunction (a) forbidding acts of physical obstruction and (b) providing a "buffer zone" forbidding further demonstrations within 15 feet of abortion clinic doorway and driveway entries [following hearings and findings of record by trial court of failure of more limited injunction effectively to restrain protestors]; but *reversing* injunction (c) securing "floating buffer zones" requiring any demonstrator or leafletter to move 15 feet from any person approaching or departing from an affected facility indicating her wish not to be confronted more closely). (Part (c) held to be overly broad restriction on first amendment right peacefully to remonstrate or persuade.) (opinion for the Court by Rehnquist, C.J.; dissent by Kennedy, Scalia, and Thomas, JJ., insofar as the Court sustained (b)).[68a]

———

2. Note that plantiffs in *Madsen* and in *Schenck* labored under the burden of having to initiate a civil action at their own expense, and having also to prove specific acts on defendants' part–acts both unprotected by the First Amendment and substantially interfering with their rights–before being entitled to any relief. Such will usually be the case, of course, at least where there is no legislation in place, pursuant to which plaintiffs might instead merely call the police and have the demonstrator(s) arrested, and held for trial under "an appropriate" law. But now suppose that plaintiffs and those strongly in sympathy with their interest seek relief from this hardship, i.e., relief

———

68a. *Schenck* is a clarifying close sequel to *Madsen*, re first amendment requirements of injunctions restricting persons or groups engaged in acts of remonstrance outside health care clinics providing abortion services. As in *Madsen*, the Court in *Schenck* held that injunctions issued to restrain public, on-site politically expressive anti-abortion activity (e.g., leafletting, sign carrying, remonstrating) are subject to "heightened scrutiny" under the first amendment. While declining to regard such injunctions as a form of prior restraint deemed presumptively forbidden by the first amendment, the Court in *Schenck* again holds they are nonetheless subject to rigorous requirements of specific fact-finding and of narrow tailoring. A close fit between the specific terms of the injunction, the specific activities it enjoins, and adequate findings of record to justify such restrictions, must be achieved to withstand heightened scrutiny appellate review. These requirements are imposed on first amendment grounds partly because of the effect of the "collateral bar" rule (briefly noted in *Madsen*). (The "collateral bar" rule may disallow one cited for contempt for violating an injunction to defend against the citation for contempt by asserting that the acts were constitutionally protected and ought not to have been enjoined. See, e.g., *Walker v. City of Birmingham*, 388 U.S. 308 (1967); *United States v. United Mine Workers of America*, 330 U.S. 258, 293 (1947).) As noted (text *supra*), the Court in *Schenck* agreed the first part of the injunction restraining physical obstruction met the appropriate standard; it divided on the part forbidding approach by protestors within 15 feet of entryways and driveways (the majority sustaining it on the strength of findings by the district court that more narrowly tailored restrictions had proven ineffective); and reversed on part (c) as overly broad.

or help from the legislature, to provide just such a law. Perhaps in the form of the following criminal statute:

> No person shall knowingly approach another person within eight feet of such person, unless such person consents, for the purpose of passing a leaflet or handbill to, displaying a sign to, or engaging in oral protest, education, or counseling, with such person in the public way or sidewalk area within a radius of one hundred feet from any entrance door to a health care facility. Any person who violates this [ordinance] commits a class 3 misdeamor.

Were this ordinance to be applied, say, to a leafletter who approached an employee as (s)he was about to enter the doorway of a health clinic offering abortion services, to try to press into her reluctant hand a leaflet with a picture (a picture of a "dismembered fetus") while displaying a small sign (a sign declaring "please don't work at this terrible place"), what would you say? Is the ordinance unconstitutional on its face?[1]

Casebook, p. 516
Add, following *Hazelwood School District v. Kuhlmeier*
ROSENBERGER V. RECTOR AND VISITORS OF THE
UNIVERSITY OF VIRGINIA
515 U.S. 819 (1995)

Justice KENNEDY delivered the opinion of the Court.[**]

---

1. *See Hill v. Colorado*, 530 U.S. ____ (June 28, 2000) (Ordinance sustained against void-in-its-face "overbreadth" challenge, six-to-three, Scalia, J., Thomas, J., and Kennedy, J. dissenting.

** [**Ed. Note**: *Rosenberger* was decided by a closely divided five-to-four vote. The dissent (Souter, Ginsburg, Stevens, and Breyer, JJ.) did not except to Justice Kennedy's general observations on forum analysis (i.e. his review of "forums," "content," and "viewpoint" discrimination re public universities and funding of various student organizations). Rather, it disagreed mainly with the Court's characterization of the facts of the case, and disagreed with its treatment of the Establishment Clause issue — an issue also present in this case. Relevant portions of the Opinions revisiting these matters and bearing on the Establishment Clause are omitted here, but included *infra*, this Supplement at pp. 122-128.

Also not considered here is any discussion of a different kind of First Amendment claim — one left over for possible consideration in light of the manner in which this case was decided. That issue is identified in one part of the concurring Opinion by Justice O'Connor, 515 U.S.at 850, where she observes: "[A]lthough the question is not presented here, I note the possibility that the student fee is susceptible to a Free Speech Clause challenge by an objecting student that she should not be compelled to pay for speech with which she disagrees." Her Opinion cites pertinent case law elaborating the bases for this kind of claim. (Those cases are considered in the casebook (*see* pp. 628-637) where this different kind of challenge is analyzed and reviewed, and with respect to which it may well be appropriate to consider the

The University of Virginia authorizes the payment of outside contractors for the printing costs of a variety of student publications. It withheld any authorization for payments on behalf of petitioners for the sole reason that their student paper "primarily promotes or manifests a particular belie[f] in or about a deity or an ultimate reality." The challenge is to the University's regulation and its denial of authorization, the case raising issues under the Speech and Establishment Clauses of the First Amendment.

I

*** Before a student group is eligible to submit bills from its outside contractors for payment by the fund described below, it must become a "Contracted Independent Organization" (CIO). CIO status is available to any group the majority of whose members are students, whose managing officers are full-time students, and that complies with certain procedural requirements. A CIO must file its constitution with the University; must pledge not to discriminate in its membership; and must include in dealings with third parties and in all written materials a disclaimer, stating that the CIO is independent of the University and that the University is not responsible for the CIO. CIO's enjoy access to University facilities, including meeting rooms and computer terminals. A standard agreement signed between each CIO and the University provides that the benefits and opportunities afforded to CIO's "should not be misinterpreted as meaning that those organizations are part of or controlled by the University, that the University is responsible for the organizations' contracts or other acts or omissions, or that the University approves of the organizations' goals or activities."

All CIO's may exist and operate at the University, but some are also entitled to apply for funds from the Student Activities Fund (SAF). The SAF receives its money from a mandatory fee of $14 per semester assessed to each full-time student. Some, but not all, CIO's may submit disbursement requests to the SAF. The Guidelines recognize 11 categories of student groups that may seek payment to third-party contractors because they "are related to the educational purpose of the University of Virginia." One of these is "student news, information, opinion, entertainment, or academic communications media groups." The Guidelines also specify, however, that the costs of certain activities of CIO's that are otherwise eligible for funding will not be reimbursed by the SAF. The student activities that are excluded from SAF support are religious activities, philanthropic contributions and activities, political activities, activities that would jeopardize the University's tax-exempt status, those which involve payment of honoraria or similar fees, or social entertainment or related expenses. The prohibition on "political activities" is defined so that it is limited to electioneering and lobbying. The Guidelines provide that "[t]hese restrictions on funding political

---

"possibility" Justice O'Connor notes.) (*See* also *Board of Regents v. Southworth*, this supplement at pp. 45 - 49)]

activities are not intended to preclude funding of any otherwise eligible student organization which ... espouses particular positions or ideological viewpoints, including those that may be unpopular or are not generally accepted." A "religious activity," by contrast, is defined as any activity that "primarily promotes or manifests a particular belie[f] in or about a deity or an ultimate reality." ***

Petitioners' organization, Wide Awake Productions (WAP), qualified as a CIO. *** WAP was established "[t]o publish a magazine of philosophical and religious expression," "[t]o facilitate discussion which fosters an atmosphere of sensitivity to and tolerance of Christian viewpoints," and "[t]o provide a unifying focus for Christians of multicultural backgrounds." WAP publishes Wide Awake: A Christian Perspective at the University of Virginia. *** The editors committed the paper to a two-fold mission: "to challenge Christians to live, in word and deed, according to the faith they proclaim and to encourage students to consider what a personal relationship with Jesus Christ means." Each page of Wide Awake, and the end of each article or review, is marked by a cross. By June 1992, WAP had distributed about 5,000 copies of Wide Awake to University students, free of charge.

WAP had acquired CIO status soon after it was organized. This is an important consideration in this case, for had it been a "religious organization," WAP would not have been accorded CIO status. As defined by the Guidelines, a "[r]eligious [o]rganization" is "an organization whose purpose is to practice a devotion to an acknowledged ultimate reality or deity." At no stage in this controversy has the University contended that WAP is such an organization.

A few months after being given CIO status, WAP requested the SAF to pay its printer $5,862 for the costs of printing its newspaper. The Appropriations Committee of the Student Council denied WAP's request on the ground that Wide Awake was a "religious activity" within the meaning of the Guidelines, i.e., that the newspaper "promote[d] or manifest[ed] a particular belie[f] in or about a deity or an ultimate reality." It made its determination after examining the first issue. WAP appealed the denial to the full Student Council, contending that WAP met all the applicable Guidelines and that denial of SAF support on the basis of the magazine's religious perspective violated the Constitution. The appeal was denied without further comment, and WAP appealed to the next level, the Student Activities Committee. In a letter signed by the Dean of Students, the committee sustained the denial of funding.

Having no further recourse within the University structure, WAP, Wide Awake, and three of its editors and members filed suit in the United States District Court for the Western District of Virginia, challenging the SAF's action as violative of 42 U.S.C. § 1983. ***

II

It is axiomatic that the government may not regulate speech based on its substantive content or the message it conveys. *** [T]he government offends the First Amendment when it imposes financial burdens on certain speakers based on the content of their expression. When the government targets not subject matter, but particular views taken by speakers on a subject, the violation of the First Amendment is all the more blatant. See *R.A.V. v. St. Paul*, 505 U.S. 377, 391 (1992). Viewpoint discrimination is thus an egregious form of content discrimination. The government must abstain from regulating speech when the specific motivating ideology or the opinion or perspective of the speaker is the rationale for the restriction.

These principles provide the framework forbidding the State to exercise viewpoint discrimination, even when the limited public forum is one of its own creation. *** The necessities of confining a forum to the limited and legitimate purposes for which it was created may justify the State in reserving it for certain groups or for the discussion of certain topics. See, e.g., *Cornelius v. NAACP Legal Defense & Ed. Fund, Inc.*, 473 U.S. 788, 806 (1985); *Perry Ed. Assn.*, at 49. Once it has opened a limited forum, however, the State must respect the lawful boundaries it has itself set. *** Thus, in determining whether the State is acting to preserve the limits of the forum it has created so that the exclusion of a class of speech is legitimate, we have observed a distinction between, on the one hand, content discrimination, which may be permissible if it preserves the purposes of that limited forum, and, on the other hand, viewpoint discrimination, which is presumed impermissible when directed against speech otherwise within the forum's limitations.

The SAF is a forum more in a metaphysical than in a spatial or geographic sense, but the same principles are applicable. *See, e.g., Perry Ed. Assn.*, at 46-47 (forum analysis of a school mail system); *Cornelius*, at 801 (forum analysis of charitable contribution program). The most recent and most apposite case is our decision in Lamb's Chapel. There, a school district had opened school facilities for use after school hours by community groups for a wide variety of social, civic, and recreational purposes. The district, however, had enacted a formal policy against opening facilities to groups for religious purposes. Invoking its policy, the district rejected a request from a group desiring to show a film series addressing various child-rearing questions from a "Christian perspective." There was no indication in the record in Lamb's Chapel that the request to use the school facilities was "denied, for any reason other than the fact that the presentation would have been from a religious perspective." Our conclusion was unanimous: "[I]t discriminates on the basis of viewpoint to permit school property to be used for the presentation of all views about family issues and childrearing except those dealing with the subject matter from a religious standpoint."

The University does acknowledge (as it must in light of our precedents) that "ideologically driven attempts to suppress a particular point of view are presumptively unconstitutional in funding, as in other contexts," but insists that this case does not present that issue because the Guidelines draw lines based on content, not viewpoint.

As we have noted, discrimination against one set of views or ideas is but a subset or particular instance of the more general phenomenon of content discrimination. And, it must be acknowledged, the distinction is not a precise one. It is, in a sense, something of an understatement to speak of religious thought and discussion as just a viewpoint, as distinct from a comprehensive body of thought. The nature of our origins and destiny and their dependence upon the existence of a divine being have been subjects of philosophic inquiry throughout human history. We conclude, nonetheless, that here, as in *Lamb's Chapel*, viewpoint discrimination is the proper way to interpret the University's objections to Wide Awake. By the very terms of the SAF prohibition, the University does not exclude religion as a subject matter but selects for disfavored treatment those student journalistic efforts with religious editorial viewpoints. Religion may be a vast area of inquiry, but it also provides, as it did here, a specific premise, a perspective, a standpoint from which a variety of subjects may be discussed and considered. The prohibited perspective, not the general subject matter, resulted in the refusal to make third-party payments, for the subjects discussed were otherwise within the approved category of publications. ***

The University tries to escape the consequences of our holding in *Lamb's Chapel* by urging that this case involves the provision of funds rather than access to facilities. The University begins with the unremarkable proposition that the State must have substantial discretion in determining how to allocate scarce resources to accomplish its educational mission. Citing our decisions in *Rust v. Sullivan, 500 U.S. 173 (1991)* and *Widmar* v. Vincent, 454 U.S. 263 (1981), the University argues that content-based funding decisions are both inevitable and lawful. Were the reasoning of *Lamb's Chapel* to apply to funding decisions as well as to those involving access to facilities, it is urged, its holding "would become a judicial juggernaut, constitutionalizing the ubiquitous content-based decisions that schools, colleges, and other government entities routinely make in the allocation of public funds."

To this end the University relies on *** *Widmar v. Vincent*. There, in the course of striking down a public university's exclusion of religious groups from use of school facilities made available to all other student groups, we stated: "Nor do we question the right of the University to make academic judgments as to how best to allocate scarce resources." The quoted language in *Widmar* was but a proper recognition of the principle that when the State is the speaker, it may make content-based choices. When the University determines the content of the education it provides, it is the University speaking, and we have permitted the government to regulate the content of what is or is not expressed when it is the speaker or when it enlists private entities to convey its own message. In the same vein, in *Rust v. Sullivan*, we upheld the government's prohibition on abortion-related advice applicable to recipients of federal funds for family planning counseling. There, the government did not create a program to encourage private speech but instead used private speakers to transmit specific information pertaining to its own program. We recognized that when the government appropriates public funds to promote a particular policy of its own it is entitled to say what it wishes. When the government disburses public funds to private entities to convey a governmental message, it may take legitimate and appropriate steps to ensure that its message is neither garbled nor distorted by the grantee.

It does not follow, however, *** that viewpoint-based restrictions are proper when the University does not itself speak or subsidize transmittal of a message it favors but instead expends funds to encourage a diversity of views from private speakers. A holding that the University may not discriminate based on the viewpoint of private persons whose speech it facilitates does not restrict the University's own speech, which is controlled by different principles. ***

The distinction between the University's own favored message and the private speech of students is evident in the case before us. The University itself has taken steps to ensure the distinction in the agreement each CIO must sign. The University declares that the student groups eligible for SAF support are not the University's agents, are not subject to its control, and are not its responsibility. Having offered to pay the third-party contractors on behalf of private speakers who convey their own messages, the University may not silence the expression of selected viewpoints.

The University urges that, from a constitutional standpoint, funding of speech differs from provision of access to facilities because money is scarce and physical facilities are not. *** The government cannot justify viewpoint discrimination among private speakers on the economic fact of scarcity. ***

Vital First Amendment speech principles are at stake here. The first danger to liberty lies in granting the State the power to examine publications to determine whether or not they are based on some ultimate idea and, if so, for the State to classify them. The second, and corollary, danger is to speech from the chilling of individual thought and expression. That danger is especially real in the University setting, where the State acts against a background and tradition of thought and experiment that is at the center of our intellectual and philosophic tradition. ***

The prohibition on funding on behalf of publications that "primarily promot[e] or manifes[t] a particular belie[f] in or about a deity or an ultimate reality," in its ordinary and commonsense meaning, has a vast potential reach. *** Were the prohibition applied with much vigor at all, it would bar funding of essays by hypothetical student contributors named Plato, Spinoza, and Descartes. And if the regulation covers, as the University says it does, those student journalistic efforts that primarily manifest or promote a belief that there is no deity and no ultimate reality, then under-graduates named Karl Marx, Bertrand Russell, and Jean-Paul Sartre would likewise have some of their major essays excluded from student publications. *** Based on the principles we have discussed, we hold that the regulation invoked to deny SAF support, both in its terms and in its application to these petitioners, is a denial of their right of free speech guaranteed by the First Amendment. ***

Casebook, p. 535
Add as new case

ARKANSAS EDUCATION TELEVISION COMMISSION V. FORBES
523 U.S. 666 (1998)

JUSTICE KENNEDY delivered the opinion of the Court, in which REHNQUIST, C. J., and O'CONNOR, SCALIA, THOMAS, and BREYER, JJ., joined.

I

Arkansas Educational Television Commission (AETC) is an Arkansas state agency owning and operating a network of five noncommercial television stations.*** In the spring of 1991, AETC staff began planning a series of debates between candidates for federal office in the November 1992 elections. On June 17, 1992, AETC invited the Republican and Democratic candidates for Arkansas' Third Congressional District to participate in the AETC debate for that seat. Two months later, after obtaining the 2,000 signatures required by Arkansas law, Ralph Forbes was certified as an independent candidate qualified to appear on the ballot for the seat. [H]e wrote to AETC requesting permission to participate in the debate for his district, scheduled for October 22, 1992. On September 4, AETC Executive Director Susan Howarth denied Forbes' request, explaining that AETC had "made a bona fide journalistic judgment that our viewers would be best served by limiting the debate" to the candidates already invited.

On October 19, 1992, Forbes filed suit against AETC, seeking injunctive and declaratory relief as well as damages.*** [T]he District Court found as a matter of law that the debate was a nonpublic forum, and the issue became whether Forbes' views were the reason for his exclusion. At trial, AETC professional staff testified Forbes was excluded because he lacked any campaign organization, had not generated appreciable voter support, and was not regarded as a serious candidate by the press covering the election. The District Court entered judgment for AETC.

The Court of Appeals*** reversed. AETC's action, the court held, made the debate a public forum, to which all candidates legally qualified to appear on the ballot had a presumptive right of access. Applying strict scrutiny, the court determined that AETC's assessment of Forbes' "political viability" was neither a "compelling nor [a] narrowly tailored" reason for excluding him from the debate.*** We now reverse.

II

At the outset, it is instructive to ask whether public forum principles apply to the case at all. Having first arisen in the context of streets and parks, the public forum doctrine should not be extended in a mechanical way to the very different context of public television broadcasting. As a general rule, the nature of editorial discretion counsels against subjecting broadcasters to claims of viewpoint discrimination. Much like a university selecting a commencement speaker, a public institution selecting speakers for a lecture series, or a public school prescribing its curriculum, a broadcaster by its nature will facilitate the expression of some viewpoints instead of others. Were the judiciary to require, and so to define and approve, pre-established criteria for access, it would risk implicating the courts in judgments that should be left to the exercise of journalistic discretion. *** In the absence of any congressional command to regiment broadcasters in this manner, we are disinclined to do so through doctrines of our own design. This is not to say the First Amendment would bar the legislative imposition of neutral rules for access to public broadcasting. Instead, we say that, in most cases, the First Amendment of its own force does not compel public broadcasters to allow third parties access to their programming.

Although public broadcasting as a general matter does not lend itself to scrutiny under the forum doctrine, candidate debates present the narrow exception to the rule. [A] candidate debate like the one at issue here is different from other programming. [U]nlike AETC's other broadcasts, the debate was by design a forum for political speech by the candidates. Consistent with the long tradition of candidate debates, the implicit representation of the broadcaster was that the views expressed were those of the candidates, not its own. The very purpose of the debate was to allow the candidates to express their views with minimal intrusion by the broadcaster. In this respect the debate differed even from a political talk show, whose host can express partisan views and then limit the discussion to those ideas.*** The special characteristics of candidate debates support the conclusion that the AETC debate was a forum of some type. The question of what type must be answered by reference to our public forum precedents, to which we now turn.

III

The parties agree the AETC debate was not a traditional public forum. The Court has rejected the view that traditional public forum status extends beyond its historic confines, and even had a more expansive conception of traditional public fora been adopted, see, *e.g.*, [*International Soc. for Krishna Consciousness v. Lee*, 505 U.S. 672, 698-699 (1992)] (KENNEDY, J., concurring in judgments), the almost unfettered access of a traditional public forum would be incompatible with the programming dictates a television broadcaster must follow. The issue, then, is whether the debate was a designated public forum or a nonpublic forum.

Under our precedents, the AETC debate was not a designated public forum. To create a forum of this type, the government must intend to make the property "generally available," *Widmar v. Vincent*, 454 U.S. 263, 264 (1981), to a class of speakers. In *Widmar*, for example, a state university created a public forum for registered student groups by implementing a policy that expressly made its meeting facilities "generally open" to such groups. A designated public forum is not created when the government allows selective access for individual speakers rather than general access for a class of speakers. In *Perry*, for example, the Court held a school district's internal mail system was not a designated public forum even though selected speakers were able to gain access to it. These cases illustrate the distinction between general access, which indicates the property is a designated public forum, and selective access, which indicates the property is a nonpublic forum. On one hand, the government creates a designated public forum when it makes its property generally available to a certain class of speakers, as the university made its facilities generally available to student groups in *Widmar*. On the other hand, the government does not create a designated public forum when it does no more than reserve eligibility for access to the forum to a particular class of speakers, whose members must then, as individuals, obtain permission.

Here AETC did not make its debate generally available to candidates for Arkansas' Third Congressional District seat.   Instead, just as the Federal Government in *Cornelius* reserved eligibility for participation in the CFC program to certain classes of voluntary agencies, AETC reserved eligibility for participation in the debate to candidates for the Third Congressional District seat (as opposed to some other seat). At that point, just as the Government in *Cornelius* made agency-by-agency determinations as to which of the eligible agencies would participate in the CFC, AETC made candidate-by-candidate determinations as to which of the eligible candidates would participate in the debate. "Such selective access, unsupported by evidence of a purposeful designation for public use, does not create a public forum." Thus the debate was a nonpublic forum.

The debate's status as a nonpublic forum, however, did not give AETC unfettered power to exclude any candidate it wished.   To be consistent with the First Amendment, the exclusion of a speaker from a nonpublic forum must not be based on the speaker's viewpoint and must otherwise be reasonable in light of the purpose of the property.

In this case, the jury found Forbes' exclusion was not based on objections or opposition to his views.   The record provides ample support for this finding, demonstrating as well that AETC's decision to exclude him was reasonable. AETC Executive Director Susan Howarth testified Forbes' views had "absolutely" no role in the decision to exclude him from the debate.   Forbes himself described his campaign organization as "bedlam" and the media coverage of his campaign as "zilch." It is, in short, beyond dispute that Forbes was excluded not because of his viewpoint but because he had generated no appreciable public interest. Nor did AETC exclude Forbes in an attempted manipulation of the political process. The evidence provided powerful support for the jury's express finding that AETC's exclusion of Forbes was not the result of "political pressure from anyone inside or outside [AETC]."*** The judgment of the Court of Appeals is [r]eversed.

JUSTICE STEVENS, with whom JUSTICE SOUTER and JUSTICE GINSBURG join, dissenting.

*** In its discussion of the law, the Court understates the constitutional importance of the distinction between state ownership and private ownership of broadcast facilities. I shall therefore first add a few words about the record in this case and the history of regulation of the broadcast media, before explaining why I believe the judgment should be affirmed.

I

Two months before Forbes was officially certified as an independent candidate qualified to appear on the ballot under Arkansas law, the AETC staff had already concluded that he "should not be invited" to participate in the televised debates because he was "not a serious candidate as determined by the voters of Arkansas." He had, however, been a serious contender for the Republican nomination for Lieutenant Governor in 1986 and again in 1990. Although he was defeated in a run-off election, in the three-way primary race conducted in 1990 — just two years before the AETC staff decision — he had received 46.88% of the statewide vote and had carried 15 of the 16 counties within the Third Congressional District by absolute majorities.

Given the fact that the Republican winner in the Third Congressional District race in 1992 received only 50.22% of the vote and the Democrat received 47.20%, it would have been necessary for Forbes, who had made a strong showing in recent Republican primaries, to divert only a handful of votes from the Republican candidate to cause his defeat. Thus, even though the AETC staff may have correctly concluded that Forbes was "not a serious candidate," their decision to exclude him from the debate may have determined the outcome of the election in the Third District.

If a comparable decision were made today by a privately owned network, it would be subject to scrutiny under the Federal Election Campaign Act unless the network used "pre-established objective criteria to determine which candidates may participate in the debate." 11 C.F.R. § 110.13(c)(1997). No such criteria governed AETC's refusal to permit Forbes to participate in the debate. Indeed, whether that refusal was based on a judgment about "newsworthiness" — as AETC has argued in this Court — or a judgment about "political viability" — as it argued in the Court of Appeals — the facts in the record presumably would have provided an adequate basis either for a decision to include Forbes in the Third District debate or a decision to exclude him, and might even have required a cancellation of two of the other debates.[6] *** The

6. Although the contest between the major-party candidates in the Third District was a relatively close one, in two of the other three districts in which both major-party candidates had been invited to debate, it was clear that one of them had virtually no chance of winning the election. *** In the Second District, Democrat Ray Thornton, the incumbent, defeated

apparent flexibility of AETC's purported standard suggests the extent to which the staff had nearly limitless discretion to exclude Forbes from the debate based on ad hoc justifications. ***

III

The dispositive issue in this case is not whether AETC created a designated public forum or a nonpublic forum, as the Court concludes, but whether AETC defined the contours of the debate forum with sufficient specificity to justify the exclusion of a ballot-qualified candidate.

No written criteria cabined the discretion of the AETC staff. Their subjective judgment about a candidate's "viability" or "newsworthiness" allowed them wide latitude either to permit or to exclude a third participant in any debate.[14] Moreover, in exercising that judgment they were free to rely on factors that arguably should favor inclusion as justifications for exclusion. Thus, the fact that Forbes had little financial support was considered as evidence of his lack of viability when that factor might have provided an independent reason for allowing him to share a free forum with wealthier candidates.[15]

The reasons that support the need for narrow, objective, and definite standards to guide licensing decisions apply directly to the wholly subjective access decisions made by the staff of AETC. The importance of avoiding arbitrary or viewpoint-based exclusions from political debates militates strongly in favor of requiring the controlling state agency to use (and adhere to) pre-established, objective criteria to determine who among qualified candidates may participate. A constitutional duty to use objective standards *** would impose only a modest requirement that would fall far short of a duty to grant every multiple-party request. Such standards would also have the benefit of providing the public with some assurance that state-owned broadcasters cannot select debate participants on arbitrary grounds.

Republican Dennis Scott and won with 74.2% of the vote. *** Scott raised only $6,000, which was less than Forbes raised; nevertheless, Scott was invited to participate in a debate while Forbes was not. ***

14. It is particularly troubling that AETC excluded the only independent candidate but invited all the major-party candidates to participate in the planned debates, regardless of their chances of electoral success. As this Court has recognized, "political figures outside the two major parties have been fertile sources of new ideas and new programs; many of their challenges to the status quo have in time made their way into the political mainstream." *Anderson v. Celebrezze*, 460 U.S. 780, 794 (1983) (citing *Illinois Bd. of Elections v. Socialist Workers Party*, 440 U.S. 173, 186 (1979)).

15. Lack of substantial financial support apparently was not a factor in the decision to invite a major-party candidate with even less financial support than Forbes.

Like the Court, I do not endorse the view of the Court of Appeals that all candidates who qualify for a position on the ballot are necessarily entitled to access to any state-sponsored debate.   I am convinced, however, that the constitutional imperatives command that access to political debates planned and managed by state-owned entities be governed by pre-established objective criteria. *** Accordingly, I would affirm the judgment of the Court of Appeals.

———

Casebook, p. 543
Add as new paragraphs to footnote 100

The "fairness doctrine" abandoned by the FCC in 1987 spoke generally to the "obligations" of broadcasters to "afford reasonable opportunity for the discussion of conflicting views on issues of public importance." See 47 C.F.R. 73.1910 (Fairness Doctrine); 2 F.C.C.R. 5043 (1987) (decision to end enforcement of Fairness Doctrine).   Although the FCC abandoned this doctrine in 1987, it continues to apply to broadcasters two other related rules, one of which reads largely like the regulations at issue in *Red Lion Broadcasting Co v. FCC.*

According to the first of these, the "political editorial rule," if a station broadcasts an editorial endorsing or opposing a candidate, it must notify the candidate's opponents (or the candidate that the editorial opposed) of the date and time of the editorial; it must provide a script or tape of the broadcast; and it must offer the affected candidate a reasonable opportunity to respond using the station's or system's facilities. 47 C.F.R. 73.1930. (As recently as the summer of 1994, the FCC admonished a station for failing to provide proper notification pursuant to this rule.)

According to the second, the "personal attack rule," if an attack on the "honesty, character, integrity, or like personal qualities" of a specific person or group is made during the presentation of views on a controversial issue of public importance, the station airing the attack must notify the attacked person or group of the date and time of the attack and the program in which it took place; provide a script, tape, or accurate summary of the attack; and offer the attacked person or group a reasonable opportunity to respond to the attack using the station's or system's facilities.   47 C.F.R. 73.1920.   In 1995, the FCC dismissed a personal attack complaint on the merits because the petitioners had failed to show that the personal attack took place during the presentation of a controversial issue of public importance but reaffirmed that broadcasters remain subject to the rule.

The FCC initiated a rulemaking in 1983 on repeal or modification of both rules. Although the pleading cycle has long since terminated, the Commissioners have repeatedly (and even as recently as spring 1998) deadlocked when attempting a vote on the issue, and thus no *Report* and *Order* has ever been issued. Accordingly, both of these rules remain in place despite the 1987 abandonment of Rule 73.1910.

———

Casebook, p. 562
**Add following NOTES AND QUESTIONS ON *TURNER*, SUBSEQUENT
REVIEW OF *TURNER BROADCASTING*   and new case, *Denver Area
Educational Telecommunications Consortium v. Federal Communications
Commission***

SUBSEQUENT REVIEW OF TURNER BROADCASTING

See also *Turner Broadcasting System, Inc. v. Federal Communications Comm'n*, 520
U.S. 180 (1997) ("*Turner II*") (*held*, §§ 4 and 5 of the Cable Television Act of 1992
requiring cable television companies with more than 12 active channels, and more than
300 subscribers, to set aside up to one-third of their channels for use by local, over-
the-air commercial broadcasters, and to set aside still additional channels for use by
local noncommercial educational stations, both without charge and without channel
repositioning, do not violate first amendment rights of cable broadcasters).

In short, in a virtual replay of *Turner Broadcasting v. FCC*, 512 U.S. 622 (1994)
("*Turner I*") (casebook at p. 548), the Cable Act's "must-carry" rules were once again
sustained. Essentially, there was no change within the Court in *Turner II*, following
the proceedings on remand; Justice Breyer provides the fifth vote for the vote previously provided by Justice Blackmun, for the same majority in *Turner I*. And in
Turner II, Justice Kennedy again wrote the majority Opinion, and Justice O'Connor
wrote the dissent. Nor did the substantive position on either side significantly change.

Just as in *Turner I*, Turner Broadcasting complained that its first amendment's rights
of editorial control, content selection, and selection of program array, were unconstitutionally abridged by the must-carry provisions of the Cable Act. Once again, however,
the majority rejected the comparison of a cable television company with a newspaper,
and reviewed the case under the far less exacting "*O'Brien* intermediate scrutiny test"
(set out in *United States v. O'Brien*, 391 U.S. 367 (1968)).[113a] Once again the
majority concluded that the must-carry rules were "content neutral"; that they were
reasonably regarded by Congress as necessary to "advance important government
interests unrelated to the suppression of free speech" (specifically, protection of free,
over-the-air local broadcasting, of assuring a multiplicity of program sources, and promoting fair competition for television programming); and that they did "not burden
substantially more speech than necessary" to serve these valid government interests.
And, as in *Turner I*, the dissent disagreed at virtually every step. It rejected the ap-

---

113a. See casebook at p. 286.

plication of the *O'Brien* test as inappropriate.[113b] Moreover, the dissent could find no sufficient justification for requiring free, enhanced cable carriage of local over-the-air broadcasters in lieu of displaced remote sources, whether as an anti-trust measure, or otherwise, especially given the availability of less editorially-intrusive measures available to Congress (e.g., subsidies), to preserve such local, over-the-air broadcasters it might deem sufficiently important so to assist.

Such clarification as *Turner II* provides over the major doctrinal differences as previously ventilated in *Turner I*, lies principally in the majority's new statement that "[t]he question is not whether Congress, as an objective matter, was correct to determine must-carry is necessary to prevent a substantial number of broadcast stations from losing cable carriage and suffering financial hardship, [but merely] whether the legislative conclusion was reasonable and supported by substantial evidence in the record before Congress." In brief, considerable deference to Congress's views, respecting the need for legislation of this sort, appears in *Turner II*. Likewise, in sustaining the act imposing the must-carry rules, the majority reiterated that it was not necessary for the government to establish that no less restrictive provisions applicable to cable television companies would suffice. Again, however, as in *Turner I*, the dissent substantially disagreed and also concluded that there was no sufficient evidence in the record establishing the must-carry obligations (including free carriage) was demonstrably "narrowly tailored" to meet any real problems allegedly meant to be addressed by the rules.[113c] Overall, however, the disagreement is pretty much the same as in *Turner I*. The principal effect of the case is largely just to lift the uncertainty as to whether the original decision would hold, despite the serious shortcomings it was thought to contain.[113d]

In the meantime, while *Turner* was on remand to the district court, a related set of questions was examined in the Supreme Court in respect to cable companies and editorial control over program content. The issue involved in these newer cases was not whether cablevision companies had been unconstitutionally restricted by the requirement that they carry certain other parties' programs against their will and carry

---

113b. Rather, the dissent insisted that the must-carry rules were not "content neutral" (since they require the forced substitution of whatever programs and advertisements merely *local* broadcasters would be transmitting for those supplied by more remote sources whose programs an affected cable company would otherwise choose to carry) and accordingly were subject to more rigorous review.

113c. In the dissent's view, there was little evidence that the problems allegedly justifying the rules were as substantial or as real as the majority avowed, or warranted the extent of the imposed must-carry rules.

113d. See, e.g., questions and footnotes, casebook at pp. 561-62.

them wholly unedited. Instead, it was whether in changing its mind, in *permitting* cable companies to *refuse* to carry certain material (even on the must-carry channels), Congress acted to abridge freedom of speech — *not* that of the cable company, rather, the freedom of speech of those the cable company was previously required to carry unedited.

So, here, suddenly, was seemingly a virtual reverse twist to the cablevision must-carry debate. When Congress merely "gives back" to cable companies *some* portion of such control as they would have had more completely if Congress had simply left them alone in the first place (i.e. had it never subjected them to any must-carry rules), and a cable company merely acts within the limits of the granted-back authority, wherein can one find grounds to frame a suitable first amendment complaint?

To be sure, anyone whose program the cable company is now permitted to turn away (and does turn away) may feel badly treated by the cable company. But so much as this would be true were there no must-carry rules at all. [113e] Even assuming the must-carry rules are not themselves an unconstitutional interference by Congress with the first amendment rights of cable companies as "publishers," to what extent would mere forbearance by Congress from requiring cable companies to carry certain types of programs (e.g., "indecent" programs)[113f] present a first amendment basis for complaint? Consider the following case.

DENVER AREA EDUCATIONAL TELECOMMUNICATIONS CONSORTIUM v. FEDERAL COMMUNICATIONS COMMISSION
518 U.S. 727 (1996)

JUSTICE BREYER announced the judgment and delivered the opinion of the Court.

These cases present First Amendment challenges to three statutory provisions that seek to regulate the broadcasting of "patently offensive" sex-related material on cable television.

113e. Note that in respect to all of its programming except that which is subject to the must-carry rules, cable companies have all along been free generally to decide what to carry or not. (Generally, a cable company is no more obliged to permit programs it disdains to carry any more than the Miami Herald need publish stories it disdains to publish, however "unfair" someone considers its policy to be.)

113f. What if the *only* programs Congress permitted cable companies to refuse to carry (over its must-carry channels) were programs "denigrative of others," or programs "the cable company deems morally objectionable"? (May there be a problem when the "giving back" of the cable company's "editorial discretion" is limited or partial, rather than in whole?)

I

Certain special channels here at issue, called "leased channels" and "public, educational, or governmental channels," carry programs provided by those to whom the law gives special cable system access rights.

A "leased channel" is a channel that federal law requires a cable system operator to reserve for commercial lease by unaffiliated third parties. About 10 to 15 percent of a cable system's channels would typically fall into this category. "[P]ublic, educational, or governmental channels" (which we shall call "public access" channels) are channels that, over the years, local governments have required cable system operators to set aside for public, educational, or governmental purposes as part of the consideration an operator gives in return for permission to install cables under city streets and to use public rights-of-way. Between 1984 and 1992 federal law *** prohibited cable system operators from exercising any editorial control over the content of any program broadcast over either leased or public access channels.

In 1992, in an effort to control sexually explicit programming conveyed over access channels, Congress enacted the three provisions before us. *** The law now permits cable operators either to allow or to forbid the transmission of "patently offensive" sex-related materials over both leased and public access channels, and requires those operators, at a minimum, to segregate and to block transmission of that same material on leased channels.

II

We turn initially to the provision that permits cable system operators to prohibit "patently offensive" (or "indecent") programming transmitted over leased access channels.

[T]he problem Congress addressed here is remarkably similar to the problem addressed by the FCC in *Pacifica* [438 U.S. 726], and the balance Congress struck is commensurate with the balance we approved there. In *Pacifica* this Court considered a governmental ban of a radio broadcast of "indecent" materials, defined in part, like the provisions before us, to include

> "'language that describes, in terms patently offensive
> as measured by contemporary community standards
> for the broadcast medium, sexual or excretory
> activities and organs, at times of the day when there
> is a reasonable risk that children may be in the
> audience.'"

The Court found this ban constitutionally permissible primarily because "broadcasting is uniquely accessible to children" and children were likely listeners to the program there at issue — an afternoon radio broadcast. *** Cable television broadcasting, including access channel broadcasting, is as "accessible to children" as over-the-air broadcasting, if not more so. Cable television systems, including access channels, "have established a uniquely pervasive presence in the lives of all Americans." *Pacifica*, [438 U.S.] at 748. ***

[T]he permissive nature of § 10(a) means that it likely restricts speech less than, not more than, the ban at issue in *Pacifica*. The provision removes a restriction as to some speakers — namely, cable operators. Moreover, although the provision does create a risk that a program will not appear, that risk is not the same as the certainty that accompanies a governmental ban. In fact, a glance at the programming that cable operators allow on their own (nonaccess) channels suggests that this distinction is not theoretical, but real. Finally, the provision's permissive nature brings with it a flexibility that allows cable operators, for example, not to ban broadcasts, but, say, to rearrange broadcast times, better to fit the desires of adult audiences while lessening the risks of harm to children.

The existence of this complex balance of interests persuades us that the permissive nature of the provision, coupled with its viewpoint-neutral application, is a constitutionally permissible way to protect children from the type of sexual material that concerned Congress, while accommodating both the First Amendment interests served by the access requirements and those served in restoring to cable operators a degree of the editorial control that Congress removed in 1984.

III

The statute's second provision significantly differs from the first ***. [T]his provision and its implementing regulations require cable system operators to place "patently offensive" leased channel programming on a separate channel; to block that channel; to unblock the channel within 30 days of a subscriber's written request for access; and to reblock the channel within 30 days of a subscriber's request for reblocking. Also, leased channel programmers must notify cable operators of an intended "patently offensive" broadcast up to 30 days before its scheduled broadcast date.

These restrictions will prevent programmers from broadcasting to viewers who select programs day by day (or, through "surfing," minute by minute); to viewers who would like occasionally to watch a few, but not many, of the programs on the "patently offensive" channel; and to viewers who simply tend to judge a program's value through channel reputation, i.e., by the company it keeps. Moreover, the "written notice" requirement will further restrict viewing by subscribers who fear for their reputations should the operator, advertently or inadvertently, disclose the list of those who wish to watch the "patently offensive" channel. *Cf. Lamont v. Postmaster General*, 381 U.S. 301, 307 (1965) (finding unconstitutional a requirement that recipients of Communist literature notify the Post Office that they wish to receive it). Further, the added costs and burdens that these requirements impose upon a cable system operator may encourage that operator to ban programming that the operator would otherwise permit to run, even if only late at night.

We agree with the Government that protection of children is a "compelling interest." But we do not agree that the "segregate and block" requirements properly accommodate the speech restrictions they impose and the legitimate objective they seek to attain.

Several circumstances lead us to this conclusion. For one thing, the law, as recently amended, uses other means to protect children from similar "patently offensive" material broadcast on unleased cable channels, i.e., broadcast over any of a system's numerous ordinary, or public access, channels. The law, as recently amended, requires cable operators to "scramble or *** block" such programming on any (unleased) channel "primarily dedicated to sexually-oriented programming." In addition, cable operators must honor a subscriber's request to block any, or all, programs on any channel to which he or she does not wish to subscribe. And manufacturers, in the future, will have to make television sets with a so-called "V-chip" — a device that will be able automatically to identify and block sexually explicit or violent programs.

Although we cannot, and do not, decide whether the new provisions are themselves lawful (a matter not before us), we note that they are significantly less restrictive than the provision here at issue. They do not force the viewer to receive (for days or weeks at a time) all "patently offensive" programming or none; they will not lead the viewer automatically to judge the few by the reputation of the many; and they will not automatically place the occasional viewer's name on a special list. They therefore inevitably lead us to ask why, if they adequately protect children from "patently offensive" material broadcast on ordinary channels, they would not offer adequate protection from similar leased channel broadcasts as well?

The record does not answer these questions. It does not explain why a simple subscriber blocking request system, perhaps a phone-call based system, would adequately protect children from "patently offensive" material broadcast on ordinary non-sex-dedicated channels (i.e., almost all channels) but a far more restrictive segregate/block/written-access system is needed to protect children from similar broadcasts on what (in the absence of the segregation requirement) would be non-sex-dedicated channels that are leased.

The record's description and discussion of a different alternative — the "lockbox" — leads, through a different route, to a similar conclusion. The Cable Communications Policy Act of 1984 required cable operators to provide "upon the request of a subscriber, a device by which the subscriber can prohibit viewing of a particular cable service during periods selected by the subscriber." 47 U.S.C. § 544(d)(2). This device — the "lockbox" — would help protect children by permitting their parents to "lock out" those programs or channels that they did not want their children to see.

No provision, we concede, short of an absolute ban, can offer certain protection against assault by a determined child. We have not, however, generally allowed this fact alone to justify reduc[ing] the adult population to only what is fit for children.

Consequently, we cannot find that the "segregate and block" restrictions on speech are a narrowly, or reasonably, tailored effort to protect children. Rather, they are overly restrictive, "sacrific[ing]" important First Amendment interests for too "speculative a gain."

IV

The statute's third provision, as implemented by FCC regulation, is similar to its first provision, in that it too *permits* a cable operator to prevent transmission of "patently offensive" programming, in this case on public access channels. But there are important differences.

The first is the historical background. As JUSTICE KENNEDY points out, cable operators have traditionally agreed to reserve channel capacity for public, governmental, and educational channels as part of the consideration they give municipalities that award them cable franchises. Significantly, these are channels over which cable operators have not historically exercised editorial control. Unlike § 10(a) therefore, § 10(c) does not restore to cable operators editorial rights that they once had, and the countervailing First Amendment interest is nonexistent, or at least much diminished.

The second difference is the institutional background that has developed as a result of the historical difference. Public access channels are normally subject to complex supervisory systems of various sorts, often with both public and private elements.

This system of public, private, and mixed nonprofit elements, through its supervising boards and nonprofit or governmental access managers, can set programming policy and approve or disapprove particular programming services. Whether these locally accountable bodies prescreen programming, promulgate rules for the use of public access channels, or are merely available to respond when problems arise, the upshot is the same: there is a locally accountable body capable of addressing the problem, should it arise, of patently offensive programming broadcast to children, making it unlikely that many children will in fact be exposed to programming considered patently offensive in that community.

Third, the existence of a system aimed at encouraging and securing programming that the community considers valuable strongly suggests that a "cable operator's veto" is less likely necessary to achieve the statute's basic objective, protecting children, than a similar veto in the context of leased channels. Of course, the system of access managers and supervising boards can make mistakes, which the operator might in some cases correct with its veto power. Balanced against this potential benefit, however, is the risk that the veto itself may be mistaken; and its use, or threatened use, could prevent the presentation of programming, that, though borderline, is not "patently offensive" to its targeted audience.

[W]e conclude that the Government cannot sustain its burden of showing that § 10(c) is necessary to protect children or that it is appropriately tailored to secure that end. Consequently, we find that this third provision violates the First Amendment.

[Concurring opinions by STEVENS and SOUTER, JJ., omitted.]

JUSTICE O'CONNOR, concurring in part and dissenting in part.

The distinctions upon which the Court relies in deciding that § 10(c) must fall while § 10(a) survives are not, in my view, constitutionally significant. The interest in protecting children remains the same, whether on a leased access channel or a public access channel, and allowing the cable operator the option of prohibiting the transmission of indecent speech seems a constitutionally permissible means of addressing that interest. Nor is the fact that public access programming may be subject to supervisory systems in addition to the cable operator, sufficient in my mind to render § 10(c) so ill-tailored to its goal as to be unconstitutional.

JUSTICE KENNEDY, with whom JUSTICE GINSBURG joins, concurring in part, concurring in the judgment in part, and dissenting in part.

Sections 10(a) and (c) are unusual. They do not require direct action against speech, but do authorize a cable operator to deny the use of its property to certain forms of speech. As a general matter, a private person may exclude certain speakers from his or her property without violating the First Amendment, *Hudgens v. NLRB*, 424 U.S. 507 (1976), and if §§ 10(a) and (c) were no more than affirmations of this principle they might be unremarkable. Access channels, however, are property of the cable operator dedicated or otherwise reserved for programming of other speakers or the government. A public access channel is a public forum, and laws requiring leased access channels create common carrier obligations. When the government identifies certain speech on the basis of its content as vulnerable to exclusion from a common carrier or public forum, strict scrutiny applies. These laws cannot survive this exacting review.

Laws removing common-carriage protection from a single form of speech based on its content should be reviewed under the same standard as content-based restrictions on speech in a public forum. Making a cable operator a common carrier does not create a public forum in the sense of taking property from private control and dedicating it to public use. A common-carriage mandate, nonetheless, serves the same function as a public forum. It ensures open, nondiscriminatory access to the means of communication.

The provisions here are content-based discriminations in the strong sense of suppressing a certain form of expression that the Government dislikes, or otherwise wishes to exclude on account of its effects, and there is no justification for anything but strict scrutiny here.

[The] concerns [for children] are weighty and will be relevant to whether the law passes strict scrutiny. They do not justify, however, a blanket rule of lesser protection for indecent speech. [T]o the extent cable operators prohibit indecent programming on access channels, not only children but adults will be deprived of it. The Government may not "reduce the adult population to [viewing] only what is fit for children." When applying strict scrutiny, we will not assume plausible alternatives will fail to protect compelling interests; there must be some basis in the record, in legislative findings or otherwise, establishing the law enacted as the least restrictive means. I dissent from the judgment of the Court insofar as it upholds the constitutionality of §10(a).

JUSTICE THOMAS, joined by the CHIEF JUSTICE and JUSTICE SCALIA, concurring in the judgment in part and dissenting in part.

I agree with the plurality's conclusion that § 10(a) is constitutionally permissible, but I disagree with its conclusion that §§ 10(b) and (c) violate the First Amendment.

The text of the First Amendment makes no distinction between print, broadcast, and cable media, but we have done so. In *Red Lion Broadcasting Co. v. FCC*, 395 U.S. 367 (1969), we held that, in light of the scarcity of broadcasting frequencies, the Government may require a broadcast licensee "to share his frequency with others and to conduct himself as a proxy or fiduciary with obligations to present those views and voices which are representative of his community and which would otherwise, by necessity, be barred from the airwaves." That public right left broadcasters with substantial, but not complete, First Amendment protection of their editorial discretion.

In contrast, we have not permitted that level of government interference in the context of the print media. In *Miami Herald Publishing Co. v. Tornillo*, 418 U.S. 241 (1974), for instance, we invalidated a Florida statute that required newspapers to allow, free of charge, a right of reply to political candidates whose personal or professional character the paper assailed.

Our First Amendment distinctions between media, dubious from their infancy, placed cable in a doctrinal wasteland in which regulators and cable operators alike could not be sure whether cable was entitled to the substantial First Amendment protections afforded the print media or was subject to the more onerous obligations shouldered by the broadcast media. Over time, however, we have drawn closer to recognizing that cable operators should enjoy the same First Amendment rights as the nonbroadcast media.

We implicitly recognized in *Turner* that the programmer's right to compete for channel space is derivative of, and subordinate to, the operator's editorial discretion. Like a free-lance writer seeking a paper in which to publish newspaper editorials, a programmer is protected in searching for an outlet for cable programming, but has no free-standing First Amendment right to have that programming transmitted.

By recognizing the general primacy of the cable operator's editorial rights over the rights of programmers and viewers, *Turner* raises serious questions about the merits of petitioners' claims. None of the petitioners in these cases are cable operators; they are all cable viewers or access programmers or their representative organizations.

Because the access provisions are part of a scheme that restricts the free speech rights of cable operators, and expands the speaking opportunities of access program-mers, who have no underlying constitutional right to speak through the cable medium, I do not believe that access programmers can challenge the scheme, or a particular part of it, as an abridgment of their "freedom of speech."

The permissive nature of §§ 10(a) and (c) is important in this regard. If Congress had forbidden cable operators to carry indecent programming on leased and public access channels, that law would have burdened the programmer's right, recognized in *Turner*, to compete for space on an operator's system. The Court would un-doubtedly strictly scrutinize such a law. But §§ 10(a) and (c) do not burden a programmer's right to seek access for its indecent programming on an operator's system. Rather, they merely restore part of the editorial discretion an operator would have absent government regulation without burdening the programmer's underlying speech rights.

Petitioners argue that public access channels are public fora in which they have First Amendment rights to speak and that § 10(c) is invalid because it imposes content-based burdens on those rights.

Our public forum cases have involved property in which the government has held at least some formal easement or other property interest permitting the government to treat the property as its own in designating the property as a public forum. That is simply not true in these cases. Pursuant to federal and state law, franchising authorities require cable operators to create public access channels, but nothing in the record suggests that local franchising authorities take any formal easement or other property interest in those channels that would permit the government to designate that property as a public forum. For this reason, and the other reasons articulated earlier, I would sustain both § 10(a) and § 10(c).

Unlike §§ 10(a) and (c), § 10(b) clearly implicates petitioners' free speech rights. Though § 10(b) by no means bans indecent speech, it clearly places content-based restrictions on the transmission of private speech by requiring cable operators to block and segregate indecent programming that the operator has agreed to carry.

Consequently, § 10(b) must be subjected to strict scrutiny and can be upheld only if it furthers a compelling governmental interest by the least restrictive means available.

The Court strikes down § 10(b) by pointing to alternatives, such as reverse- blocking and lockboxes, that it says are less restrictive than segregation and blocking. Though these methods attempt to place in parents' hands the ability to permit their children to watch as little, or as much, indecent programming as the parents think proper, they do not effectively support parents' authority to direct the moral upbringing of their children. Rather than being able to simply block out certain channels at certain times, a subscriber armed with only a lockbox must carefully monitor all leased-access programming and constantly reprogram the lockbox to keep out undesired programming. Thus, even assuming that cable subscribers generally have the technical proficiency to properly operate a lockbox, by no means a given, this distinguishing characteristic of leased access channels makes lockboxes and reverse- blocking largely ineffective.

The FCC regulation requires only that the cable operator receive written consent. Other statutory provisions make clear that the cable operator may not share that, or any other, information with any other person, including the Government.

The segregation and blocking requirement was not intended to be a replacement for lockboxes, V-chips, reverse-blocking, or other subscriber-initiated measures. Once a subscriber requests access to blocked programming, the subscriber remains free to use other methods, such as lockboxes, to regulate the kind of programming shown on those channels in that home.

The United States has carried its burden of demonstrating that § 10(b) and its implementing regulations are narrowly tailored to satisfy a compelling governmental interest. Accordingly, I would affirm the judgment of the Court of Appeals in its entirety.

_____

QUESTIONS AND PROBLEMS

1. Note how sharply five members of the Court divided in defining the threshold first amendment issues — i.e. how to characterize the case for purposes of determining *which* first amendment test to apply. Two justices (Kennedy and Ginsburg) contended that all three sections of the 1992 Act were subject to "strict scrutiny," and that all three sections failed that test. (What made "strict scrutiny" appropriate in their view? Did they have the matter right?)[113g] By way of contrast, three others (Thomas, Scalia,

_____

113g. With respect to § 10(a) of the Act, which applied to "leased access channels," and with respect to the "common carrier" model suppose an Act of Congress designated certain kinds of major interstate freight haulers (railroads) as common carriers, then forbade them to reject any safely packaged and lawful goods, but permitted them to refuse to carry materials "unsuitable for minors." Why might this be unconstitutional? (Note that seven of the justices

and Rehnquist) voted to sustain all three sections, but only after concluding that the first amendment *barely* applied to sections 10(a) and 10(c). (On what basis did they so thoroughly disagree as to the proper way to view the case?)[113h]

In contrast, none of the remaining justices agreed with either of the sharply differing models offered by their colleagues. But neither did they offer an alternative description, one providing a better fit (in their view). Granted that they may have had good reason to be wary of appropriating pre-existing "models," still — how would you describe the method of first amendment review as explained and applied by them?[113i]

2. To move beyond cable television, suppose restrictions were imposed by Congress on users of the Internet, and on owners of certain Internet service providers, to forbid the knowing transmission of sexually-explicit, indecent, patently offensive material (as defined by the statute in *Denver Area* or as defined in the FCC regulation in

---

voted to sustain § 10(a) of the Act involved in *Denver Area*. Is there any reason to think some of them might not sustain this variation?)

113h. The dissent relied heavily on the "editorial discretion" of the cable operator. The New York Times may decline to publish what it does not regard as "fit to print." Can a cable television company appropriately be compared with the New York Times? Why or why not? The concurring/dissenting opinion by Kennedy and Ginsburg distinguished leased access channels and public access channels from conventional privately owned property, even while otherwise agreeing that, "[a]s a general matter, a private person *may* exclude certain speakers from his or her property without violating the first amendment," citing *Hudgens v. NLRB*, 424 U.S. 507 (1976) (emphasis added). Further consideration of the extent to which "private property" may be subject (or not subject) to third party first amendment claims of access and speech-use is provided *infra*, ch. III, § 9, pp. 589-614 ("The Blurred Boundary Between Private and Public Property"). The *Hudgens* case is included as a principal case (casebook at pp. 595-599).

113i. Note the observation in the plurality opinion by Justice Breyer that sections 10(a) and (c) are "viewpoint neutral" (even if not "content neutral") — a matter obviously critical for Justice Breyer's vote to sustain even § 10(a) (which six of the other eight also voted to uphold). Is it altogether "viewpoint neutral"? No doubt it is, in comparison with the type of ordinance held invalid in the *Hudnut* case (sexually explicit material depicting women in positive ways permitted, sexually explicit material depicting women as "subordinate" or as "objects" forbidden) (see casebook at pp. 252-258) But is it "viewpoint neutral" in a larger sense? May not one's choice of words (four-letter or otherwise) capture and offer "viewpoints" very distinctive from depictions or descriptions composed from an abridged dictionary? If one is equally forbidden to use four-letter expletives whether to praise the draft or to condemn the draft, is "viewpoint neutrality" preserved — or, rather, are certain "viewpoints" thereby banished on *both* sides, as it were, by stripping out certain features of expression (and thus also certain competing perspectives) as well? Cf. *Cohen v. California*, 403 U.S. 15 (1971) (Harlan, J.) (casebook at pp. 154-56).

Pacifica)[113j] over networks readily accessed by minors.[113k]

NOTE

Section 505 of the Communications Decency Act, 47 U.S.C. § 561, requires every multisystem operator either to fully scramble or to time channel (i.e. to "safe harbor hours") "sexually explicit adult programming or other programming that is indecent" on any channels that are "primarily dedicated to sexually-oriented programming" (e.g., the Playboy network or Spice). The purpose of the provision is to eliminate "signal bleed" (partial reception of audio or video) when children may be watching. There are also a number of technologies available to consumers to ensure that their households do not receive signal bleed; § 504 of the CDA, for instance, requires a multisystem operator to fully scramble or fully block both audio and video, free of charge, upon request by the consumer (i.e. a subscriber-blocking request system similar to that described in *Denver Area*). Enforcement of section 505 was stayed for fourteen months, during which time several hundred lock-boxes were ordered, nationwide. (Estimates place the number of households capable of receiving signal bleed at 38-39 million homes.) Upon challenge to the constitutionality of section 505, the government argued that the subscriber-blocking request system is not an "effective" alternative, among other reasons because consumers are ("apparently") unaware of the option. *See United States v. Playboy Entertainment Group*, 530 U.S.____ (2000), this supplement at pp. 105-110, *infra*.

Casebook, p. 614
Add to footnote 137

See also New York Magazine v. Metropolitan Transportation Authority, 136 F.3d 123 (2nd Cir. 1998), *cert. denied*, 119 S. Ct. 68 (1998). (The New York MTA leases commercial and political advertising space on outsides of public buses in New York City. All contracts contain an indemnity clause to hold MTA harmless in respect to liability arising from any ads placed with MTA. New York Magazine contracted, for $85,000, for ads to be carried on seventy-five city buses, each prominently featuring the magazine logo and the following eye-catching caption: "Possibly the only good thing in New York Rudy hasn't taken credit for." The name reference ("Rudy") was to Rudolph W. Giuliani, Mayor of New York City. Shortly after the first ads appeared on the buses pursuant to the contract, however, MTA removed them. It did so following complaint to MTA from the mayor's office, requesting prompt removal, and

---

113j. *FCC v. Pacifica Found.*, 438 U.S. 726 (1978) (reviewed in the principal opinion in *Denver Area*, and see also casebook at p. 543, n.99).

113k. For a first response to the problem, see *Reno v. ACLU*, 521 U.S. 844 (1997), this Supplement at pp. 94-102, *infra*.

calling to MTA's attention § 50 of N.Y. Civil Rights Law. §50 of the N.Y. Civil Rights Law makes it a misdemeanor and an actionable tort for "any person, firm, or corporation [to] use for advertising purposes...the name, portrait, or picture of any living person without having obtained the consent of such person." In response to MTA's action, New York Magazine at once brought suit in federal court to enjoin MTA, asserting first amendment claims for entitlement to requested relief to have the ads displayed.) (Consider the case in relation to *Lebron*; cases on privacy and misappropriation of personal likeness for commercial gain, casebook, pp. 212-13, n. 97; and with *Hustler*, casebook at p. 243.)

———

Casebook, p. 567
Add as new case

BOY SCOUTS OF AMERICA v. JAMES DALE[*]
530 U.S. ___[June 28, 2000]

CHIEF JUSTICE REHNQUIST delivered the opinion of the Court.

The Boy Scouts asserts that homosexual conduct is inconsistent with the values it seeks to instill. Respondent is James Dale, a former Eagle Scout whose adult membership in the Boy Scouts was revoked when the Boy Scouts learned that he is an avowed homosexual and gay rights activist. The New Jersey Supreme Court held that New Jersey's public accommodations law requires that the Boy Scouts admit Dale. This case presents the question whether applying New Jersey's public accommodations law in this way violates the Boy Scouts' First Amendment right of expressive association. We hold that it does.

I

James Dale became a Boy Scout in 1981 and remained a Scout until he turned 18. By all accounts, Dale was an exemplary Scout. In 1988, he achieved the rank of Eagle Scout, one of Scouting's highest honors. [H]e applied for adult membership in the Boy Scouts in 1989. The Boy Scouts approved his application for the position of assistant scoutmaster of Troop 73. Around the same time, Dale left home to attend Rutgers University. After arriving at Rutgers, Dale first acknowledged to himself and others that he is gay. He quickly became involved with, and eventually became the co-

———

*[Ed. Note: See also and compare, *California Democratic Party et al. v. Bill Jones, Secretary of State of California*, 530 U.S. ____ (June 26, 2000). (First amendment right of "expressive association" of political parties to select their candidates to appear on the general election ballot, recognized and applied; state "blanket primary" election law authorizing non-party members–including members of parties with ideology different from or even opposite of that the party espouses –to vote to determine each political party's nominees for election for statewide offices, held unconstitutional.)

president of, the Rutgers University Lesbian/Gay Alliance. In 1990, Dale attended a seminar addressing the psychological and health needs of lesbian and gay teenagers. A newspaper covering the event interviewed Dale about his advocacy of homosexual teenagers' need for gay role models. [I]t published the interview and Dale's photograph over a caption identifying him as the co-president of the Lesbian/Gay Alliance.

Later that month, Dale received a letter from Monmouth Council Executive James Kay revoking his adult membership. Dale wrote to Kay requesting the reason for Monmouth Council's decision. Kay responded by letter that the Boy Scouts "specifically forbid membership to homosexuals."

In 1992, Dale filed a complaint against the Boy Scouts in the New Jersey Superior Court. The complaint alleged that the Boy Scouts had violated New Jersey's public accommodations statute and its common law by revoking Dale's membership based solely on his sexual orientation. New Jersey's public accommodations statute prohibits, among other things, discrimination on the basis of sexual orientation in places of public accommodation.

The New Jersey Superior Court's Chancery Division granted summary judgment in favor of the Boy Scouts. The New Jersey Superior Court's Appellate Division reversed [and] rejected the Boy Scouts' federal constitutional claims. The New Jersey Supreme Court affirmed the judgment of the Appellate Division.*** With respect to the right of expressive association, the court "agree[d] that Boy Scouts expresses a belief in moral values and uses its activities to encourage the moral development of its members." But the court concluded that it was "not persuaded...that a shared goal of Boy Scout members is to associate in order to preserve the view that homosexuality is immoral." Accordingly, the court held "that Dale's membership does not violate the Boy Scouts' right of expressive association because his inclusion would not affect in any significant way [the Boy Scouts'] existing members' ability to carry out their various purposes. The court also determined that New Jersey has a compelling interest in eliminating "the destructive consequences of discrimination from our society," and that its public accommodations law abridges no more speech than is necessary to accomplish its purpose.***We granted the Boy Scouts' petition for certiorari to determine whether the application of New Jersey's public accommodations law violated the First Amendment.

II

In *Roberts* v. *United States Jaycees,* 468 U. S. 609 (1984), we observed that "implicit in the right to engage in activities protected by the First Amendment" is "a corresponding right to associate with others in pursuit of a wide variety of political, social, economic, educational, religious, and cultural ends." This right is crucial in preventing the majority from imposing its views on groups that would rather express other, perhaps unpopular, ideas. See *ibi*d. (stating that protection of the right to expressive association is "especially important in preserving political and cultural diversity and in shielding dissident expression from suppression by the majority"). Government actions that may unconstitutionally burden this freedom may take many forms, one of which is "intrusion into the internal structure or affairs of an association" like a "regulation that forces the group to accept members it does not desire." Forcing a group to accept certain members may impair the ability of the group to express those views, and only those views, that it intends to express. Thus, "[f]reedom of association ...plainly presupposes a freedom not to associate."

The forced inclusion of an unwanted person in a group infringes the group's freedom of expressive association if the presence of that person affects in a significant way the group's ability to advocate public or private viewpoints. *New York State Club Assn., Inc.* v. *City of New York*, 487 U. S. 1, 13 (1988). But the freedom of expressive association, like many freedoms, is not absolute. We have held that the freedom could be overridden "by regulations adopted to serve compelling state interests, unrelated to the suppression of ideas, that cannot be achieved through means significantly less restrictive of associational freedoms." *Roberts,* at 623.

To determine whether a group is protected by the First Amendment's expressive associational right, we must determine whether the group engages in "expressive association." The First Amendment's protection of expressive association is not reserved for advocacy groups. But to come within its ambit, a group must engage in some form of expression, whether it be public or private.

Because this is a First Amendment case where the ultimate conclusions of law are virtually inseparable from findings of fact, we are obligated to independently review the factual record to ensure that the state court' s judgment does not unlawfully intrude on free expression. See *Hurley,* at 567–568. The record reveals the following. The Boy Scouts is a private, nonprofit organization. According to its mission statement: "It is the mission of the Boy Scouts of America to serve others by helping to instill values in young people and, in other ways, to prepare them to make ethical choices over their lifetime in achieving their full potential. The values we strive to instill are based on those found in the Scout Oath and Law:

Scout Oath	Scout Law
"On my honor I will do my best To do my duty to God and my country and to obey the Scout Law; To help other people at all times; To keep myself physically strong, mentally, awake, and morally straight	A Scout is: Trustworthy, Obedient, Loyal, Cheerful, Helpful, Thrifty, Friendly, Brave, Courteous, Clean, Kind, Reverent."

Thus, the general mission of the Boy Scouts is clear: "[T]o instill values in young people." The Boy Scouts seeks to instill these values by having its adult leaders spend time with the youth members, instructing and engaging them in activities like camping, archery, and fishing. During the time spent with the youth members, the scoutmasters and assistant scoutmasters inculcate them with the Boy Scouts' values—both expressly and by example. It seems indisputable that an association that seeks to transmit such a system of values engages in expressive activity. Given that the Boy Scouts engages in expressive activity, we must determine whether the forced inclusion of Dale as an assistant scoutmaster would significantly affect the Boy Scouts' ability to advocate public or private viewpoints. This inquiry necessarily requires us first to explore, to a limited extent, the nature of the Boy Scouts' view of homosexuality.

The Boy Scouts explains that the Scout Oath and Law provide "a positive moral code for living; they are a list of 'do's' rather than 'don'ts.'" Brief for Petitioners 3. The Boy Scouts asserts that homosexual conduct is inconsistent with the values embodied in the Scout Oath and Law, particularly with the values represented by the terms "morally straight" and "clean."

Obviously, the Scout Oath and Law do not expressly mention sexuality or sexual orientation. And the terms "morally straight" and "clean" are by no means self-defining. Different people would attribute to those terms very different meanings. For example, some people may believe that engaging in homosexual conduct is not at odds with being "morally straight" and "clean." And others may believe that engaging in homosexual conduct is contrary to being "morally straight" and "clean." The Boy Scouts says it falls within the latter category.

The New Jersey Supreme Court analyzed the Boy Scouts' beliefs and found that the "exclusion of members solely on the basis of their sexual orientation is inconsistent with Boy Scouts' commitment to a diverse and 'representative' membership... [and] contradicts Boy Scouts' overarching objective to reach 'all eligible youth.'" The court concluded that the exclusion of members like Dale "appears antithetical to the organization's goals and philosophy." But our cases reject this sort of inquiry; it is not the role of the courts to reject a group's expressed values because they disagree with those values or find them internally inconsistent. See *Thomas* v. *Review Bd. of Indiana Employment Security Div.,* ("[R]eligious beliefs need not be acceptable, logical, consistent, or comprehensible to others to merit First Amendment protection").

The Boy Scouts asserts that it "teach[es] that homosexual conduct is not morally straight," Brief for Petitioners 39, and that it does "not want to promote homosexual conduct as a legitimate form of behavior," Reply Brief for Petitioners 5. We accept the Boy Scouts' assertion. We need not inquire further to determine the nature of the Boy Scouts' expression with respect to homosexuality. But because the record before us contains written evidence of the Boy Scouts' viewpoint, we look to it as instructive, if only on the question of the sincerity of the professed beliefs.

A 1978 position statement to the Boy Scouts' Executive Committee, signed by Downing B. Jenks, the President of the Boy Scouts, and Harvey L. Price, the Chief

Scout Executive, expresses the Boy Scouts' "official position" with regard to "homosexuality and Scouting":

> "Q. May an individual who openly declares himself to be a homosexual be a volunteer Scout leader?

> "A. No. The Boy Scouts of America is a private, membership organization and leadership therein is a privilege and not a right. We do not believe that homosexuality and leadership in Scouting are appropriate. We will continue to select only those who in our judgment meet our standards and qualifications for leadership."

Thus, at least as of 1978—the year James Dale entered Scouting—the official position of the Boy Scouts was that avowed homosexuals were not to be Scout leaders. A position statement promulgated by the Boy Scouts in 1991 (after Dale's membership was revoked but before this litigation was filed) also supports its current view:

> "We believe that homosexual conduct is inconsistent with the requirement in the Scout Oath that a Scout be morally straight and in the Scout Law that a Scout be clean in word and deed, and that homosexuals do not provide a desirable role model for Scouts."

This position statement was redrafted numerous times but its core message remained consistent. For example, a 1993 position statement, the most recent in the record, reads, in part:

> "The Boy Scouts of America has always reflected the expectations that Scouting families have had for the organization. We do not believe that homosexuals provide a role model consistent with these expectations. Accordingly, we do not allow for the registration of avowed homosexuals as members or as leaders of the BSA."

The Boy Scouts publicly expressed its views with respect to homosexual conduct by its assertions in prior litigation. For example, throughout a California case with similar facts filed in the early 1980's, the Boy Scouts consistently asserted the same position with respect to homosexuality that it asserts today. We cannot doubt that the Boy Scouts sincerely holds this view.

We must then determine whether Dale's presence as an assistant scoutmaster would significantly burden the Boy Scouts' desire to not "promote homosexual conduct as a legitimate form of behavior." Reply Brief for Petitioners 5. As we give deference to an association' s assertions regarding the nature of its expression, we must also give deference to an association's view of what would impair its expression. That is not to say that an expressive association can erect a shield against anti-discrimination laws simply by asserting that mere acceptance of a member from a particular group would impair its message. But here Dale, by his own admission, is one of a group of gay

Scouts who have "become leaders in their community and are open and honest about their sexual orientation." Dale was the copresident of a gay and lesbian organization at college and remains a gay rights activist. Dale's presence in the Boy Scouts would, at the very least, force the organization to send a message, both to the youth members and the world, that the Boy Scouts accepts homosexual conduct as a legitimate form of behavior.

Hurley is illustrative on this point. There we considered whether the application of Massachusetts' public accommodations law to require the organizers of a private St. Patrick's Day parade to include among the marchers an Irish-American gay, lesbian, and bisexual group, GLIB, violated the parade organizers' First Amendment rights. We noted that the parade organizers did not wish to exclude the GLIB members because of their sexual orientations, but because they wanted to march behind a GLIB banner.*** As the presence of GLIB in Boston's St. Patrick's Day parade would have interfered with the parade organizers' choice not to propound a particular point of view, the presence of Dale as an assistant scoutmaster would just as surely interfere with the Boy Scout's choice not to propound a point of view contrary to its beliefs.

The New Jersey Supreme Court determined that the Boy Scouts' ability to disseminate its message was not significantly affected by the forced inclusion of Dale as an assistant scoutmaster because of the following findings: "Boy Scout members do not associate for the purpose of disseminating the belief that homosexuality is immoral; Boy Scouts discourages its leaders from disseminating *any* views on sexual issues; and Boy Scouts includes sponsors and members who subscribe to different views in respect of homosexuality." We disagree with the New Jersey Supreme Court's conclusion drawn from these findings.

First, associations do not have to associate for the "purpose" of disseminating a certain message in order to be entitled to the protections of the First Amendment. An association must merely engage in expressive activity that could be impaired in order to be entitled to protection. For example, the purpose of the St. Patrick's Day parade in *Hurley* was not to espouse any views about sexual orientation, but we held that the parade organizers had a right to exclude certain participants nonetheless.

Second, even if the Boy Scouts discourages Scout leaders from disseminating views on sexual issues—a fact that the Boy Scouts disputes with contrary evidence—the First Amendment protects the Boy Scouts' method of expression. If the Boy Scouts wishes Scout leaders to avoid questions of sexuality and teach only by example, this fact does not negate the sincerity of its belief discussed above.

Third, the First Amendment simply does not require that every member of a group agree on every issue in order for the group's policy to be "expressive association." The Boy Scouts takes an official position with respect to homosexual conduct, and that is sufficient for First Amendment purposes. In this same vein, Dale makes much of the claim that the Boy Scouts does not revoke the membership of heterosexual Scout leaders that openly disagree with the Boy Scouts' policy on sexual orientation. But if this is true, it is irrelevant. The presence of an avowed homosexual and gay rights activist in an assistant scoutmaster's uniform sends a distinctly different message from the presence of a heterosexual assistant scoutmaster who is on record as disagreeing with Boy Scouts policy. The Boy Scouts has a First Amendment right to choose to send one message but not the other. The fact that the organization does not trumpet its views from the housetops, or that it tolerates dissent within its ranks, does not mean that its views receive no First Amendment protection.

Having determined that the Boy Scouts is an expressive association and that the forced inclusion of Dale would significantly affect its expression, we inquire whether the application of New Jersey's public accommodations law to require that the Boy Scouts accept Dale as an assistant scoutmaster runs afoul of the Scouts' freedom of expressive association. We conclude that it does.

State public accommodations laws were originally enacted to prevent discrimination in traditional places of public accommodation—like inns and trains. Over time, the public accommodations laws have expanded to cover more places.[1] New Jersey' s statutory definition of "' [a] place of public accommodation'" is extremely broad. In this case, the New Jersey Supreme Court went a step further and applied its public accommodations law to a private entity without even attempting to tie the term "place" to a physical location.[2] As the definition of "public accommodation" has expanded from clearly commercial entities, such as restaurants, bars, and hotels, to membership organizations such as the Boy Scouts, the potential for conflict between state public accommodations laws and the First Amendment rights of organizations has increased.

***

Dale contends that we should apply the intermediate standard of review enunciated in *United States* v. *O' Brien,* 391 U. S. 367 (1968), to evaluate the competing interests. There the Court enunciated a four-part test for review of a governmental regulation that has only an incidental effect on protected speech—in that case the symbolic burning of a draft card. A law prohibiting the destruction of draft cards only incidentally affects the free speech rights of those who happen to use a violation of that law as a symbol of protest. But New Jersey' s public accommodations law directly and immediately

---

1. Public accommodations laws have also broadened in scope to cover more groups; they have expanded beyond those groups that have been given heightened equal protection scrutiny under our cases. Some municipal ordinances have even expanded to cover criteria such as prior criminal record, prior psychiatric treatment, military status, personal appearance, source of income, place of residence, and political ideology.

2. Four State Supreme Courts and one United States Court of Appeals have ruled that the Boy Scouts is not a place of public accommodation. No federal appellate court or state supreme court—except the New Jersey Supreme Court in this case—has reached a contrary result.

affects associational rights, in this case associational rights that enjoy First Amendment protection. Thus, *O' Brien* is inapplicable.

In *Hurley,* we applied traditional First Amendment analysis to hold that the application of the Massachusetts public accommodations law to a parade violated the First Amendment rights of the parade organizers. Although we did not explicitly deem the parade in *Hurley* an expressive association, the analysis we applied there is similar to the analysis we apply here. We have already concluded that a state requirement that the Boy Scouts retain Dale as an assistant scoutmaster would significantly burden the organization's right to oppose or disfavor homosexual conduct. The state interests embodied in New Jersey's public accommodations law do not justify such a severe intrusion on the Boy Scouts' rights to freedom of expressive association. That being the case, we hold that the First Amendment prohibits the State from imposing such a requirement through the application of its public accommodations law.[3]

We are not, as we must not be, guided by our views of whether the Boy Scouts' teachings with respect to homosexual conduct are right or wrong; public or judicial disapproval of a tenet of an organization's expression does not justify the State's effort to compel the organization to accept members where such acceptance would derogate from the organization's expressive message. "While the law is free to promote all sorts of conduct in place of harmful behavior, it is not free to interfere with speech for no better reason than promoting an approved message or discouraging a disfavored one, however enlightened either purpose may strike the government." *Hurley,* 515 U. S., at 579.

The judgment of the New Jersey Supreme Court is reversed, and the cause remanded for further proceedings not inconsistent with this opinion.

It is so ordered.

JUSTICE STEVENS, with whom JUSTICE SOUTER, JUSTICE GINSBURG and JUSTICE BREYER join, dissenting.

The majority holds that New Jersey law violates BSA's right to associate and its right to free speech. But that law does not "impos[e] any serious burdens" on BSA's "collective effort on behalf of [its] shared goals," *Roberts* v. *United States Jaycees,* 468

---

3. We anticipated this result in *Hurley* when we illustrated the reasons for our holding in that case by likening the parade to a private membership organization. 515 U. S., at 580. We stated: "Assuming the parade to be large enough and a source of benefits (apart from its expression) that would generally justify a mandated access provision, GLIB could nonetheless be refused admission as an expressive contingent with its own message just as readily as a private club could exclude an applicant whose manifest views were at odds with a position taken by the club's existing members." *Id.,* at 580–581.

U. S. 609, 622 (1984), nor does it force BSA to communicate any message that it does not wish to endorse. New Jersey's law, therefore, abridges no constitutional right of the Boy Scouts.

I
***

BSA's mission statement reads as follows: "It is the mission of the Boy Scouts of America to serve others by helping to instill values in young people and, in other ways, to prepare them to make ethical choices over their lifetime in achieving their full potential." Its federal charter declares its purpose is "to promote, through organization, and cooperation with other agencies, the ability of boys to do things for themselves and others, to train them in scoutcraft, and to teach them patriotism, courage, self-reliance, and kindred values, using the methods which were in common use by Boy Scouts on June 15, 1916." In particular, the group emphasizes that "[n]either the charter nor the bylaws of the Boy Scouts of America permits the exclusion of any boy...."

To bolster its claim that its shared goals include teaching that homosexuality is wrong, BSA directs our attention to two terms[,] the phrase "morally straight," in the Oath, [and] the word "clean," which appears in a list of 12 characteristics comprising the Scout Law.

The Boy Scout Handbook defines "morally straight," as such:
> [G]uide your life with honesty, purity, and justice. Respect and defend the rights of all people. Your relationships with others should be honest and open. Be clean in your speech and actions, and faithful in your religious beliefs. The values you follow as a Scout will help you become virtuous and self-reliant.

As for the term "clean," the Boy Scout Handbook offers the following:
> A Scout is CLEAN. A Scout keeps his body and mind fit and clean. He chooses the company of those who live by these same ideals. He helps keep his home and community clean. You never need to be ashamed of dirt that will wash off.*** There's another kind of dirt that won't come off by washing. It is the kind that shows up in foul language and harmful thoughts. Swear words, profanity, and dirty stories are weapons that ridicule other people and hurt their feelings. A Scout knows there is no kindness or honor in such mean-spirited behavior. He avoids it in his own words and deeds. He defends those who are targets of insults.

It is plain as the light of day that neither one of these principles—"morally straight" and "clean"—says the slightest thing about homosexuality. Indeed, neither term in the Boy Scouts' Law and Oath expresses any position whatsoever on sexual matters.

BSA's published guidance on that topic underscores this point. *** More specifically, BSA has set forth a number of rules for Scoutmasters when these types of issues come up:

You may have boys asking you for information or advice about sexual matters.... How should you handle such matters?

Rule number 1: *You do not undertake to instruct Scouts, in any formalized manner, in the subject of sex and family life. The reasons are that it is not construed to be Scouting's proper area*, and that you are probably not well qualified to do this.

(Emphasis added.)

II

The Court seeks to fill the void by pointing to a statement of "policies and procedures relating to homosexuality and Scouting" signed by BSA's President and Chief Scout Executive in 1978 and addressed to the members of the Executive Committee of the national organization. The letter says that the BSA does "not believe that homosexuality and leadership in Scouting are appropriate." But when the *entire* 1978 letter is read, BSA's position is far more equivocal:

4. Q. May an individual who openly declares himself to be a homosexual be employed by the Boy Scouts of America as a professional or non-professional?

A. Boy Scouts of America does not knowingly employ homosexuals as professionals or non-professionals. We are unaware of any present laws which would prohibit this policy.

5. Q. Should a professional or non-professional individual who openly declares himself to be a homosexual be terminated?

A. Yes, *in the absence of any law to the contrary.***In the event that such a law was applicable, it would be necessary for the Boy Scouts of America to obey it, in this case as in Paragraph 4 above.* It is our position, however, that homosexuality and professional or non-professional employment in Scouting are not appropriate.

(Emphasis added.)

[A]t most this letter simply adopts an exclusionary membership policy. But simply adopting such a policy has never been considered sufficient, by itself, to prevail on a right to associate claim. Second, the 1978 policy [itself] was never publicly expressed— unlike, for example, the Scout's duty to be "obedient." It was an internal memorandum, never circulated beyond the few members of BSA's Executive Committee. It remained, in effect, a secret Boy Scouts policy. [T]he 1978 policy appears to be no more than a private statement of a few BSA executives that the organization wishes to exclude gays—and that wish has nothing to do with any expression BSA actually engages in.

The majority also relies on four other policy statements that were issued between 1991 and 1993. All of them were written and issued *after* BSA revoked Dale's membership. Accordingly, they have little, if any, relevance to the legal question before this Court.*** In any event, they do not bolster BSA' s claim.*** BSA never took any clear and unequivocal position on homosexuality. Though the 1991 and 1992 policies state one interpretation of "morally straight" and "clean," the group's published definitions appearing in the Boy Scout and Scoutmaster Handbooks take quite another view. And BSA's broad religious tolerance combined with its declaration that sexual matters are not its "proper area" render its views on the issue equivocal at best and incoherent at worst.   [A]t most the 1991 and 1992 statements declare only that BSA believed "homosexual *conduct* is inconsistent with the requirement in the Scout Oath that a Scout be morally straight and in the Scout Law that a Scout be clean in word and deed." (Emphasis added.) But New Jersey's law prohibits discrimination on the basis of sexual *orientatio*n. And when Dale was expelled from the Boy Scouts, BSA said it did so because of his sexual orientation, not because of his sexual conduct.[4]

III

Several principles are made perfectly clear by *Jaycees* and *Rotary Club*. First, to prevail on a claim of expressive association in the face of a State's anti-discrimination law, it is not enough simply to engage in *some kind* of expressive activity. Both the Jaycees and the Rotary Club engaged in expressive activity protected by the First Amendment, yet that fact was not dispositive. Second, it is not enough to adopt an openly avowed exclusionary membership policy. Both the Jaycees and the Rotary Club did that as well. Third, it is not sufficient merely to articulate *some* connection between the group's expressive activities and its exclusionary policy.

Rather, in *Jaycees*, we asked whether Minnesota's Human Rights Law requiring the admission of women "impose[d] any *serious burden*s" on the group's "collective effort on behalf of [its] *shared goals*."***The relevant question is whether the mere inclusion of the person at issue would "impose any serious burden," "affect in any significant way," or be "a substantial restraint upon" the organization's "shared goals," "basic goals," or "collective effort to foster beliefs." Accordingly, it is necessary to examine what, exactly, are BSA's shared goals and the degree to which its expressive activities would be burdened, affected, or restrained by including homosexuals.

The evidence before this Court makes it exceptionally clear that BSA has, at most, simply adopted an exclusionary membership policy and has no shared goal of disapproving of homosexuality.*** There is simply no evidence that BSA otherwise teaches anything in this area, or that it instructs Scouts on matters involving homosexuality in ways not conveyed in the Boy Scout or Scoutmaster Handbooks. In short, Boy Scouts of America is simply silent on homosexuality. There is no shared goal or collective effort to foster a belief about homosexuality at all—let alone one that is significantly burdened by admitting homosexuals.

---

4. At oral argument, BSA's counsel was asked: "[W]hat if someone is homosexual in the sense of having a sexual orientation in that direction but does not engage in any homosexual conduct?" Counsel answered: "[I]f that person also were to take the view that the reason they didn't engage in that conduct [was because] it would be morally wrong . . . that person would not be excluded." Tr. of Oral Arg. 8.

IV

The majority pretermits this entire analysis. It finds that BSA in fact "teach[es] that homosexual conduct is not morally straight." This conclusion, remarkably, rests entirely on statements in BSA's briefs. Moreover, the majority insists that we must "give deference to an association's assertions regarding the nature of its expression" and "we must also give deference to an association's view of what would impair its expression." So long as the record "contains written evidence" to support a group's bare assertion, "[w]e need not inquire further."***

[N]othing in our cases calls for this Court to do any such thing. An organization can adopt the message of its choice, and it is not this Court's place to disagree with it. But we must inquire whether the group is, in fact, expressing a message (whatever it may be) and whether that message (if one is expressed) is significantly affected by a State's anti-discrimination law.***There is, of course, a valid concern that a court's independent review may run the risk of paying too little heed to an organization's sincerely held views. ***In this case, no such concern is warranted. It is entirely clear that BSA in fact expresses no clear, unequivocal message burdened by New Jersey's law.

V

Even if BSA's right to associate argument fails, it nonetheless might have a First Amendment right to refrain from including debate and dialogue about homosexuality as part of its mission to instill values in Scouts. It can, for example, advise Scouts who are entering adulthood and have questions about sex to talk "with your parents, religious leaders, teachers, or Scoutmaster," and, in turn, it can direct Scoutmasters who are asked such questions "not undertake to instruct Scouts, in any formalized manner, in the subject of sex and family life" because "it is not construed to be Scouting's proper area." ***

The majority, though, does not rest its conclusion on the claim that Dale will use his position as a bully pulpit. Rather, it contends that Dale's mere presence among the Boy Scouts will itself force the group to convey a message about homosexuality—even if Dale has no intention of doing so. The majority holds that "[t]he presence of an avowed homosexual and gay rights activist in an assistant scoutmaster's uniform sends a distinc[t] ...message," and, accordingly, BSA is entitled to exclude that message.

The majority's argument relies exclusively on *Hurley* v. *Irish-American Gay, Lesbian and Bisexual Group of Boston, Inc.****Dale's inclusion in the Boy Scouts is nothing like the case in *Hurley*. His participation sends no cognizable message to the Scouts or to the world. Unlike GLIB, Dale did not carry a banner or a sign; he did not distribute any fact sheet; and he expressed no intent to send any message. If there is any kind of message being sent, then, it is by the mere act of joining the Boy

Scouts. Such an act does not constitute an instance of symbolic speech under the First Amendment.[5]

Furthermore, it is not likely that BSA would be understood to send any message, either to Scouts or to the world, simply by admitting someone as a member. In 1992 over one million adults were active BSA members. The notion that an organization of that size and enormous prestige implicitly endorses the views that each of those adults may express in a non-Scouting context is simply mind boggling.***

VI

Unfavorable opinions about homosexuals "have ancient roots." *Bowers* v. *Hardwick*, 478 U. S. 186, 192 (1986). Like equally atavistic opinions about certain racial groups, those roots have been nourished by sectarian doctrine. That such prejudices are still prevalent and that they have caused serious and tangible harm to countless members of the class New Jersey seeks to protect are established matters of fact that neither the Boy Scouts nor the Court disputes. That harm can only be aggravated by the creation of a constitutional shield for a policy that is itself the product of a habitual way of thinking about strangers.*** If we would guide by the light of reason, we must let our minds be bold.

I respectfully dissent.

JUSTICE SOUTER, with whom JUSTICE GINSBURG and JUSTICE BREYER join, dissenting.

I join JUSTICE STEVENS's dissent but add this further word on the significance of Part VI of his opinion.***The right of expressive association does not, of course, turn on the popularity of the views advanced by a group that claims protection. Whether the group appears to this Court to be in the vanguard or rearguard of social thinking is irrelevant to the group's rights. I conclude that BSA has not made out an expressive association claim, therefore, not because of what BSA may espouse, but because of its failure to make sexual orientation the subject of any unequivocal advocacy, using the channels it customarily employs to state its message. ***If, on the other hand, an expressive association claim has met the conditions JUSTICE STEVENS describes as

---

5. The majority might have argued (but it did not) that Dale had become so publicly and pervasively identified with a position advocating the moral legitimacy of homosexuality (as opposed to just being an individual who openly stated he is gay) that his leadership position in BSA would necessarily amount to using the organization as a conduit for publicizing his position. But as already noted, when BSA expelled Dale, it had nothing to go on beyond the one newspaper article quoted above, and one newspaper article does not convert Dale into a public symbol for a message. BSA simply has not provided a record that establishes the factual premise for this argument.

necessary, there may well be circumstances in which the antidiscrimination law must yield.

F.   Coerced Expression and Freedom Not to Speak

Casebook, p. 628
Add as *[Ed. Note] to caption for *Abood v. Detroit Board of Education*

* [**Ed. Note:** But see *Glickman v. Wileman Bros. & Elliott, Inc.*, 521 U.S. 457 (1997) (*infra*, pp. 80-88 of this Supplement) (agricultural producer compelled to render financial support to commercial advertisements in order lawfully to produce, process, and market agricultural products promoted by the advertisements, fails to state a first amendment claim to resist the Secretary's assessment of the pro rata fee — *Abood* compared and distinguished by the Court).]

Casebook, p. 636
Add at beginning of footnote 138

This question has now been addressed by the court in the following case.

———

BOARD OF REGENTS OF THE UNIVERSITY OF WISCONSIN v. SOUTHWORTH
2000 WL 293217 (March 22, 2000)

JUSTICE KENNEDY delivered the opinion of the Court.

Respondents are a group of students at the University of Wisconsin. They brought a First Amendment challenge to a mandatory student activity fee imposed by petitioner Board of Regents of the University of Wisconsin and used in part by the University to support student organizations engaging in political or ideological speech. Respondents object to the speech and expression of some of the student organizations. Relying upon our precedents which protect members of unions and bar associations from being required to pay fees used for speech the members find objectionable, both the District Court and the Court of Appeals invalidated the University's student fee program.

We reverse. The First Amendment permits a public university to charge its students an activity fee used to fund a program to facilitate extracurricular student speech if the program is viewpoint neutral. We do not sustain, however, the student referendum mechanism of the University's program, which appears to permit the exaction of fees in violation of the viewpoint neutrality principle. As to that aspect of the program, we remand for further proceedings.

I

[S]ince its founding the University has required full-time students enrolled at its Madison campus to pay a nonrefundable activity fee. For the 1995-1996 academic year, when this suit was commenced, the activity fee amounted to $331.50 per year.***The allocable portion of the fee supports extracurricular endeavors pursued by the University's registered student organizations or RSO's. To qualify for RSO status students must organize as a not-for-profit group, limit membership primarily to students, and agree to undertake activities related to student life on campus. As one would expect, the expressive activities undertaken by RSO's are diverse in range and content, from displaying posters and circulating newsletters throughout the campus, to hosting campus debates and guest speakers, and to what can best be described as political lobbying.

RSO's obtain funding support on a reimbursement basis by submitting receipts or invoices to the University. Guidelines identify expenses appropriate for reimbursement. Permitted expenditures include, in the main, costs for printing, postage, office supplies, and use of University facilities and equipment. Materials printed with student fees must contain a disclaimer that the views expressed are not those of the [Associated Students of Madison]. In March 1996, respondents, each of whom attended or still attend the University's Madison campus, filed suit in the United States District Court for the Western District of Wisconsin against members of the board of regents.***On cross-motions for summary judgment, the District Court ruled in their favor, declaring the University's segregated fee program invalid under *Abood v. Detroit Bd. of Ed.*, 431 U.S. 209 (1977), and *Keller v. State Bar of Cal.*, 496 U.S. 1 (1990).

II

We must begin by recognizing that the complaining students are being required to pay fees which are subsidies for speech they find objectionable, even offensive.***The proposition that students who attend the University cannot be required to pay subsidies for the speech of other students without some First Amendment protection follows from the *Abood* and *Keller* cases. Students enroll in public universities to seek fulfillment of their personal aspirations and of their own potential. If the University conditions the opportunity to receive a college education, an opportunity comparable in importance to joining a labor union or bar association, on an agreement to support objectionable, extracurricular expression by other students, the rights acknowledged in Abood and Keller become implicated. It infringes on the speech and beliefs of the individual to be required, by this mandatory student activity fee program, to pay subsidies for the objectionable speech of others without any recognition of the State's corresponding duty to him or her. Yet recognition must be given as well to the important and substantial purposes of the University, which seeks to facilitate a wide range of speech.

In *Abood* and *Keller* the constitutional rule took the form of limiting the required subsidy to speech germane to the purposes of the union or bar association. The standard of germane speech as applied to student speech at a university is unworkable, however, and gives insufficient protection both to the objecting students and to the University program itself. Even in the context of a labor union, whose functions are, or so we might have thought, well known and understood by the law and the courts after a long history of government regulation and judicial involvement, we have encountered difficulties in deciding what is germane and what is not. The difficulty manifested itself in our decision in *Lehnert v. Ferris Faculty Assn.*, 500 U.S. 507 (1991), where different members of the Court reached varying conclusions regarding what expressive activity was or was not germane to the mission of the association. If it is difficult to define germane speech with ease or precision where a union or bar association is the party, the standard becomes all the more unmanageable in the public university setting, particularly where the State undertakes to stimulate the whole universe of speech and ideas.

Just as the vast extent of permitted expression makes the test of germane speech inappropriate for intervention, so too does it underscore the high potential for intrusion on the First Amendment rights of the objecting students. It is all but inevitable that the fees will result in subsidies to speech which some students find objectionable and offensive to their personal beliefs. If the standard of germane speech is inapplicable, then, it might be argued the remedy is to allow each student to list those causes which he or she will or will not support. If a university decided that its students' First Amendment interests were better protected by some type of optional or refund system it would be free to do so. We decline to impose a system of that sort as a constitutional requirement, however. The restriction could be so disruptive and expensive that the program to support extracurricular speech would be ineffective. The First Amendment does not require the University to put the program at risk.

The University may determine that its mission is well served if students have the means to engage in dynamic discussions of philosophical, religious, scientific, social, and political subjects in their extracurricular campus life outside the lecture hall. If the University reaches this conclusion, it is entitled to impose a mandatory fee to sustain an open dialogue to these ends.

The University must provide some protection to its students' First Amendment interests, however. The proper measure, and the principal standard of protection for objecting students, we conclude, is the requirement of viewpoint neutrality in the allocation of funding support. Viewpoint neutrality was the obligation to which we gave substance in *Rosenberger v. Rector and Visitors of Univ. of Va.*, 515 U.S. 819 (1995).***While *Rosenberger* was concerned with the rights a student has to use an extracurricular speech program already in place, today's case considers the antecedent question, acknowledged but unresolved in *Rosenberger*: whether a public university may require its students to pay a fee which creates the mechanism for the extracurricular speech in the first instance. When a university requires its students to pay fees to support the extracurricular speech of other students, all in the interest of open discussion, it may not prefer some viewpoints to others. There is symmetry then in our holding here and in *Rosenberger*: Viewpoint neutrality is the justification for requiring the student to pay the fee in the first instance and for ensuring the integrity of the program's operation once the funds have been collected. We conclude that the University of Wisconsin may sustain the extracurricular dimensions of its programs by using mandatory student fees with viewpoint neutrality as the operational principle.***If the rule of viewpoint neutrality is respected, our holding affords the University latitude to adjust its extracurricular student speech program to accommodate these advances and opportunities.

Our decision ought not to be taken to imply that in other instances the University, its agents or employees, or--of particular importance--its faculty, are subject to the First Amendment analysis which controls in this case. Where the University speaks, either in its own name through its regents or officers, or in myriad other ways through its diverse faculties, the analysis likely would be altogether different.***In the instant case, the speech is not that of the University or its agents. It is not, furthermore, speech by an instructor or a professor in the academic context, where principles applicable to government speech would have to be considered. Cf.. Rosenberger at 833 (discussing the discretion universities possess in deciding matters relating to their educational mission).

III

It remains to discuss the referendum aspect of the University's program. While the record is not well developed on the point, it appears that by majority vote of the student body a given RSO may be funded or defunded. It is unclear to us what protection, if any, there is for viewpoint neutrality in this part of the process. To the extent the referendum substitutes majority determinations for viewpoint neutrality it would undermine the constitutional protection the program requires. The whole theory of viewpoint neutrality is that minority views are treated with the same respect as are majority views. Access to a public forum, for instance, does not depend upon majoritarian consent. That principle is controlling here. A remand is necessary and appropriate to resolve this point; and the case in all events must be reexamined in light of the principles we have discussed.

It is so ordered.

JUSTICE SOUTER, with whom JUSTICE STEVENS AND JUSTICE BREYER join, concurring in the judgment.

The majority today validates the University's student activity fee after recognizing a new category of First Amendment interests and a new standard of viewpoint neutrality protection. I agree that the University's scheme is permissible, but do not believe that the Court should take the occasion to impose a cast-iron viewpoint neutrality requirement to uphold it.

***Our understanding of academic freedom has included not merely liberty from restraints on thought, expression, and association in the academy, but also the idea that universities and schools should have the freedom to make decisions about how and what to teach. In *Regents of Univ. of Mich. v. Ewing*, 474 U.S. (1985), we recognized these related conceptions: "Academic freedom thrives not only on the independent and uninhibited exchange of ideas among teachers and students, but also, and somewhat inconsistently, on autonomous decisionmaking by the academy itself." Some of the opinions in our books emphasize broad conceptions of academic freedom that if accepted by the Court might seem to clothe the University with an immunity to any challenge to regulations made or obligations imposed in the discharge of its educational mission......

[Even so] our cases on academic freedom thus far have dealt with more limited subjects, and do not compel the conclusion that the objecting university student is without a First Amendment claim here.[4] While we have spoken in terms of a wide protection for the academic freedom and autonomy that bars legislatures (and courts) from imposing conditions on the spectrum of subjects taught and viewpoints expressed in college teaching (as the majority recognizes), we have never held that universities lie entirely beyond the reach of students' First Amendment rights. Thus our prior cases do not go so far as to control the result in this one, and going beyond those cases would be out of order, simply because the University has not litigated on grounds of academic freedom. As to that freedom and university autonomy, then, it is enough to say that protecting a university's discretion to shape its educational mission may prove to be an important consideration in First Amendment analysis of objections to student fees.

G.   Equalizing Freedom of Speech by Leveling Expenditures and Contributions — Regulating the Uses of Money and Speech

Casebook, p. 672
Add as new case following NOTE

COLORADO REPUBLICAN FEDERAL CAMPAIGN COMMITTEE v.
FEDERAL ELECTION COMMISSION
518 U.S. 604 (1996)

JUSTICE BREYER announced the judgment of the Court and delivered an opinion, in which JUSTICE O'CONNOR and JUSTICE SOUTER join.

---

4. Our university cases have dealt with restrictions imposed from outside the academy on individual teachers' speech or associations, and cases dealing with the right of teaching institutions to limit expressive freedom of students have been confined to high schools [citations omitted], whose students and their schools' relation to them are different and at least arguably distinguishable from their counterparts in college education.

In April 1986, before the Colorado Republican Party had selected its senatorial candidate for the fall's election, that Party's Federal Campaign Committee bought radio advertisements attacking Timothy Wirth, the Democratic Party's likely candidate. The Federal Election Commission (FEC) charged that this "expenditure" exceeded the dollar limits that a provision of the Federal Election Campaign Act of 1971 (FECA) imposes upon political party "expenditure[s] in connection with" a "general election campaign" for congressional office. This case focuses upon the constitutionality of those limits as applied to this case. We conclude that the First Amendment prohibits the application of this provision to the kind of expenditure at issue here — an expenditure that the political party has made independently, without coordination with any candidate.

I

To understand the issues and our holding, one must begin with FECA as it emerged from Congress in 1974. ***

Most of the provisions this Court found unconstitutional imposed expenditure limits. Those provisions limited candidates' rights to spend their own money, limited a candidate's campaign expenditures, limited the right of individuals to make "independent" expenditures (not coordinated with the candidate or candidate's campaign), and similarly limited the right of political committees to make "independent" expenditures [*Federal Election Comm'n v. National Conservative Political Action Comm.*, 470 U.S. 480, 497 (1985)]. The provisions that the Court found constitutional mostly imposed contribution limits — limits that apply both when an individual or political committee contributes money directly to a candidate and also when they indirectly contribute by making expenditures that they coordinate with the candidate. See *Buckley*, [424 U.S.] at 23-36. See also *California Medical Assn. [v. Federal Election Comm'n*, 453 U.S.], at 193-199 (limits on contributions to political committees). Consequently, for present purposes, the Act now prohibits individuals and political committees from making direct, or indirect, contributions that exceed the [specified] limits.

FECA also has a special provision, directly at issue in this case, that governs contributions and expenditures by political parties. § 441a(d).

*** After exempting political parties from the general contribution and expenditure limitations of the statute, the Party Expenditure Provision then imposes a substitute limitation upon party "expenditures" in a senatorial campaign equal to the greater of $20,000 or "2 cents multiplied by the voting age population of the State," § 441a(d)(3)(A)(I), adjusted for inflation since 1974, § 441a(c). The Provision permitted a political party in Colorado in 1986 to spend about $103,000 in connection with the general election campaign of a candidate for the United States Senate. ***

II

The summary judgment record indicates that the expenditure in question is what this Court in Buckley called an "independent" expenditure, not a "coordinated" expenditure that other provisions of FECA treat as a kind of campaign "contribution." The record describes how the expenditure was made. In a deposition, the Colorado Party's Chairman, Howard Callaway, pointed out that, at the time of the expenditure, the Party had not yet selected a senatorial nominee from among the three individuals vying for the nomination. He added that he arranged for the development of the script at his own initiative, that he, and no one else, approved it, that the only other politically relevant individuals who might have read it were the party's executive director and political director, and that all relevant discussions took place at meetings attended only by party staff. *** We can find no "genuine" issue of fact in this respect. And we therefore treat the expenditure, for constitutional purposes, as an "independent" expenditure, not an indirect campaign contribution.

So treated, the expenditure falls within the scope of the Court's precedents that extend First Amendment protection to independent expenditures. Beginning with *Buckley*, the Court's cases have found a "fundamental constitutional difference between money spent to advertise one's views independently of the candidate's campaign and money contributed to the candidate to be spent on his campaign." *** At the same time, reasonable contribution limits directly and materially advance the Government's interest in preventing exchanges of large financial contributions for political favors.

In contrast, the Court has said that restrictions on independent expenditures significantly impair the ability of individuals and groups to engage in direct political advocacy and "represent substantial *** restraints on the quantity and diversity of political speech." And at the same time, the Court has concluded that limitations on independent expenditures are less directly related to preventing corruption, since "[t]he absence of prearrangement and coordination of an expenditure with the candidate *** not only undermines the value of the expenditure to the candidate, but also alleviates the danger that expenditures will be given as a *quid pro quo* for improper commitments from the candidate."

Given these established principles, we do not see how a provision that limits a political party's independent expenditures can escape their controlling effect. A political party's independent expression not only reflects its members' views about the philosophical and governmental matters that bind them together, it also seeks to convince others to join those members in a practical democratic task, the task of creating a government that voters can instruct and hold responsible for subsequent success or failure. The independent expression of a political party's views is "core" First Amendment activity no less than is the independent expression of individuals, candidates, or other political committees. ***

We recognize that FECA permits individuals to contribute more money ($20,000) to a party than to a candidate ($1,000) or to other political committees ($5,000). We also recognize that FECA permits unregulated "soft money" contributions to a party for certain activities, such as electing candidates for state office, see § 431(8)(A)(I), or for voter registration and "get out the vote" drives, see § 431(8)(B)(xii). But the opportunity for corruption posed by these greater opportunities for contributions is, at best, attenuated. *** If anything, an independent expenditure made possible by a $20,000 donation, but controlled and directed by a party rather than the donor, would seem less likely to corrupt than the same (or a much larger) independent expenditure made directly by that donor. In any case, the constitutionally significant fact, present equally in both instances, is the lack of coordination between the candidate and the source of the expenditure. ***

The Government does not point to record evidence or legislative findings suggesting any special corruption problem in respect to independent party expenditures. *** In fact, rather than indicating a special fear of the corruptive influence of political parties, the legislative history demonstrates Congress' general desire to enhance what was seen as an important and legitimate role for political parties in American elections.

We therefore believe that this Court's prior case law controls the outcome here. We do not see how a Constitution that grants to individuals, candidates, and ordinary political committees the right to make unlimited independent expenditures could deny the same right to political parties.

IV

The Colorado Party and supporting *amici* have argued a broader question than we have decided, for they have claimed that, in the special case of political parties, the First Amendment forbids congressional efforts to limit coordinated expenditures as well as independent expenditures. Because the expenditure before us is an independent expenditure we have not reached this broader question in deciding the Party's "as applied" challenge. ***

[T]he judgment of the Court of Appeals is vacated, and the case is remanded for further proceedings.

JUSTICE KENNEDY, with whom THE CHIEF JUSTICE and JUSTICE SCALIA join, concurring in the judgment and dissenting in part.

In agreement with JUSTICE THOMAS, I would hold that the Colorado Republican Party, in its pleadings in the District Court and throughout this litigation, has preserved its claim that the constraints imposed by the Federal Election Campaign Act of 1971 (FECA), both on its face and as interpreted by the Federal Elections Commission (FEC), violate the First Amendment. ***

The central holding in *Buckley v. Valeo*, 424 U.S. 1 (1976), is that spending money on one's own speech must be permitted, and this is what political parties do when they make the expenditures FECA restricts. FECA calls spending of this nature a "contribution," § 441a(a)(7)(B)(I), and it is true that contributions can be restricted consistent with *Buckley*. *** In my view, we should not transplant the reasoning of cases upholding ordinary contribution limitations to a case involving FECA's restrictions on political party spending.

The First Amendment embodies a "profound national commitment to the principle that debate on public issues should be uninhibited, robust, and wide- open." *New York Times Co. v. Sullivan*, 376 U.S. 254, 270 (1964). Political parties have a unique role in serving this principle; they exist to advance their members' shared political beliefs. *** Having identified its members, however, a party can give effect to their views only by selecting and supporting candidates. A political party has its own traditions and principles that transcend the interests of individual candidates and campaigns; but in the context of particular elections, candidates are necessary to make the party's message known and effective, and vice versa.

It makes no sense, therefore, to ask, as FECA does, whether a party's spending is made "in cooperation, consultation, or concert with" its candidate. The answer in most cases will be yes, but that provides more, not less, justification for holding unconstitutional the statute's attempt to control this type of party spending, which bears little resemblance to the contributions discussed in *Buckley*. Party spending "in cooperation, consultation, or concert with" its candidates of necessity "communicate[s] the underlying basis for the support," i.e., the hope that he or she will be elected and will work to further the party's political agenda.

The problem is not just the absence of a basis in our First Amendment cases for treating the party's spending as contributions. The greater difficulty posed by the statute is its stifling effect on the ability of the party to do what it exists to do. ***

We have a constitutional tradition of political parties and their candidates engaging in joint First Amendment activity; we also have a practical identity of interests between the two entities during an election. Party spending "in cooperation, consultation, or concert with" a candidate therefore is indistinguishable in substance from expenditures by the candidate or his campaign committee. We held in *Buckley* that the First Amendment does not permit regulation of the latter, and it should not permit this regulation of the former. Congress may have authority, consistent with the First Amendment, to restrict undifferentiated political party contributions which satisfy the constitutional criteria we discussed in *Buckley*, but that type of regulation is not at issue here. ***

JUSTICE THOMAS, concurring in the judgment and dissenting in part, with whom THE CHIEF JUSTICE and JUSTICE SCALIA join in Parts I and III.

I agree that petitioners' rights under the First Amendment have been violated, but I think we should reach the facial challenge in this case in order to make clear the circumstances under which political parties may engage in political speech without running afoul of 2 U.S.C. § 441a(d)(3). In resolving that challenge, I would reject the framework established by *Buckley v. Valeo*, 424 U.S. 1 (1976), for analyzing the constitutionality of campaign finance laws and hold that § 441a(d)(3)'s limits on independent and coordinated expenditures fail strict scrutiny. But even under *Buckley*, § 441a(d)(3) cannot stand, because the anti-corruption rationale that we have relied upon in sustaining other campaign finance laws is inapplicable where political parties are the subject of such regulation. ***

II
A

[U]nlike the *Buckley* Court, I believe that contribution limits infringe as directly and as seriously upon freedom of political expression and association as do expenditure limits. The protections of the First Amendment do not depend upon so fine a line as that between spending money to support a candidate or group and giving money to the candidate or group to spend for the same purpose. In principle, people and groups give money to candidates and other groups for the same reason that they spend money in support of those candidates and groups: because they share social, economic, and political beliefs and seek to have those beliefs affect governmental policy. I think that the *Buckley* framework for analyzing the constitutionality of campaign finance laws is deeply flawed. Accordingly, I would not employ it, as JUSTICE BREYER and JUSTICE KENNEDY do.

B

Instead, I begin with the premise that there is no constitutionally significant difference between campaign contributions and expenditures: both forms of speech are central to the First Amendment. Curbs on protected speech, we have repeatedly said, must be strictly scrutinized. ***

The formula for strict scrutiny is, of course, well-established. It requires both a compelling governmental interest and legislative means narrowly tailored to serve that interest. In the context of campaign finance reform, the only governmental interest that we have accepted as compelling is the prevention of corruption or the appearance of corruption, see *Federal Election Commission v. NCPAC*, 470 U.S., at 496-497, and we have narrowly defined "corruption" as a "financial quid pro quo: dollars for political favors," id., at 497. ***

In my opinion, FECA's monetary caps fail the narrow tailoring test. Addressing the constitutionality of FECA's contribution caps, the *Buckley* appellants argued:

> "If a small minority of political contributions are given
> to secure appointments for the donors or some other
> quid pro quo, that cannot serve to justify prohibiting
> all large contributions, the vast majority of which are
> given not for any such purpose but to further the ex-
> pression of political views which the candidate and
> donor share. Where First Amendment rights are in-

> volved, a blunderbuss approach which prohibits mostly innocent speech cannot be held a means narrowly and precisely directed to the governmental interest in the small minority of contributions that are not innocent." ***

*** As one commentator has observed, "it must not be forgotten that a large number of contributions are made without any hope of specific gain: for the promotion of a program, because of enthusiasm for a candidate, or to promote what the giver vaguely conceives to be the national interest." L. Overacker, Money in Elections 192 (1974).

In contrast, federal bribery laws are designed to punish and deter the corrupt conduct the Government seeks to prevent under FECA, and disclosure laws work to make donors and donees accountable to the public for any questionable financial dealings in which they may engage. In light of these alternatives, wholesale limitations that cover contributions having nothing to do with bribery — but with speech central to the First Amendment — are not narrowly tailored. ***

III

Were I convinced that the *Buckley* framework rested on a principled distinction between contributions and expenditures, which I am not, I would nevertheless conclude that § 441a(d)(3)'s limits on political parties violate the First Amendment. *** [A]s long as the Court continues to permit Congress to subject individuals to limits on the amount they can give to parties, and those limits are uniform as to all donors, there is little risk that an individual donor could use a party as a conduit for bribing candidates.

*** And insofar as it appears that Congress did not actually enact § 441a(d)(3) in order to stop corruption by political parties "but rather for the constitutionally insufficient purpose of reducing what it saw as wasteful and excessive campaign spending," [*ante* citing *Buckley*] the statute's ceilings on coordinated expenditures are as unwarranted as the caps on independent expenditures.

In sum, there is only a minimal threat of "corruption," as we have understood that term, when a political party spends to support its candidate or to oppose his competitor, whether or not that expenditure is made in concert with the candidate. Parties and candidates have traditionally worked together to achieve their common goals, and when they engage in that work, there is no risk to the Republic. To the contrary, the danger to the Republic lies in Government suppression of such activity. ***

JUSTICE STEVENS, with whom JUSTICE GINSBURG joins, dissenting.

In my opinion, all money spent by a political party to secure the election of its candidate for the office of United States Senator should be considered a "contribution" to his or her campaign. I therefore disagree with the conclusion reached in Part III of the Court's opinion.

I am persuaded that three interests provide a constitutionally sufficient predicate for federal limits on spending by political parties. First, such limits serve the interest in avoiding both the appearance and the reality of a corrupt political process. A party shares a unique relationship with the candidate it sponsors because their political fates are inextricably linked. That interdependency creates a special danger that the party — or the persons who control the party — will abuse the influence it has over the candidate by virtue of its power to spend. The provisions at issue are appropriately aimed at reducing that threat. ***

Second, these restrictions supplement other spending limitations embodied in the Act, which are likewise designed to prevent corruption. Individuals and certain organizations are permitted to contribute up to $1,000 to a candidate. Since the same donors can give up to $5,000 to party committees, § 441a(a)(1)(C), if there were no limits on party spending, their contributions could be spent to benefit the candidate and thereby circumvent the $1,000 cap. We have recognized the legitimate interest in blocking similar attempts to undermine the policies of the Act. See *California Medical Assn. v. Federal Election Comm'n.*, 453 U.S. 182, 197-199 (1981) (plurality opinion) (approving ceiling on contributions to political action committees to prevent circumvention of limitations on individual contributions to candidates).

Finally, I believe the Government has an important interest in leveling the electoral playing field by constraining the cost of federal campaigns. As Justice White pointed out in his opinion in *Buckley*, "money is not always equivalent to or used for speech, even in the context of political campaigns." It is quite wrong to assume that the net effect of limits on contributions and expenditures — which tend to protect equal access to the political arena, to free candidates and their staffs from the interminable burden of fund-raising, and to diminish the importance of repetitive 30-second commercials — will be adverse to the interest in informed debate protected by the First Amendment.***

Accordingly, I would affirm the judgment of the Court of Appeals.

NOTE

In 1999, the Court granted certiorari in a case involving the constitutionality of a state limit on contributions to candidates for state political office, set at $1000 in 1996 (and adjusted for inflation, since then, to $1075). Although the contribution limit was set to equal the limit sustained (in 1976) in *Buckley*, counsel for a candidate and a PAC successfully argued before the United States Court of Appeals for the Eighth Circuit that the State of Missouri had not justified the burden imposed by the limit. *See Shrink Missouri Government PAC v. Nixon*, 161 F.3d 519 (8th Cir. 1998) (striking contribution limit). The Supreme Court reversed. *See Nixon v. Shrink Missouri Government PAC*, 528 U.S. ____ 120 S.Ct. 897 (2000) (opinion of the court by Souter, J., dissent by Justices Kennedy, Scalia, and Thomas.)

H.   Anonymity and the First Amendment

Casebook, p. 680
Add, as new material following QUESTION

ADDITIONAL QUESTIONS AND DEVELOPMENTS ON *McINTYRE* AND ANONYMOUS POLITICAL SPEECH

As noted by the Court in *McIntyre*, Ohio explained its statute forbidding the distribution of any anonymous publication "designed to promote the…election or defeat of [any] candidate … or to promote the adoption or defeat of any issue," as a proper measure to prevent "fraud" (— the "fraud," for example, of making knowingly false descriptions of the "tax proposal" voters were asked to approve on the referendum ballot). The statute was also defended as a proper measure to aid members of the public to assess the value of such information as is presented in the publication, by being informed of the identity and address of its author. As to this latter matter, however, where, as here, a "handbill [is] written by a private citizen who is not known to the recipient," it was the Court's view that requiring "the name and address of the author adds little, if anything to the reader's ability to evaluate the document's message." So this part of the state's justification was regarded as marginal, at best, and not sufficient to support the disclosure requirement.

In contrast, the Court declared (see casebook at p. 678) that the "state interest in preventing fraud stands on a different footing." Moreover, it agreed that "this interest carries special weight during election campaigns when false statements, if credited, may have serious adverse consequences for the public at large." But two countervailing observations were offered to defeat that justification.

First, the Court noted that Mrs. McIntyre's anonymous leaflets were not alleged to contain any such false or misleading misrepresentations. Second, and perhaps more to the point, it observed that Ohio's "Election Code includes detailed and specific prohibitions against making or disseminating false statements during political campaigns. *** Thus, Ohio's prohibition of anonymous leaflets plainly is not its principal weapon against fraud." In the Court's view, the ban on all anonymous leaflets was not a necessary measure, given the other means it had at hand. Of course, the implicit suggestion is that these other means do not present the same constitutional problems present in the ban on anonymous handbills per se. And on the face of things, that surely would seem to be right.

Still, before finally leaving this subject, perhaps one might want to consider such a statute concretely. They are not all of a piece. Here is one recently in litigation, subsequent to *McIntyre*, in the Washington Supreme Court.[156] Section 2.17.530 of the Revised Code of Washington, titled "False Political Advertising," provides:

> (1) It is a violation of this chapter for a person
> to sponsor with actual malice:
> (a) Political advertising that contains a false
> statement of material fact; ***
>
> (2) Any violation of this section shall be
>
> proven by clear and convincing evidence.

Is there some reason to think this provision may itself be vulnerable to First Amendment objection? — That despite the passing observations made to such laws, favorably, in *McIntyre,* that even this provision, such as it is, could be "void on its face?"[157]

––––––––

In the 1998 Term, the Supreme Court again addressed the effect of the First Amendment on balancing claims of anonymity (freedom from coerced speech) against state interests in the fair regulation of elections and public referenda ballot measures. It did so in the following case, discussing and applying *McIntyre* along the way.

––––––––

BUCKLEY V. AMERICAN CONSTITUTIONAL LAW FOUNDATION, INC.
119 S. Ct. 636 (1999)

––––––––––––––––––

156. *See State of Washington Public Disclosure Comm'n v. 119 Vote NO! Committee*, 135 Wash.2d 618 (1998) (acting on complaint of proponents of Initiative Proposal 119, a "Death With Dignity" ballot measure which would permit physician-assisted suicide under described circumstances and procedures, the state commission filed state court action seeking $10,000 fine plus costs, attorney fees, and treble damages from The 119 Vote NO! Committee, and from named individuals, responsible for authoring and distributing leaflets describing the measure as one to "let doctors end patients' lives without benefit of safeguards" and other statements in leaflet the Commission charged were false in fact and made with "malice"; the Committee and ACLU (as intervenor) moved to dismiss, challenging the "facial constitutionality" of § 2.17.530(a)).

157. Is this statute readily susceptible to an interpretation saving it from such a conclusion? Is there some basis to think that a statute drawn (and enforced) as this one, is significantly distinguishable from a common law provision merely enabling a private civil libel action to be brought by a candidate for office? Might one distinguish such laws as will reach false statements made with "malice" to mislead voters in some respect about a candidate for office, from such laws as will equally reach false statements of issues on the ballot? (*See* the case, and discussion therein, n. 156 *supra.*)

JUSTICE GINSBURG delivered the opinion of the Court.

Colorado allows its citizens to make laws directly through initiatives placed on election ballots. We review in this case three conditions Colorado places on the ballot-initiative process: (1) the requirement that initiative-petition circulators be registered voters; (2) the requirement that they wear an identification badge bearing the circulator's name; and (3) the requirement that proponents of an initiative report the names and addresses of all paid circulators and the amount paid to each circulator.

In *Meyer v. Grant*, 486 U.S. 414 (1988), we struck down Colorado's prohibition of payment for the circulation of ballot-initiative petitions.* *** We have also recognized, however, that "there must be a substantial regulation of elections if they are to be fair and honest and if some sort of order, rather than chaos, is to accompany the democratic processes." *Storer v. Brown*, 415 U.S. 724, 730 (1974). Taking careful account of these guides, the Court of Appeals for the Tenth Circuit upheld some of the

---

* **[Ed. Note**: The decision in *Meyer v. Grant* was unanimous. The Court held that the state had no credible evidence that *paid* petition circulators were per se more likely than *volunteer* circulators to falsify voter signatures, or mislead those asked to sign the petition re the nature of the proposed measure; moreover, the Court noted, alternative means of policing the integrity of such soliciting (e.g, felony penalties for falsification, disclosure requirements on the petition itself) were readily available to the states insofar as there was some bona fide concern.

Note, too, however, that the Court has not held that "the right of the people...to petition the Government for a redress of grievances" (as provided in the First Amendment) requires the national government — or any state government — to provide *any* kind of initiative-and-referendum mechanism by means of which laws may be made directly "by the people" rather than solely through some elected, legislative branch of government. (Indeed, far from the First Amendent or any other clause having been construed to guarantee some form of direct law-making power in "the people," as through an initiative-and-referendum mechanism, it has been vigorously argued that the Constitution forbids, rather than requires (or even permits) direct law-making "by the people" as such. *See*, e.g., *Pacific States Tel. Co. v. Oregon*, 223 U.S. 118 (1912) (argument that the provision in Art. I, § 4 ("The United States shall guarantee to every State in this Union a *Republican* Form of Government") distinguishes republican (representative) government from direct — or mere plebiscite — democracies, and therefore only laws made by representative bodies — not by the indiscriminate citizenry at large — should be accepted as valid by courts). *But see* William Mayton, *Direct Democracy, Federalism and the Guarantee Clause*, 2 The Green Bag 269 (1999) (Art. I, § 4 does not prohibit a state, rather, it guarantees to every state, a prerogative to provide means for direct law-making by the people of that state, insofar as a state may wish so to provide). *Query*: At the national level, were Congress to authorize some form of citizen initiative-and-referendum mechanism, to enable "the people" to make laws for the United States; would it be sustainable pursuant to the "necessary and proper" clause in Article I, § 8, or is it forbidden by Art. I, §1 ("All legislative Powers herein granted shall be vested in a Congress of the United States")?]

State's regulations, but found the three controls at issue excessively restrictive of political speech, and therefore declared them invalid. [We] now affirm that judgment. ***

II

As the Tenth Circuit recognized, *** States allowing ballot initiatives have considerable leeway to protect the integrity and reliability of the initiative process, as they have with respect to election processes generally. We have several times said no litmus-paper test will separate valid ballot-access provisions from invalid interactive speech restrictions.... But the First Amendment requires us to be vigilant in making those judgments, to guard against undue hindrances to political conversations and the exchange of ideas. We therefore detail why we are satisfied that, as in *Meyer*, the restrictions in question significantly inhibit communication with voters about proposed political change, and are not warranted by the state interests (administrative efficiency, fraud detection, informing voters) alleged to justify those restrictions.[12] Our judgment is informed by other means Colorado employs to accomplish its regulatory purposes.

III

When this case was before the District Court, registered voters in Colorado numbered approximately 1.9 million. At least 400,000 persons eligible to vote were not registered. Trial testimony complemented the statistical picture. Typical of the submissions, initiative proponent Paul Grant testified: "Trying to circulate an initiative petition, you're drawing on people who are not involved in normal partisan politics for the most part.... [L]arge numbers of these people, our natural support, are not registered voters."***

The Tenth Circuit reasoned that the registration requirement placed on Colorado's voter-eligible population produces a speech diminution of the very kind produced by the ban on paid circulators at issue in *Meyer*. We agree. The requirement that circulators be not merely voter eligible, but registered voters, decreases the pool of potential circulators as certainly as that pool is decreased by the prohibition of payment to circulators. Both provisions "limi[t] the number of voices who will convey [the initiative proponents'] message" and, consequently, cut down "the size of the audience [proponents] can reach." In this case, as in *Meyer*, the requirement "imposes a burden on political expression that the State has failed to justify."***

The State's dominant justification appears to be its strong interest in policing lawbreakers among petition circulators. Colorado seeks to ensure that circulators will be amenable to the Secretary of State's subpoena power, which in these matters does not extend beyond the State's borders. *** ACLF did not challenge Colorado's right

---

12. Our decision is entirely in keeping with the "now-settled approach" that state regulations "impos[ing] 'severe burdens' on speech ... [must] be narrowly tailored to serve a compelling state interest." See post, at 649 (THOMAS, J., concurring in judgment).

to require that all circulators be residents, a requirement that, the Tenth Circuit said, "more precisely achieved" the State's subpoena service objective. Colorado maintains that it is more difficult to determine who is a state resident than it is to determine who is a registered voter. The force of that argument is diminished, however, by the affidavit attesting to residence that each circulator must submit with each petition section.

In sum, assuming that a residence requirement would be upheld as a needful integrity-policing measure — a question we, like the Tenth Circuit, have no occasion to decide because the parties have not placed the matter of residence at issue — the added registration requirement is not warranted. That requirement cuts down the number of message carriers in the ballot-access arena without impelling cause.

IV

Colorado enacted the provision requiring initiative-petition circulators to wear identification badges in 1993, five years after our decision in *Meyer*. The Tenth Circuit held the badge requirement invalid insofar as it requires circulators to display their names. The Court of Appeals did not rule on the constitutionality of other elements of the badge provision, namely the "requirements that the badge disclose whether the circulator is paid or a volunteer, and if paid, by whom." Nor do we.

The badge requirement, a veteran ballot-initiative-petition organizer stated, "very definitely limited the number of people willing to work for us and the degree to which those who were willing to work would go out in public." Another witness told of harassment he personally experienced as circulator of a hemp initiative petition. He also testified to the reluctance of potential circulators to face the recrimination and retaliation that bearers of petitions on "volatile" issues sometimes encounter: "[W]ith their name on a badge, it makes them afraid." Other petition advocates similarly reported that "potential circulators were not willing to wear personal identification badges."

Colorado urges that the badge enables the public to identify, and the State to apprehend, petition circulators who engage in misconduct. Here again, the affidavit requirement, unsuccessfully challenged below, is responsive to the State's concern. This notarized submission, available to law enforcers, renders less needful the State's provision for personal names on identification badges. *** As the Tenth Circuit explained, the name badge requirement "forces circulators to reveal their identities at the same time they deliver their political message"; it operates when reaction to the circulator's message is immediate and "may be the most intense, emotional, and unreasoned." The affidavit, in contrast, does not expose the circulator to the risk of "heat of the moment" harassment. *** In sum, we conclude, as did the Court of Appeals, that Colorado's current badge requirement discourages participation in the petition circulation process by forcing name identification without sufficient cause.

V

Like the badge requirement, Colorado's disclosure provisions were enacted post-*Meyer* in 1993. The Tenth Circuit trimmed these provisions. Colorado requires ballot-initiative proponents who pay circulators to file both a final report when the initiative petition is submitted to the Secretary of State, and monthly reports during the circulation period. The Tenth Circuit invalidated the[se] report provision[s] only insofar as [they] compelled disclosure of information specific to each paid circulator, in particular, the circulators' names and addresses and the total amount paid to each circulator.***

In ruling on Colorado's disclosure requirements for paid circulations, the Court of Appeals looked primarily to our decision in *Buckley v. Valeo*, 424 U.S. 1(1976) (per curiam).*** Mindful of *Buckley*, the Tenth Circuit did not upset Colorado's disclosure requirements as a whole. Notably, the Court of Appeals upheld the State's requirements for disclosure of payors, in particular, proponents' names and the total amount they have spent to collect signatures for their petitions. In this regard, the State and supporting amici stress the importance of disclosure as a control or check on domination of the initiative process by affluent special interest groups. Disclosure of the names of initiative sponsors, and of the amounts they have spent gathering support for their initiatives, responds to that substantial state interest.***

Through the disclosure requirements that remain in place, voters are informed of the source and amount of money spent by proponents to get a measure on the ballot; in other words, voters will be told who has proposed a measure, and who has provided funds for its circulation. The added benefit of revealing the names of paid circulators and amounts paid to each circulator, the lower courts fairly determined from the record as a whole, is hardly apparent and has not been demonstrated.[22]

In addition, as we stated in *Meyer*, *** absent evidence to the contrary, "we are not prepared to assume that a professional circulator — whose qualifications for similar future assignments may well depend on a reputation for competence and integrity — is any more likely to accept false signatures than a volunteer who is motivated entirely by an interest in having the proposition placed on the ballot." [23]

---

22. JUSTICE O'CONNOR states that "[k]nowing the names of paid circulators and the amounts paid to them [will] allo[w] members of the public to evaluate the sincerity or, alternatively, the potential bias of any circulator that approaches them." It is not apparent why or how this is so, for the reports containing the names of paid circulators would be filed with the Secretary of State and would not be at hand at the moment the circulators approach.

23. *** Far from making any ultimate finding to that effect, the District Court determined that neither the State's interest in preventing fraud, nor its interest in informing the public concerning the "financial resources ... available to [initiative proponents]" or the "special interests" supporting a ballot measure, is "significantly advanced by disclosure of the names

In sum, we agree with the Court of Appeals appraisal: Listing paid circulators and their income from circulation "forc[es] paid circulators to surrender the anonymity enjoyed by their volunteer counterparts"; no more than tenuously related to the substantial interests disclosure serves, Colorado's reporting requirements, to the extent that they target paid circulators, fail exacting scrutiny." *** Affirmed.*

---

and addresses of each person paid to circulate any section of [a] petition." Such disclosure in proponents' reports, the District Court also observed, risked exposing the paid circulators "to intimidation, harassment and retribution in the same manner as the badge requirement."

* [**Ed. Note.** Thomas, J., concurred in the judgment, but wrote separately. O'Connor and Breyer, JJ., dissented in part as did Rehnquist, C.J., in a separate opinion. They voted to sustain the reporting requirements imposed upon proponents disclosing all paid circulators' names and addresses, both in the required monthly and their final reports, as serving legitimate public interests to determine who such persons were and how much each was paid. They voted also to sustain the registered voter requirement. But they agreed with the Court's application of *McIntyre* in invalidating the badge information requirement — as failing "strict scrutiny" re the protection of anonymity from forced disclosure in direct political speech. (The Court was thus unanimous in holding the badge-disclosure provision invalid on First Amendment grounds, applying and extending *McIntyre*.)]

Chapter 4

THE FIRST AMENDMENT AND THE LESSER PROTECTION OF NONPOLITICAL SPEECH IN THE UNITED STATES

A.   Commercial Speech

Casebook, p. 754
Add as a new case following *Rubin v. Coors Brewing Co.*

44 LIQUORMART, INC. v. RHODE ISLAND
517 U.S. 484 (1996)

[JUSTICE STEVENS announced the judgment of the Court and delivered the opinion of the Court with respect to Parts I, II, VII, and VIII.]

I

In 1956, the Rhode Island Legislature enacted two separate prohibitions against advertising the retail price of alcoholic beverages. The first *** prohibits *** "advertising in any manner whatsoever" the price of any alcoholic beverage offered for sale in the State; the only exception is for price tags or signs displayed with the merchandise within licensed premises and not visible from the street. The second statute applies to the Rhode Island news media. It contains a categorical prohibition against the publication or broadcast of any advertisements — even those referring to sales in other States — that "make reference to the price of any alcoholic beverages." ***

II

Petitioners 44 Liquormart, Inc., and Peoples Super Liquor Stores, Inc. , are licensed retailers of alcoholic beverages. Petitioner 44 Liquormart operates a store in Rhode Island and petitioner Peoples operates several stores in Massachusetts that are patronized by Rhode Island residents. Peoples uses alcohol price advertising extensively in Massachusetts, where such advertising is permitted, but Rhode Island newspapers and other media outlets have refused to accept such ads. ***

*** 44 Liquormart, joined by Peoples, filed this action against the administrator in the Federal District Court seeking a declaratory judgment that the two statutes and the administrator's implementing regulations violate the First Amendment ***. The Rhode Island Liquor Stores Association was allowed to intervene as a defendant and in due course the State of Rhode Island replaced the administrator as the principal defendant. The parties stipulated that the price advertising ban is vigorously enforced, that Rhode Island permits "all advertising of alcoholic beverages excepting references to price outside the licensed premises," and that petitioners' proposed ads do not concern an illegal activity and presumably would not be false or misleading. The parties disagreed, however, about the impact of the ban on the promotion of temperance in Rhode Island. ***

In his findings of fact, the District Judge first noted that there was a pronounced lack of unanimity among researchers who have studied the impact of advertising on the level of consumption of alcoholic beverages. After summarizing the testimony of the expert witnesses for both parties, he found "as a fact that Rhode Island's off-premises liquor price advertising ban has no significant impact on levels of alcohol consumption in Rhode Island."

*** Acknowledging that it might have been reasonable for the state legislature to "assume a correlation between the price advertising ban and reduced consumption," he held that more than a rational basis was required to justify the speech restriction, and that the State had failed to demonstrate a reasonable "fit" between its policy objectives and its chosen means.

The Court of Appeals reversed. It found "inherent merit" in the State's submission that competitive price advertising would lower prices and that lower prices would produce more sales. Moreover, it agreed with the reasoning of the Rhode Island Supreme Court that the Twenty-first Amendment gave the statutes an added presumption of validity. *** We granted certiorari [and now reverse the Court of Appeals].

III*

*** In *Central Hudson*, we took stock of our developing commercial speech jurisprudence. [W]e considered a regulation "completely" banning all promotional advertising by electric utilities. Our decision acknowledged the special features of commercial speech but identified the serious First Amendment concerns that attend blanket advertising prohibitions that do not protect consumers from commercial harms.

Five Members of the Court recognized that the state interest in the conservation of energy was substantial, and that there was "an immediate connection between advertising and demand for electricity." Nevertheless, they concluded that the regulation was invalid because the Commission had failed to make a showing that a more limited speech regulation would not have adequately served the State's interest.[9]

In reaching its conclusion, the majority explained that although the special nature of commercial speech may require less than strict review of its regulation, special concerns arise from "regulations that entirely suppress commercial speech in order to pursue a nonspeech-related policy." In those circumstances, "a ban on speech could screen from public view the underlying governmental policy." As a result, the Court concluded that "special care" should attend the review of such blanket bans, and it pointedly remarked that "in recent years this Court has not approved a blanket ban on

---

* [**Ed. Note.** Stevens, Kennedy, Souter, Ginsburg, JJ.]

9. In other words, the regulation failed the fourth step in the four-part inquiry that the majority announced in its opinion. ***

commercial speech unless the speech itself was flawed in some way, either because it was deceptive or related to unlawful activity."[10]

IV*

As our review of the case law reveals, Rhode Island errs in concluding that all commercial speech regulations are subject to a similar form of constitutional review simply because they target a similar category of expression. The mere fact that messages propose commercial transactions does not in and of itself dictate the constitutional analysis that should apply to decisions to suppress them. See *Rubin v. Coors Brewing Co.*, (STEVENS, J., concurring in judgment).

When a State regulates commercial messages to protect consumers from misleading, deceptive, or aggressive sales practices, or requires the disclosure of beneficial consumer information, the purpose of its regulation is consistent with the reasons for according constitutional protection to commercial speech and therefore justifies less than strict review. However, when a State entirely prohibits the dissemination of truthful, nonmisleading commercial messages for reasons unrelated to the preservation of a fair bargaining process, there is far less reason to depart from the rigorous review that the First Amendment generally demands. ***

Precisely because bans against truthful, nonmisleading commercial speech rarely seek to protect consumers from either deception or overreaching, they usually rest solely on the offensive assumption that the public will respond "irrationally" to the truth. The First Amendment directs us to be especially skeptical of regulations that seek to keep people in the dark for what the government perceives to be their own good. ***

V*

*** The State argues that the price advertising prohibition should nevertheless be upheld because it directly advances the State's substantial interest in promoting temperance, and because it is no more extensive than necessary. Although there is some confusion as to what Rhode Island means by temperance, we assume that the State asserts an interest in reducing alcohol consumption.

We can agree that common sense supports the conclusion that a prohibition against price advertising, like a collusive agreement among competitors to refrain from such

---

10. The Justices concurring in the judgment adopted a somewhat broader view. They expressed "doubt whether suppression of information concerning the availability and price of a legally offered product is ever a permissible way for the State to 'dampen' the demand for or use of the product." Indeed, Justice Blackmun believed that even "though 'commercial' speech is involved, such a regulation strikes at the heart of the First Amendment."

* [**Ed. Note.** Stevens, Kennedy, Ginsburg, JJ.]

* [**Ed. Note.** Stevens, Kennedy, Souter, Ginsburg, JJ.]

advertising, will tend to mitigate competition and maintain prices at a higher level than would prevail in a completely free market. Despite the absence of proof on the point, we can even agree with the State's contention that it is reasonable to assume that demand, and hence consumption throughout the market, is somewhat lower whenever a higher, noncompetitive price level prevails. However, without any findings of fact, or indeed any evidentiary support whatsoever, we cannot agree with the assertion that the price advertising ban will significantly advance the State's interest in promoting temperance.

Although the record suggests that the price advertising ban may have some impact on the purchasing patterns of temperate drinkers of modest means, the State has presented no evidence to suggest that its speech prohibition will significantly reduce market-wide consumption.[16] Indeed, the District Court's considered and uncontradicted finding on this point is directly to the contrary. Moreover, the evidence suggests that the abusive drinker will probably not be deterred by a marginal price increase, and that the true alcoholic may simply reduce his purchases of other necessities.[17] ***

The State also cannot satisfy the requirement that its restriction on speech be no more extensive than necessary. It is perfectly obvious that alternative forms of regulation that would not involve any restriction on speech would be more likely to achieve the State's goal of promoting temperance. As the State's own expert conceded, higher prices can be maintained either by direct regulation or by increased taxation. Per capita purchases could be limited as is the case with prescription drugs. Even educational campaigns focused on the problems of excessive, or even moderate, drinking might prove to be more effective.

As a result, even under the less than strict standard that generally applies in commercial speech cases, the State has failed to establish a "reasonable fit" between its abridgment of speech and its temperance goal. It necessarily follows that the price advertising ban cannot survive the more stringent constitutional review that *Central Hudson* itself concluded was appropriate for the complete suppression of truthful, nonmisleading commercial speech.

---

16. The appellants' stipulation that they each expect to realize a $100,000 benefit per year if the ban is lifted is not to the contrary. The stipulation shows only that the appellants believe they will be able to compete more effectively for existing alcohol consumers if there is no ban on price advertising. It does not show that they believe either the number of alcohol consumers, or the number of purchases by those consumers, will increase in the ban's absence. ***

17. Although the Court of Appeals concluded that the regulation directly advanced the State's interest, it did not dispute the District Court's conclusion that the evidence suggested that, at most, a price advertising ban would have a marginal impact on overall alcohol consumption.

VI*

The State responds by arguing that it merely exercised appropriate "legislative judgment" in determining that a price advertising ban would best promote temperance. Relying on the *Central Hudson* analysis set forth in *Posadas de Puerto Rico Associates v. Tourism Co. of P. R.*, 478 U.S. 328 (1986), and *United States v. Edge Broadcasting Co.*, 509 U.S. 418 (1993), Rhode Island first argues that, because expert opinions as to the effectiveness of the price advertising ban "go both ways," the Court of Appeals correctly concluded that the ban constituted a "reasonable choice" by the legislature. The State next contends that precedent requires us to give particular deference to that legislative choice because the State could, if it chose, ban the sale of alcoholic beverages outright. ***

In *Edge*, we upheld a federal statute that permitted only those broadcasters located in States that had legalized lotteries to air lottery advertising. The statute was designed to regulate advertising about an activity that had been deemed illegal in the jurisdiction in which the broadcaster was located. Here, by contrast, the commercial speech ban targets information about entirely lawful behavior.

Posadas is more directly relevant. There, a five-Member majority held that, under the *Central Hudson* test, it was "up to the legislature" to choose to reduce gambling by suppressing in-state casino advertising rather than engaging in educational speech. Rhode Island argues that this logic demonstrates the constitutionality of its own decision to ban price advertising in lieu of raising taxes or employing some other less speech-restrictive means of promoting temperance.

The reasoning in *Posadas* does support the State's argument, but, on reflection, we are now persuaded that *Posadas* erroneously performed the First Amendment analysis. The casino advertising ban was designed to keep truthful, nonmisleading speech from members of the public for fear that they would be more likely to gamble if they received it. As a result, the advertising ban served to shield the State's antigambling policy from the public scrutiny that more direct, nonspeech regulation would draw. ***

Because the 5-to-4 decision in *Posadas* marked such a sharp break from our prior precedent, and because it concerned a constitutional question about which this Court is the final arbiter, we decline to give force to its highly deferential approach.

Instead, in keeping with our prior holdings, we conclude that a state legislature does not have the broad discretion to suppress truthful, nonmisleading information for paternalistic purposes that the *Posadas* majority was willing to tolerate. ***

We also cannot accept the State's second contention, which is premised entirely on the "greater-includes-the-lesser" reasoning endorsed toward the end of the majority's opinion in *Posadas*. There, the majority stated that "the greater power to completely

---

* [**Ed. Note.** Stevens, Kennedy, Thomas, Ginsburg, JJ.]

ban casino gambling necessarily includes the lesser power to ban advertising of casino gambling." *** The majority concluded that it would "surely be a strange constitutional doctrine which would concede to the legislature the authority to totally ban a product or activity, but deny to the legislature the authority to forbid the stimulation of demand for the product or activity through advertising on behalf of those who would profit from such increased demand." On the basis of these statements, the State reasons that its undisputed authority to ban alcoholic beverages must include the power to restrict advertisements offering them for sale. ***

The text of the First Amendment makes clear that the Constitution presumes that attempts to regulate speech are more dangerous than attempts to regulate conduct. That presumption accords with the essential role that the free flow of information plays in a democratic society. As a result, the First Amendment directs that government may not suppress speech as easily as it may suppress conduct, and that speech restrictions cannot be treated as simply another means that the government may use to achieve its ends.

These basic First Amendment principles clearly apply to commercial speech; indeed, the *Posadas* majority impliedly conceded as much by applying the *Central Hudson* test. *** The distinction that our cases have consistently drawn between these two types of governmental action is fundamentally incompatible with the absolutist view that the State may ban commercial speech simply because it may constitutionally prohibit the underlying conduct.[20] ***

Thus, just as it is perfectly clear that Rhode Island could not ban all obscene liquor ads except those that advocated temperance, we think it equally clear that its power to ban the sale of liquor entirely does not include a power to censor all advertisements that contain accurate and nonmisleading information about the price of the product. As the entire Court apparently now agrees, the statements in the *Posadas* opinion on which Rhode Island relies are no longer persuasive.

Finally, we find unpersuasive the State's contention that, under *Posadas* and *Edge*, the price advertising ban should be upheld because it targets commercial speech that pertains to a "vice" activity. *** [T]he scope of any "vice" exception to the protection

---

20. It is also no answer to say that it would be "strange" if the First Amendment tolerated a seemingly "greater" regulatory measure while forbidding a "lesser" one. We recently held that although the government had the power to proscribe an entire category of speech, such as obscenity or so-called fighting words, it could not limit the scope of its ban to obscene or fighting words that expressed a point of view with which the government disagrees. *R.A.V. v. St. Paul*, 505 U.S. 377 (1992). Similarly, in *Cincinnati v. Discovery Network, Inc.*, 507 U.S. 410 (1993), we assumed that States could prevent all newsracks from being placed on public sidewalks, but nevertheless concluded that they could not ban only those newsracks that contained certain commercial publications.

afforded by the First Amendment would be difficult, if not impossible, to define. Almost any product that poses some threat to public health or public morals might reasonably be characterized by a state legislature as relating to "vice activity." ***

VII

*** [A]lthough the Twenty-first Amendment limits the effect of the dormant Commerce Clause on a State's regulatory power over the delivery or use of intoxicating beverages within its borders, "the Amendment does not license the States to ignore their obligations under other provisions of the Constitution." That general conclusion reflects our specific holdings that the Twenty-first Amendment does not in any way diminish the force of the Supremacy Clause, the Establishment Clause, or the Equal Protection Clause. We see no reason why the First Amendment should not also be included in that list. *** The Twenty-first Amendment, therefore, cannot save Rhode Island's ban on liquor price advertising.

VIII

Because Rhode Island has failed to carry its heavy burden of justifying its complete ban on price advertising, we conclude that R.I. Gen. Laws §§ 3-8-7 and 3-8-8.1, as well as Regulation 32 of the Rhode Island Liquor Control Administration, abridge speech in violation of the First Amendment as made applicable to the States by the Due Process Clause of the Fourteenth Amendment. The judgment of the Court of Appeals is therefore reversed. ***

JUSTICE SCALIA, concurring in part and concurring in the judgment.

I share JUSTICE THOMAS's discomfort with the *Central Hudson* test, which seems to me to have nothing more than policy intuition to support it. I also share JUSTICE STEVENS' aversion towards paternalistic governmental policies that prevent men and women from hearing facts that might not be good for them. ***

Since I do not believe we have before us the wherewithal to declare *Central Hudson* wrong — or at least the wherewithal to say what ought to replace it — I must resolve this case in accord with our existing jurisprudence, which all except JUSTICE THOMAS agree would prohibit the challenged regulation. I am not disposed to develop new law, or reinforce old, on this issue, and accordingly I merely concur in the judgment of the Court. ***

JUSTICE THOMAS, concurring in Parts I, II, VI, and VII, and concurring in the judgment.

In cases such as this, in which the government's asserted interest is to keep legal users of a product or service ignorant in order to manipulate their choices in the marketplace, the balancing test adopted in *Central Hudson* should not be applied, in my view. Rather, such an "interest" is *per se* illegitimate and can no more justify regulation of "commercial" speech than it can justify regulation of "noncommercial" speech. ***

I do not join the principal opinion's application of the *Central Hudson* balancing test because I do not believe that such a test should be applied to a restriction of "commercial" speech, at least when, as here, the asserted interest is one that is to be achieved through keeping would-be recipients of the speech in the dark.[5] Application of the advancement-of-state-interest prong of *Central Hudson* makes little sense to me in such circumstances. Faulting the State for failing to show that its price advertising ban decreases alcohol consumption "significantly," as JUSTICE STEVENS does, seems to imply that if the State had been more successful at keeping consumers ignorant and thereby decreasing their consumption, then the restriction might have been upheld. This contradicts *Virginia Pharmacy Bd.*'s rationale for protecting "commercial" speech in the first instance.

Both JUSTICE STEVENS and JUSTICE O'CONNOR appear to adopt a stricter, more categorical interpretation of the fourth prong of *Central Hudson* than that suggested in some of our other opinions, one that could, as a practical matter, go a long way toward the position I take. In their application of the fourth prong, both JUSTICE STEVENS and JUSTICE O'CONNOR hold that because the State can ban the sale of lower priced alcohol altogether by instituting minimum prices or levying taxes, it cannot ban advertising regarding lower priced liquor. Although the tenor of JUSTICE O'CONNOR's opinion (and, to a lesser extent, that of JUSTICE STEVENS's opinion) might suggest that this is just another routine case-by-case application of *Central Hudson*'s fourth prong, the Court's holding will in fact be quite sweeping if applied consistently in future cases. The opinions would appear to commit the courts to striking down restrictions on speech whenever a direct regulation (i.e., a regulation involving no restriction on speech regarding lawful activity at all) would be an equally effective method of dampening demand by legal users. But it would seem that directly banning a product (or rationing it, taxing it, controlling its price, or otherwise restricting its sale in specific ways) would virtually always be at least as effective in discouraging consumption as merely restricting advertising regarding the product would be, and thus virtually all restrictions with such a purpose would fail the fourth prong of the *Central Hudson* test. This would be so even if the direct regulation is, in one sense, more restrictive of conduct generally. ***

---

5. In other words, I do not believe that a *Central Hudson*-type balancing test should apply when the asserted purpose is like the one put forth by the government in *Central Hudson* itself. Whether some type of balancing test is warranted when the asserted state interest is of a different kind is a question that I do not consider here.

The upshot of the application of the fourth prong in the opinions of JUSTICE STEVENS and of JUSTICE O'CONNOR seems to be that the government may not, for the purpose of keeping would-be consumers ignorant and thus decreasing demand, restrict advertising regarding commercial transactions — or at least that it may not restrict advertising regarding commercial transactions except to the extent that it outlaws or otherwise restricting it or otherwise directly restricts the same transactions within its own borders.[7] I welcome this outcome; but, rather than "applying" the fourth prong of *Central Hudson* to reach the inevitable result that all or most such advertising restrictions must be struck down, I would adhere to the doctrine adopted in *Virginia Pharmacy Bd.* and in Justice Blackmun's *Central Hudson* concurrence, that all attempts to dissuade legal choices by citizens by keeping them ignorant are impermissible. ***

JUSTICE O'CONNOR, with whom THE CHIEF JUSTICE, JUSTICE SOUTER, and JUSTICE BREYER join, concurring in the judgment. ***

Both parties agree that the first two prongs of the *Central Hudson* test are met. Even if we assume arguendo that Rhode Island's regulation also satisfies the requirement that it directly advance the governmental interest, Rhode Island's regulation fails the final prong; that is, its ban is more extensive than necessary to serve the State's interest. ***

Rhode Island says that the ban is intended to keep alcohol prices high as a way to keep consumption low. By preventing sellers from informing customers of prices, the regulation prevents competition from driving prices down and requires consumers to spend more time to find the best price for alcohol. The higher cost of obtaining alcohol, Rhode Island argues, will lead to reduced consumption.

---

7. The two most obvious situations in which no equally effective direct regulation will be available for discouraging consumption (and thus, the two situations in which the Court and I might differ on the outcome) are: (1) When a law directly regulating conduct would violate the Constitution (e.g., because the item is constitutionally protected), or (2) when the sale is to occur outside the State's borders. As to the first situation: Although the Court's application of the fourth prong today does not specifically foreclose regulations or bans of advertising regarding items that cannot constitutionally be banned, it would seem strange to hold that the government's power to interfere with transmission of information regarding these items, in order to dampen demand for them, is more extensive than its power to restrict, for the same purpose, advertising of items that are not constitutionally protected. As to the second situation: When a State seeks to dampen consumption by its citizens of products or services outside its borders, it does not have the option of direct regulation. *** Perhaps JUSTICE STEVENS and JUSTICE O'CONNOR would distinguish a situation in which a State had actually banned sales of lower priced alcohol within the State and had then, through a ban of advertising by out-of-state sellers, sought to keep residents ignorant of the fact that lower priced alcohol was legally available in other States. The outcome in *Edge* may well be in conflict with the principles espoused in *Virginia Pharmacy Bd.* and ratified by me today.

The fit between Rhode Island's method and this particular goal is not reasonable. If the target is simply higher prices generally to discourage consumption, the regulation imposes too great, and unnecessary, a prohibition on speech in order to achieve it. The State has other methods at its disposal — methods that would more directly accomplish this stated goal without intruding on sellers' ability to provide truthful, nonmisleading information to customers. *** The ready availability of such alternatives — at least some of which would far more effectively achieve Rhode Island's only professed goal, at comparatively small additional administrative cost — demonstrates that the fit between ends and means is not narrowly tailored. ***

Respondents point for support to *Posadas*. The Court there accepted as reasonable the legislature's belief that the regulation would be effective, and concluded that, because the restriction affected only advertising of casino gambling aimed at residents of Puerto Rico, not that aimed at tourists, the restriction was narrowly tailored to serve Puerto Rico's interest. The Court accepted without question Puerto Rico's account of the effectiveness and reasonableness of its speech restriction. Respondents ask us to make a similar presumption here to uphold the validity of Rhode Island's law.

It is true that Posadas accepted as reasonable, without further inquiry, Puerto Rico's assertions that the regulations furthered the government's interest and were no more extensive than necessary to serve that interest. Since *Posadas*, however, this Court has examined more searchingly the State's professed goal, and the speech restriction put into place to further it, before accepting a State's claim that the speech restriction satisfies First Amendment scrutiny. In *** these cases we declined to accept at face value the proffered justification for the State's regulation, but examined carefully the relationship between the asserted goal and the speech restriction used to reach that goal. The closer look that we have required since *Posadas* comports better with the purpose of the analysis set out in *Central Hudson*, by requiring the State to show that the speech restriction directly advances its interest and is narrowly tailored. Under such a closer look, Rhode Island's price-advertising ban clearly fails to pass muster.

Because Rhode Island's regulation fails even the less stringent standard set out in *Central Hudson*, nothing here requires adoption of a new analysis for the evaluation of commercial speech regulation. The principal opinion acknowledges that "even under the less than strict standard that generally applies in commercial speech cases, the State has failed to establish a reasonable fit between its abridgement of speech and its temperance goal." Because we need go no further, I would not here undertake the question whether the test we have employed since *Central Hudson* should be displaced.

————

NOTES

1. Does *Liquormart* stand for the proposition that a "lesser" restriction is invalid where a "greater" restriction would serve the end to be achieved with equal (or, indeed, with

far greater) direct effect? Is this also Justice Thomas's summary of the majority opinion? Is it correct?

2. Note that in *Liquormart,* promotional advertising was not forbidden — to the contrary, only price terms were forbidden. Neither was there any dollar restriction on how much money might be spent on promotional advertising, whether to encourage general consumer awareness of liquor's ready availability, or of particular brands, or of particular stores. Doesn't the effect of failing to limit or forbid promotional advertising make the mere ban on price terms sufficiently problematic (in terms of having a "substantial" effect to reduce intemperance) to raise a fair question whether "temperance" as such was, after all, really the main object of this law? Or does nothing turn on this?

3. Suppose, to follow up on the implications of the preceding question, the state defended the ban on price advertising not on the basis of encouraging "temperance."[16a] Suppose, rather, Rhode Island defended the ban on liquor price advertising as part of a legislative policy to favor small retailers as such.[16b] — And suppose the evidence were compelling that it had just that effect (albeit, to be sure, as any such legislative preference may tend to do, at consumer expense). *Now* will the ban be sustained? Why or why not? (Is the "governmental interest" in the maintenance of small retailers permissible? May it also be "substantial"? (Who says it cannot be said to be a "substantial" interest of the state?) Is it "directly" advanced? Does the price advertising ban have a "reasonable fit" to *that* end?

———

GREATER NEW ORLEANS BROADCASTING ASS'N INC.
V. UNITED STATES
527 U.S. 173 (1999)

JUSTICE STEVENS delivered the opinion of the Court.

I

Through most of the 19th and the first half of the 20th centuries, Congress adhered to a policy that not only discouraged the operation of lotteries and similar schemes, but forbade the dissemination of information concerning such enterprises by use of the

———

16a. How direct was the ban in relation to encouraging "temperance" as the desired end? Very direct? Or only highly indirect, and even then additionally attenuated (note the ban on price advertising does not in so many words, or otherwise, affirmatively encourage "temperance" in any way; note, too, that the least temperate are among the least likely to be affected (i.e. least "in the dark" about price)).

16b. May it not in fact have a far closer fit with this objective (the product of successful lobbying by a trade association of small retail liquor stores) than with the objective of "temperance"?

mails, even when the lottery in question was chartered by a state legislature. Consistent with this Court's earlier view that commercial advertising was unprotected by the First Amendment, see *Valentine v. Chrestensen*, 316 U.S. 52, 54 (1942), we found that the notion that "lotteries ... are supposed to have a demoralizing influence upon the people" provided sufficient justification for excluding circulars concerning such enterprises from the federal postal system. *Ex parte Jackson*, 96 U.S. 727, 736-737 (1878). We likewise deferred to congressional judgment in upholding the similar exclusion for newspapers that contained either lottery advertisements or prize lists.

[In 1934,] Congress extended its restrictions on lottery-related information to broadcasting. Now codified at 18 U.S.C. § 1304, the statute prohibits radio and television broadcasting, by any station for which a license is required, of "any advertisement of or information concerning any lottery, gift enterprise, or similar scheme, offering prizes dependent in whole or in part upon lot or chance, or any list of the prizes drawn or awarded by means of any such lottery, gift enterprise, or scheme." ***

During the second half of this century, Congress dramatically narrowed the scope of the broadcast prohibition in § 1304. [In 1975], advertisements of State-conducted lotteries [were exempted] from the nationwide postal restrictions and from the broadcast restriction, when "broadcast by a radio or television station licensed to a location in...a State which conducts such a lottery."***In 1988, 25 U.S.C. § 2701 et seq., authorized Native American tribes to conduct various forms of gambling — including casino gambling — [and] exempted any gaming conducted by an Indian tribe pursuant to the Act from both the postal and transportation restrictions in 18 U.S.C. §§ 1301-1302, and the broadcast restriction in § 1304. [And] 18 U.S.C. §1307(a(2)] extended the exemption from §§ 1301-1304 for state-run lotteries to include any other lottery, gift enterprise, or similar scheme — not prohibited by the law of the State in which it operates — when conducted by: (I) any governmental organization; (ii) any not-for-profit organization; or (iii) a commercial organization as a promotional activity "clearly occasional and ancillary to the primary business of that organization." *** [T]he exemptions in both of these 1988 statutes are not geographically limited; they shield messages from § 1304's reach in States that do not authorize such gambling as well as those that do.***

III

In a number of cases involving restrictions on speech that is "commercial" in nature, we have employed *Central Hudson*'s four-part test to resolve First Amendment challenges[.] ***Partly because of [its] intricacies, petitioners as well as certain judges, scholars, and amici curiae have advocated repudiation of the *Central Hudson* standard and implementation of a more straightforward and stringent test for assessing the validity of governmental restrictions on commercial speech. As the opinions in *44 Liquormart* demonstrate, reasonable judges may disagree about the merits of such proposals. It is, however, an established part of our constitutional jurisprudence that we do not ordinarily reach out to make novel or unnecessarily broad pronouncements on constitutional issues when a case can be fully resolved on a narrower ground. In this case, there is no need to break new ground. *Central Hudson*, as applied in our more recent commercial speech cases, provides an adequate basis for decision.

IV

All parties to this case agree that the messages petitioners wish to broadcast constitute commercial speech, and that these broadcasts would satisfy the first part of the *Central Hudson* test: Their content is not misleading and concerns lawful activities, i.e., private casino gambling in Louisiana and Mississippi. As well, the proposed commercial messages would convey information — whether taken favorably unfavorably by the audience — about an activity that is the subject of intense public debate in many communities. In addition, petitioners' broadcasts presumably would disseminate accurate information as to the operation of market competitors, such as pay-out ratios, which can benefit listeners by informing their consumption choices and fostering price competition. Thus, even if the broadcasters' interest in conveying these messages is entirely pecuniary, the interests of, and benefit to, the audience may be broader.

The second part of the *Central Hudson* test asks whether the asserted governmental interest served by the speech restriction is substantial. The Solicitor General identifies two such interests: (1) reducing the social costs associated with "gambling" or "casino gambling," and (2) assisting States that "restrict gambling" or "prohibit casino gambling" within their own borders. Underlying Congress' statutory scheme, the Solicitor General contends, is the judgment that gambling contributes to corruption and organized crime; underwrites bribery, narcotics trafficking, and other illegal conduct; imposes a regressive tax on the poor; and "offers a false but sometimes irresistible hope of financial advancement."

We can accept the characterization of these two interests as "substantial," but that conclusion is by no means self-evident. No one seriously doubts that the Federal Government may assert a legitimate and substantial interest in alleviating the societal ills recited above, or in assisting like-minded States to do the same. But in the judgment of both the Congress and many state legislatures, the social costs that support the suppression of gambling are offset, and sometimes outweighed, by countervailing policyconsiderations, primarily in the form of economic benefits.[5] Despite its

---

5. Some form of gambling is legal in nearly every State. 37 States and the District of Columbia operate lotteries. As of 1997, commercial casino gambling existed in 11 States, and at least 5 authorize state-sponsored video gambling. About half the States in the Union host Class III Indian gaming (which may encompass casino gambling), including Louisiana, Mississippi, and four other States that had private casinos. One count by the Bureau of Indian Affairs tallied 60 tribes that advertise their casinos on television and radio. By the mid-1990's, tribal casino-style gambling generated over $3 billion in gaming revenue — increasing its share to 18% of all casino gaming revenue, matching the total for the casinos in Atlantic City, New

awareness of the potential social costs, Congress has not only sanctioned casino gambling for Indian tribes through tribal-state compacts, but has enacted other statutes that reflect approval of state legislation that authorizes a host of public and private gambling activities.*** Whatever its character in 1934 when §1304 was adopted, the federal policy of discouraging gambling in general, and casino gambling in particular, is now decidedly equivocal.***[W]e cannot ignore Congress' unwillingness to adopt a single national policy that consistently endorses either interest asserted by the Solicitor General. Even though the Government has identified substantial interests, when we consider both their quality and the information sought to be suppressed, the crosscurrents in the scope and application of §1304 become more difficult for the Government to defend.

V

The third part of the *Central Hudson* test asks whether the speech restriction directly and materially advances the asserted governmental interest. "This burden is not satisfied by mere speculation or conjecture; rather, a governmental body seeking to sustain a restriction on commercial speech must demonstrate that the harms it recites are real and that its restriction will in fact alleviate them to a material degree." *Edenfield v. Fane*, 507 U.S. 761, 770-71 (1993). Consequently, "the regulation may not be sustained if it provides only ineffective or remote support for the government's purpose." *Central Hudson*, 447 U.S., at 564. We have observed that "this requirement is critical; otherwise, 'a State could with ease restrict commercial speech in the service of other objectives that could not themselves justify a burden on commercial expression.'" *Rubin*, 514 U.S., at 487, quoting *Edenfield*, 507 U.S., at 771.

The fourth part of the test complements the direct-advancement inquiry of the third, asking whether the speech restriction is not more extensive than necessary to serve the interests that support it. The Government is not required to employ the least restrictive means conceivable, but it must demonstrate narrow tailoring of the challenged regulation to the asserted interest — "a fit that is not necessarily perfect, but reasonable; that represents not necessarily the single best disposition but one whose scope is in proportion to the interest served." *Fox*, 492 U.S. at 480. [T]he challenged regulation should indicate that its proponent "'carefully calculated' the costs and benefits associated with the burden on speech imposed by its prohibition." *Discovery Network*, 507 U.S. at 417 (1993).

As applied to petitioners' case, § 1304 cannot satisfy these standards. With regard to the first asserted interest — alleviating the social costs of casino gambling by limiting demand — the Government contends that its broadcasting restrictions directly advance that interest because "promotional" broadcast advertising concerning casino gambling

---

Jersey, and reaching about half the figure for Nevada's casinos. ***

increases demand for such gambling, which in turn increases the amount of casino gambling that produces those social costs. Additionally, the Government believes that compulsive gamblers are especially susceptible to the pervasiveness and potency of broadcast advertising. Assuming the accuracy of this causal chain, it does not necessarily follow that the Government's speech ban has directly and materially furthered the asserted interest. While it is no doubt fair to assume that more advertising would have some impact on overall demand for gambling, it is also reasonable to assume that much of that advertising would merely channel gamblers to one casino rather than another. More important, any measure of the effectiveness of the Government's attempt to minimize the social costs of gambling cannot ignore Congress' simultaneous encouragement of tribal casino gambling, which may well be growing at a rate exceeding any increase in gambling or compulsive gambling that private casino advertising could produce.

We need not resolve the question whether any lack of evidence in the record fails to satisfy the standard of proof under *Central Hudson*, however, because the flaw in the Government's case is more fundamental: The operation of § 1304 and its attendant regulatory regime is so pierced by exemptions and inconsistencies that the Government cannot hope to exonerate it. Under current law, a broadcaster may not carry advertising about privately operated commercial casino gambling, regardless of the location of the station or the casino. On the other hand, advertisements for tribal casino gambling authorized by state compacts — whether operated by the tribe or by a private party pursuant to a management contract — are subject to no such broadcast ban, even if the broadcaster is located in or broadcasts to a jurisdiction with the strictest of antigambling policies. Government-operated, nonprofit, and "occasional and ancillary" commercial casinos are likewise exempt.***

Even putting aside the broadcast exemptions for arguably distinguishable sorts of gambling that might also give rise to social costs about which the Federal Government is concerned — such as state lotteries and parimutuel betting on horse and dog races, the Government presents no convincing reason for pegging its speech ban to the identity of the owners or operators of the advertised casinos. The Government***admits that tribal casinos offer precisely the same types of gambling as private casinos. Further, the Solicitor General does not maintain that government-operated casino gaming is any different, that States cannot derive revenue from taxing private casinos, or that any one class of casino operators is likely to advertise in a meaningfully distinct manner than the others.

Ironically, the most significant difference identified by the Government between tribal and other classes of casino gambling is that the former are "heavily regulated." If such direct regulation provides a basis for believing that the social costs of gambling in tribal casinos are sufficiently mitigated to make their advertising tolerable, one would have thought that Congress might have at least experimented with comparable regulation before abridging the speech rights of federally unregulated casinos. While Congress' failure to institute such direct regulation of private casino gambling does not necessarily compromise the constitutionality of § 1304, it does undermine the asserted justifications for the restriction before us. There surely are practical and nonspeech-related forms of regulation — including a prohibition or supervision of gambling on credit; limitations on the use of cash machines on casino premises; controls on admissions; pot or betting limits; location restrictions; and licensing requirements — that could more directly and effectively alleviate some of the social costs of casino gambling.***

Given the special federal interest in protecting the welfare of Native Americans, we recognize that there may be valid reasons for imposing commercial regulations on non-Indian businesses that differ from those imposed on tribal enterprises. It does not follow, however, that those differences also justify abridging non-Indians' freedom of speech more severely than the freedom of their tribal competitors. For the power to prohibit or to regulate particular conduct does not necessarily include the power to prohibit or regulate speech about that conduct. It is well settled that the First Amendment mandates closer scrutiny of government restrictions on speech than of its regulation of commerce alone. And to the extent that the purpose and operation of federal law distinguishes among information about tribal, governmental, and private casinos based on the identity of their owners or operators, the Government presents no sound reason why such lines bear any meaningful relationship to the particular interest asserted: minimizing casino gambling and its social costs by way of a (partial) broadcast ban. [D]ecisions that select among speakers conveying virtually identical messages are in serious tension with the principles undergirding the First Amendment.

The second interest asserted by the Government — the derivative goal of "assisting" States with policies that disfavor private casinos — adds little to its case. We cannot see how this broadcast restraint, ambivalent as it is, might directly and adequately further any *state* interest in dampening consumer demand for casino gambling if it cannot achieve the same goal with respect to the similar *federal* interest.***[T]he Government's second asserted interest provides no more convincing basis for upholding the regulation than the first.

VI

Accordingly, respondents cannot overcome the presumption that the speaker and the audience, not the Government, should be left to assess the value of accurate and nonmisleading information about lawful conduct. Had the Federal Government adopted a more coherent policy, or accommodated the rights of speakers in States that have legalized the underlying conduct, this might be a different case. But under current federal law, as applied to petitioners and the messages that they wish to convey, the broadcast prohibition in 18 U.S.C. §1304 and 47 CFR §73.1211 (1998) violates the First Amendment. The judgment of the Court of Appeals is therefore reversed.

CHIEF JUSTICE REHNQUIST, concurring.

I agree with the Court that "[t]he operation of § 1304 and its attendant regulatory regime is so pierced by exemptions and inconsistencies," that it violates the First Amendment.***

Were Congress to undertake substantive regulation of the gambling industry, rather than simply the manner in which it may broadcast advertisements, "exemptions and inconsistencies" such as those in §1304 might well prove constitutionally tolerable.*** But when Congress regulates commercial speech, the *Central Hudson* test imposes a more demanding standard of review. I agree with the Court that that standard has not been met here and I join its opinion.

JUSTICE THOMAS, concurring in the judgment.

I continue to adhere to my view that "[i]n cases such as this, in which the government's asserted interest is to keep legal users of a product or service ignorant in order to manipulate their choices in the marketplace," the *Central Hudson* test should not be applied because "such an 'interest' is per se illegitimate and can no more justify regulation of 'commercial speech' than it can justify regulation of 'noncommercial' speech." *44 Liquormart, Inc. v. Rhode Island*, 517 U.S. 484, 518 (1996) (concurring in part and concurring in the judgment). Accordingly, I concur only in the judgment.

———

GLICKMAN v. WILEMAN BROTHERS & ELLIOTT, INC.*
521 U.S. 457 (1997)

JUSTICE STEVENS delivered the opinion of the Court.

A number of growers, handlers, and processors of California tree fruits (respondents) brought this proceeding to challenge the validity of various regulations contained in marketing orders promulgated by the Secretary of Agriculture. The orders impose assessments that cover the cost of generic advertising of California nectarines, plums, and peaches. The question presented is whether the requirement that respondents

———

* [Ed. Note: This new "commercial speech" case concerns forced financial contributions for promotional advertising. It is thus also closely related to the cases and materials in ch. 3, pt. F of the casebook at pp 614-638 ("The First Amendment in Specific Environments — Coerced Expression and Freedom Not to Speak"), and particularly to *Abood v. Detroit Bd. of Educ.* (casebook at p. 628). The Court acknowledges the connection of this case with these earlier cases which the reader may wish to review. Because the case is also treated as a "commercial speech" case which allegedly should therefore also be reviewed under the *Central Hudson* standards for commercial speech (rather than under *Abood*), however, the case appears here. (As the reader will see, the Court sharply contests the applicability of *Central Hudson* to the case — albeit, assuredly, a case of "commercial" speech).]

finance such generic advertising is a law "abridging the freedom of speech" within the meaning of the First Amendment.

I

Congress enacted the Agricultural Marketing Agreement Act of 1937 in order to establish and maintain orderly marketing conditions and fair prices for agricultural commodities. Marketing orders promulgated pursuant to the AMAA are a species of economic regulation that has displaced competition in a number of discrete markets; they are expressly exempted from the antitrust laws. *** Marketing orders must be approved by either two-thirds of the affected producers or by producers who market at least two-thirds of the volume of the commodity. ***

Among the collective activities that Congress authorized for certain specific commodities is "any form of marketing promotion including paid advertising." *** The central message of the generic advertising at issue in this case is that "California Summer Fruits" are wholesome, delicious, and attractive to discerning shoppers. ***

[II-V]

Respondent Wileman Bros. & Elliott, Inc., is a large producer of these fruits that packs and markets its own output as well as that grown by other farmers. [Wileman, along with 15 other handlers] challenged the generic advertising provisions of the orders as violative of both the First Amendment. ***

The Court of Appeals concluded that government enforced contributions to pay for generic advertising violated the First Amendment rights of the handlers. Relying on our decision in *Abood v. Detroit Bd. of Ed.*, the court began by stating that the "First Amendment right of freedom of speech includes a right not to be compelled to render financial support for others' speech." It then reviewed the generic advertising regulations under "the test for restrictions on commercial speech set out in *Central Hudson Gas & Elec. Corp. v. Public Serv. Comm'n of N.Y.* Although it was satisfied that the government interest in enhancing returns to peach and nectarine growers was substantial, it was not persuaded that the generic advertising passed either the second or third "prongs" of *Central Hudson*. With respect to the former, even though the generic advertising "undoubtedly" has increased peach and nectarine sales, the government failed to prove that it did so more effectively than individualized advertising. The court also concluded that the program was not "narrowly tailored" because it did not give the handlers any credit for their own advertising and because California was the only state in which such programs were in place. ***

In challenging the constitutionality of the generic advertising program in the Court of Appeals, respondents relied, in part, on their claimed disagreement with the content of some of the generic advertising. The District Court had found no merit to this aspect of their claim,[10] and the Court of Appeals did not rely on it for its conclusion that the program was unconstitutional. Rather, the Court of Appeals invalidated the entire program on the theory that the program could not survive *Central Hudson* because the Government had failed to prove that generic advertising was more effective than individual advertising in increasing consumer demand for California nectarines, plums, and peaches. *** Although respondents have continued in this Court to argue about their disagreement with particular messages, those arguments, while perhaps calling into question the administration of portions of the program, have no bearing on the validity of the entire program.

For purposes of our analysis, we neither accept nor reject the factual assumption underlying the Court of Appeals' invalidation of the program-namely that generic advertising may not be the most effective method of promoting the sale of these commodities. The legal question that we address is whether being compelled to fund this advertising raises a First Amendment issue for us to resolve, or rather is simply a question of economic policy for Congress and the Executive to resolve. ***

The Court of Appeals apparently accepted respondents' argument that the assessments infringe First Amendment rights because they constitute compelled speech. Our compelled speech case law, however, is clearly inapplicable to the regulatory scheme at issue here. The use of assessments to pay for advertising does not require respondents to repeat an objectionable message out of their own mouths, cf. *West Virginia Bd. of Ed. v. Barnette*, require them to use their own property to convey an antagonistic ideological message, cf. *Wooley v. Maynard*, *** or require them to be publicly identified or associated with another's message, cf. *Prune Yard Shopping Center v. Robins*. Respondents are not required themselves to speak, but are merely required to make contributions for advertising. *** [T]he advertising is attributed not to them, but to the California Tree Fruit Agreement or "California Summer Fruits."

*** As the Court of Appeals read our decision in *Abood*, just as the First Amendment prohibits compelled speech, it prohibits — at least without sufficient justification by the government — compelling an individual to "render financial support for others' speech." However, *Abood*, and the cases that follow it, did not announce a broad First Amendment right not to be compelled to provide financial support for any organization that conducts expressive activities. Rather, *Abood* merely recognized a First Amendment interest in not being compelled to contribute to an organization whose

---

10. The District Court stated: "Scattered throughout plaintiffs' briefs are additional objections which are difficult to characterize or quantify. They assert that the advertising condones 'lying' in that it promotes the 'lie' that red colored fruit is superior, that it rewards mediocrity by advertising all varieties of California fruit to be of equal quality, that it promotes sexually subliminal messages as evidenced by an ad depicting a young girl in a wet bathing suit, and that it promotes the 'socialistic programs' of the Secretary. It is impossible from these 'vague claims' to determine that plaintiffs' first amendment rights have been significantly infringed."

expressive activities conflict with one's "freedom of belief." We considered, in *Abood*, whether it was constitutional for the State of Michigan to require government employees who objected to unions or union activities to contribute to an "agency shop" arrangement requiring all employees to pay union dues as a condition of employment. We held that compelled contributions to support activities related to collective bargaining were "constitutionally justified by the legislative assessment of the important contribution of the union shop" to labor relations. Relying on our compelled-speech cases, however, the Court found that compelled contributions for political purposes unrelated to collective bargaining implicated First Amendment interests because they interfere with the values lying at the "heart of the First Amendment[—]the notion that an individual should be free to believe as he will, and that in a free society one's beliefs should be shaped by his mind and his conscience rather than coerced by the State."

Here, however, requiring respondents to pay the assessments cannot be said to engender any crisis of conscience. None of the advertising in this record promotes any particular message other than encouraging consumers to buy California tree fruit. Neither the fact that respondents may prefer to foster that message independently in order to promote and distinguish their own products, nor the fact that they think more or less money should be spent fostering it, makes this case comparable to those in which an objection rested on political or ideological disagreement with the content of the message. ***

Moreover, rather than suggesting that mandatory funding of expressive activities always constitutes compelled speech in violation of the First Amendment, our cases provide affirmative support for the proposition that assessments to fund a lawful collective program may sometimes be used to pay for speech over the objection of some members of the group. Thus, in *Lehnert v. Ferris Faculty Assn.*, while we held that the cost of certain publications that were not germane to collective-bargaining activities could not be assessed against dissenting union members, we squarely held that it was permissible to charge them for those portions of "the Teachers' Voice that concern teaching and education generally, professional development, unemployment, job opportunities, award programs, and other miscellaneous matters." That holding was an application of the rule announced in *Abood* and further refined in *Keller v. State Bar of Cal.*, a case involving bar association activities.***

As we pointed out in *Keller*, "*Abood* held that a union could not expend a dissenting individual's dues for ideological activities not 'germane' to the purpose for which compelled association was justified: collective bargaining. Here the compelled association and integrated bar are justified by the State's interest in regulating the legal profession and improving the quality of legal services. The State Bar may therefore constitutionally fund activities germane to those goals out of the mandatory dues of all members. It may not, however, in such manner fund activities of an ideological nature which fall outside of those areas of activity." This test is clearly satisfied in this case because (1) the generic advertising of California peaches and nectarines is unquestionably germane to the purposes of the marketing orders and, (2) in any event, the assessments are not used to fund ideological activities.

We are not persuaded that any greater weight should be given to the fact that some producers do no wish to foster generic advertising than to the fact that many of them may well object to the marketing orders themselves because they might earn more money in an unregulated market. Similar criticisms might be directed at other features of the regulatory orders that impose restraints on competition that arguably disadvantage particular producers for the benefit of the entire market. Although one may indeed question the wisdom of such a program, its debatable features are insufficient to warrant special First Amendment scrutiny. It was therefore error for the Court of Appeals to rely on *Central Hudson* for the purpose of testing the constitutionality of market order assessments for promotional advertising.[18]

*** While the First Amendment unquestionably protects the individual producer's right to advertise its own brands, the statute is designed to further the economic interests of the producers as a group. *** Appropriate respect for the power of Congress to regulate commerce among the States provides abundant support for the constitutionality of these marketing orders on the following reasoning.

Generic advertising is intended to stimulate consumer demand for an agricultural product in a regulated market. That purpose is legitimate and consistent with the regulatory goals of the overall statutory scheme. At least a majority of the producers in each of the markets in which such advertising is authorized must be persuaded that it is effective, or presumably the programs would be discontinued. Whether the benefits from the advertising justify its cost is a question that not only might be answered differently in different markets, but also involves the exercise of policy judgments that are better made by producers and administrators than by judges.

*** In sum, what we are reviewing is a species of economic regulation that should enjoy the same strong presumption of validity that we accord to other policy judgments made by Congress.

The judgment of the Court of Appeals is reversed.

JUSTICE SOUTER, with whom THE CHIEF JUSTICE and JUSTICE SCALIA join, and with whom JUSTICE THOMAS joins except as to Part II, dissenting.

---

18. The Court of Appeals fails to explain why the *Central Hudson* test, which involved a restriction on commercial speech, should govern a case involving the compelled funding of speech. Given the fact that the Court of Appeals relied on *Abood* for the proposition that the program implicates the First Amendment, it is difficult to understand why the Court of Appeals did not apply *Abood*'s "germaneness" test.

The Court today finds no First Amendment right to be free of coerced subsidization of commercial speech, for two principal reasons. First, the Court finds no discernible element of speech in the implementation of the Government's marketing orders, beyond what it sees as "germane" to the undoubtedly valid, nonspeech elements of the orders. Second, the Court in any event takes the position that a person who is neither barred from saying what he wishes, nor subject to personal attribution of speech he dislikes, has no First Amendment objection to mandatory subsidization of speech unless it is ideological or political or contains a message with which the objecting person disagrees. I part company with the Court on each of these closely related points. I respectfully dissent.

[I-II]

Even before we first recognized commercial speech protection in *Virginia Bd. of Pharmacy*, we had stated a basic proposition of First Amendment protection, that "[a]ll ideas having even the slightest redeeming social importance *** have the full protection of the guaranties [of the First Amendment]," *Roth v. United States*. *** Since commercial speech is not subject to any categorical exclusion from First Amendment protection, and indeed is protectible as a speaker's chosen medium of commercial enterprise, it becomes subject to a second First Amendment principle: that compelling cognizable speech officially is just as suspect as suppressing it, and is typically subject to the same level of scrutiny.

As a familiar corollary to the principle that what may not be suppressed may not be coerced, we have recognized (thus far, outside the context of commercial speech) that individuals have a First Amendment interest in freedom from compulsion to subsidize speech and other expressive activities undertaken by private and quasi-private organizations.[2] We first considered this issue in *Abood v. Detroit Bd. of Ed.* [As] in this case, the sole imposition upon nonmembers was the assessment to help pay for the union's activities. And yet, purely financial as the imposition was, we held that the union's use of dissenters' service fees for expressive purposes unrelated to collective bargaining violated the First Amendment rights of those employees. ***

Decisions postdating *Abood* have made clear that its limited sanction for laws affecting First Amendment interests may not be expanded to cover every imposition that is in some way "germane" to a regulatory program in the sense of relating sympathetically to it. Rather, to survive scrutiny under *Abood*, a mandatory fee must not only be germane to some otherwise legitimate regulatory scheme; it must also be justified by vital policy interests of the government and not add significantly to the burdening of

---

2. The Secretary of Agriculture does not argue that the advertisements at issue represent so-called "government speech," with respect to which the government may have greater latitude in selecting content than otherwise permissible under the First Amendment.

free speech inherent in achieving those interests. *Lehnert v. Ferris Faculty Assn.* [500 U.S. 507 (1991)].

Thus, in *Lehnert* eight Justices concluded that a teachers' union could not constitutionally charge objecting employees for a public relations campaign meant to raise the esteem for teachers in the public mind and so increase the public's willingness to pay for public education. The advertising campaigns here suffer from the same defect as the public relations effort to stimulate demand for the teachers' product. *** Thus, the *Abood* line does not permit this program merely because it is germane to the marketing orders.

The Court's second misemployment of *Abood* and its successors is its reliance on them for the proposition that when government neither forbids speech nor attributes it to an objector, it may compel subsidization for any objectionable message that is not political or ideological. But this, of course, is entirely at odds with the principle that speech significant enough to be protected at some level is outside the government's power to coerce or to support by mandatory subsidy without further justification. ***

An apparent third ground for the Court's conclusion that the First Amendment is not implicated here is its assumption that respondents do not disagree with the advertisements they object to subsidizing. But this assumption is doubtful and would be beside the point even if true. [R]espondents do claim to disagree with the messages of some promotions they are being forced to fund. *** In any event, the requirement of disagreement finds no legal warrant in our compelled-speech cases. *** What counts here, then, is not whether respondents fail to disagree with the generalized message of the generic ads that California fruit is good, but that they do indeed deny that the general message is as valuable and worthy of their support as more particular claims about the merits of their own brands. One need not "disagree" with an abstractionist when buying a canvas from a representational painter; one merely wishes to support a different act of expression. ***

For the reasons discussed above, none of the Court's grounds suffices for discounting respondents' interests in expression here and treating these compelled advertising schemes as regulations of purely economic conduct instead of commercial speech. I would therefore adhere to the principle laid down in our compelled-speech cases: laws requiring an individual to engage in or pay for expressive activities are reviewed under the same standard that applies to laws prohibiting one from engaging in or paying for such activities. Under the test for commercial speech, the law may be held constitutional only if (1) the interest being pursued by the government is substantial, (2) the regulation directly advances that interest and (3) is narrowly tailored to serve it. *** In this case, the Secretary has failed to establish that the challenged advertising programs satisfy any of these three prongs of the *Central Hudson* test. ***

*** The record indicates merely that numerous commodity groups have come to the Congress and asked for authority to provide for [market development and advertising] activities under the terms of their agreement and it has always been granted. *** [T]he most reasonable inference is not of a substantial government interest, but effective politics on the part of producers who see the chance to spread their advertising costs. Nothing more appears. ***

Even if the Secretary could establish a sufficiently substantial interest, he would need also to show how the compelled advertising programs directly advance that interest, that is, how the schemes actually contribute to stabilizing agricultural markets and maintaining farm income by stimulating consumer demand. *** The Secretary argues that though respondents have voiced the desire to do more individual advertising if the system of mandatory assessments were ended, other handlers who benefit from the Government's program might well become "free riders" if promotion were to become wholly voluntary, to the point of cutting the sum total of advertising done. That might happen. It is also reasonably conceivable, though, that pure self-interest would keep the level of voluntary advertising high enough that the mandatory program could only be seen as affecting the details of the ads or shifting their costs, in either event without effect on market stability or income to producers as a group. We, of course, do not know, but these possibilities alone should be fatal to the Government here, which has the burden to establish the factual justification for ordering a subsidy for commercial speech.***

Finally, a regulation of commercial speech must be narrowly tailored to achieving the government's interests; there must be a "'fit' between the legislature's ends and the means chosen to accomplish those ends, — a fit *** that represents not necessarily the single best disposition but one whose scope is in proportion to the interest served." Respondents argue that the mandatory advertising schemes for California peaches, plums, and nectarines fail this narrow tailoring requirement, because they deny handlers any credit toward their assessments for some or all of their individual advertising expenditures. The point is well-taken. *** Indeed, the remarkable thing is that the AMAA itself provides for exactly such credits for individual advertising expenditures under marketing orders for almonds, filberts, raisins, walnuts, olives, and Florida Indian River grapefruit, but not for other commodities. ***

Although the government's obligation is not a heavy one in *Central Hudson* and the cases that follow it, we have understood it to call for some showing beyond plausibility, and there has been none here. I would accordingly affirm the judgment of the Ninth Circuit.

JUSTICE THOMAS, with whom JUSTICE SCALIA joins as to Part II, dissenting.

I write separately to note my disagreement with the majority's conclusion that coerced funding of advertising by others does not involve "speech" at all and does not even raise a First Amendment "issue." ***

In numerous cases, this Court has recognized that paying money for the purposes of advertising involves speech. The Court also has recognized that compelling speech raises a First Amendment issue just as much as restricting speech. Given these two elemental principles of our First Amendment jurisprudence, it is incongruous to suggest that forcing fruit-growers to contribute to a collective advertising campaign does not even involve speech, while at the same time effectively conceding that forbidding a fruit-grower from making those same contributions voluntarily would violate the First Amendment. ***

What we are now left with, if we are to take the majority opinion at face value, is one of two disturbing consequences: Either (1) paying for advertising is not speech at all, while such activities as draft card burning, flag burning, armband wearing, public sleeping, and nude dancing are, or (2) compelling payment for third party communication does not implicate speech, and thus the Government would be free to force payment for a whole variety of expressive conduct that it could not restrict. In either case, surely we have lost our way.

NOTES

1. Does the Court hold that Wileman's claim fails because the AMAA provision for forced contributions to generic advertising satisfies *Central Hudson*'s first amendment standards and does not transgress *Abood*'s first amendment limitations? Or does it hold, rather, that the provision is merely an "economic" regulation not even subject to First Amendment review?

2. If, pursuant to an authorizing act of Congress, the Department of Agriculture itself spent funds from its budget to buy radio and tv ads promoting California peaches and nectarines, would Wileman (or anyone else) have a first amendment claim? If not according to the majority in *Glickman*, then according to the dissent? If not (i.e. if not even according to the dissent in *Glickman*), why not? How is this different from the situation in *Glickman* itself? (See n.2 of the dissent. See also casebook at pp. 636–37).

3. In *Abood*, suppose a portion of the teachers' union dues (which nonmembers were also required to pay pursuant to the agency shop provision of the collective bargaining contract) were spent on advertisements to promote public confidence in teachers, e.g., to pay for bumper strips, declaring: "Teachers Are Our Children's Most Precious Resource." How, if at all, would this differ from an advertising campaign approved by the designated producers group in *Glickman*, paying for and distributing bumper strips declaring: "Hardly Anything Is Sweeter than a California Peach"?

4. In *Glickman*, the Court reversed the court of appeals in its holding that "the entire program" was invalid (i.e. that it failed to meet the requirements of *Central Hudson*, and that Wileman could thus not be made to contribute to it *at all*). Insofar as Wileman also objected to *particular* advertisements on the basis that they conveyed

messages contrary to his own beliefs, the Court acknowledged the point but observed that "those arguments, while perhaps calling into question the administration of portions of the program, have no bearing on the validity of the entire program."

However, might they have a bearing were Wileman now not to attack "the entire program," but to seek to be excused only from that portion of the advertising assessment representing merely the fraction of the advertising devoted to such messages as he declares to be "false" in his own view, or "offensive to" his beliefs? Suppose, in the previous hypothetical involving the bumper strip declaring that "Hardly Anything is Sweeter than a California Peach," Wileman objects, declaring: "Here, again, just as in the ad depicting a young girl in a wet bathing suit [see n.10 in majority opinion], this ad carries a prurient sexualized suggestion I resent, reject, and find humiliating." May he successfully demand a rebate from his advertising assessment in fair proportion to the costs of these kinds of ads as a fraction of the whole?

———

B.   The Uncertainties of Regulating or Criminalizing the "Obscene"

Casebook, p. 827
Add as Notes, Developments, and Questions Subsequent to *New York v. Ferber*

1.   As noted in *Ferber*, "[t]hirty-five States and the United States Congress" have enacted statutes forbidding the production, reproduction, distribution, dissemination or (under some of these laws) possession of any visual depiction of an underage person taking part in some described act (e.g. "actual or simulated sexual intercourse"), or depicted in some sexually explicit way (e.g., with "lewd exhibition of genitals"). That the performance or visual depiction — or the work of which it is a part — is not "obscene"[49a] is treated as irrelevant. It is the "exploitation" of youngsters featured in sexual performances or pictures with which these laws is concerned — a concern the Court agrees a legislature may conclude may not be adequately met by forbidding their use only in such depictions as would also qualify as "obscene."[49b] In keeping with that

———

49a.   [i.e. that it does not meet the *Roth-Miller-Slayton-Ginsberg-Mishkin* standards of obscenity]

49b.   Note, nevertheless, the Court's admission these laws are facially directed to "speech" (pictures, visual depictions) and, on their face, bring within immediate threat of severe criminal sanction some material which the First Amendment may well protect despite the sexually explicit (but nonobscene) manner in which a particular young person may be shown (e.g., in a particular issue of National Geographic). Moreover, the Court sustained the New York statute despite the absence of any provision providing for *any* exceptions, dismissing the "unconstitutional chilling effect" complaint. (By denying that the degree of facial overbreadth was "substantial," it disallowed a "void on its face" challenge, even while reserving an "as applied" challenge as it might arise in a case suitably presenting the question in a specific

rationale, however, the Court also notes that none of these statutes applies where the depicted persons are not in fact underage, however they may have been selected and featured for their very youthful look.[49c]

2. As noted also in *Ferber*, there is a parallel act of Congress, 18 U.S.C.§ 2252. Titled "The Protection of Children Against Sexual Exploitation Act of 1977," the federal statute differs from the New York statute principally in extending the critical age of any "performer" forbidden to be featured in any visual depiction of "sexually explicit conduct" to anyone under eighteen (rather than only to those under sixteen). In this respect, the federal statute does sweep more widely than the New York act. (Additionally, the sanctions for violations of this federal act are quite severe — up to fifteen years imprisonment for a single offense, up to thirty years for two or more.)[49d]

---

factual context.)

49c. As might be the case, for example, in casting the lead female role in a stage or film version of Vladimir Nabokov's Lolita, or in preparing copy for a magazine apparently featuring prepubescent girls and boys in various sexually explicit depictions. (If "obscene," such depictions might put the producer, distributor or buyer at risk but, if so, presumably only under the more stringent requirements of being "obscene"). Nor do these statutes apply to essays, novels, or other forms of speech describing, whether clinically or alluringly, varieties or qualities of sexuality or sensuality of the young, nor to "visual depictions" that are themselves graphic illustrations but of no actual underage person (i.e., an artist's imaginative renderings are not reached). So, "ideological pedophilia" (books, films, plays, etc., presenting the "affirmative case" for "freer sexual liberality involving pubescent or prepubescent 'minors'") is not, as such, affected by the New York law. (See and compare *Kingsley International Pictures Corp. v. Regents of The University of The State of New York*, casebook at p. 781.)

49d. The 1977 act was enacted by Congress pursuant to its express power to "regulate Commerce...among the several states" (U.S. Const. Art. I §8, cl. 3). Note, however, under the 1977 act, it is not necessary that there be any sale, or purchase, or commercial exchange — whether in interstate commerce or otherwise — to trigger the act. Rather, the act applies in respect to any visual depiction of the described forbidden kind (i.e., of a person under eighteen depicted in certain sexually-explicit acts or poses) produced (or intended to be produced) for distribution via any medium of interstate commerce, as it likewise applies to any such depiction distributed or received by means of any such medium (including receiving by computer). Moreover, the act also applies if the visual depiction of the described forbidden kind is produced (whether "produced" by the sender or "produced" by the receiver) by means merely "*using* materials that have been mailed or shipped or transported in interstate or foreign commerce by any means." In brief, the federal statute is extremely far-reaching in its application and effect, substantially overlapping most of the state laws of the same general kind. (For example, a lower federal court has held that the statute applies even if the only connection with interstate commerce is that the camera (or some component thereof) used to produce the picture, or the film, or the photographic paper used to print the picture, had an

This 1977 federal act was initially held unconstitutional, however, for lack of any scienter requirement respecting the age of the person or persons depicted in the sexually explicit material. That is, as the ninth circuit understood the matter, this act (unlike the New York statute upheld in *Ferber*) applied whether or not one charged under the act neither knew or had reason to know that anyone featured in any of the sexually explicit visual depictions was in fact under eighteen.[49e] The Supreme Court reversed this ninth circuit decision, but only after it substantially narrowed the statute by implying a scienter requirement. According to the Court's ruling, to pursue a successful prosecution under § 2252, the government must in each case prove — by evidence convincing to a jury beyond reasonable doubt — that: (a) the defendant was aware of the sexually explicit nature of the material; and (b) was also aware that one or more of the persons depicted in the material was underage (i.e., under eighteen years of age).[49f] And so matters stood, as of 1994.

3. Shortly thereafter, however, Congress enacted an additional measure, 18 U.S.C. § 2252A.[49g] Dissatisfied with the limited reach of the 1977 Act insofar as it only

---

out-of-state origin; nor is it consequential that the defendant did not know the statute would thus apply.)

49e. Applying the Supreme Court's earlier decision in *Smith v. California* (casebook at p. 777), the ninth circuit held the act to be "void on its face."

49f. *See United States v. X-Citement Video, Inc.*, 513 U.S. 64, 78 (1994) (emphasis added) ("[W]e conclude that the term 'knowingly' in § 2252 extends *both* to the sexually explicit nature of the material *and to the age of the performers*.") (*Query* whether actual knowledge, rather than some lesser scienter standard (e.g., "reason to know") is constitutionally required of such statutes according to *Smith*.)

49g. The 1977 Act was enacted to halt the use of underage persons in the production and circulation of sexually explicit performances or material depicting such performances, on a finding by Congress like that relied upon by New York in *Ferber* — that "the use of children as subjects of pornographic materials is harmful to the physiological, emotional, and mental health of the child," i.e. the health of the child or children thus used or identifiably featured in the production. (Thus the very title of the 1977 Act as "The Protection of Children Against Sexual Exploitation Act of 1977.") The 1996 additions include this concern, but go well beyond, even as made quite clear by the much blunter title of the 1996 Act ("The Child Pornography Prevention Act"). What is sought to be "prevented" is "child pornography," neither more nor less. The phrase refers to a certain kind of material (just as the phrase "racist speech" refers to a certain kind of speech). Such material may typically involve underage persons in its presentation but need not involve any such person still to *be* "child pornography" in Congress's view.

Indeed, the phrase "child pornography" has been used from time to time to describe three different things, although some who use the term may think it properly applies (or should be applied) to all three of the varieties hereinafter described. For purposes of first amendment analysis in the assessment of different particular statutes, however, it may be useful to

reached sexually explicit visual depictions (or "performances") of actual minors (i.e., of persons under eighteen), Congress extended the definition of "child pornography" in a new section (§2256), to include any visual depiction[49h] where

> (A) the production of such visual depiction involves the use of a minor engaging in sexually explicit conduct;[49i] [or]
>
> (B) such visual depiction is, or appears to be, of a minor engaging in sexually explicit conduct;[49j] [or]
>
> (C) such visual depiction has been created, adapted, or modified to appear that an identifiable minor is engaging in sexually explicit conduct; [or]
>
> (D) such visual depiction is advertised, promoted, presented, described, or distributed in such a manner that conveys the impression that the material is or contains [such a visual depiction].

Under new subsections (B) and (D) of § 2252A, even if the "performer" (i.e., the person visually depicted as engaged in "sexually explicit conduct") is an adult and *not* a person under eighteen, if the visual depiction "appears" to be of such a person, or if

---

distinguish or separate these several strands: (a) "child pornography" as sexually explicit suggestive material *meant to appeal to minors* (see, e.g., *Ginsberg v. New York*, 390 U.S. 629 (1968) (sustaining restrictions on sales or distributions to minors of sexually explicit material the first amendment protects in respect to adults), and compare *Butler v. Michigan* (casebook at p. 760 n. 40), *Reno v. American Civil Liberties Union* (the next principal case in this Supplement); (b) "child pornography" as sexually explicit materials not particularly (and sometimes not at all) *meant to appeal to minors*, but *using* minors as performers, or *using* minors in sexually explicit depictions (e.g., as reviewed in *Ferber*); (c) "child pornography" as any sexually explicit material *conducive to exciting, promoting, encouraging, or gratifying a sexual interest in children.*

49h. [Including "undeveloped film and videotape, and data stored on computer disk or by electronic means which is capable of conversion into a visual image."] (Note, however, that *"verbal depictions"* are evidently excluded from the act, e.g., alluring, even graphic, sexual descriptions of minors as willing and/or desirable objects of sexual desire, are per se not subject to the act.) (Cf. The Indianapolis ordinance in *American Booksellers v. Hudnut*, casebook at p. 252 (actionable "pornography" defined as "the graphic sexually explicit subordination of women, whether in pictures or in words...." [etc.].)

49i. [This part may be but a restatement from the pre-existing statute.]

49j. [I.e. "appears to be...of a minor," though it is not, rather, it is actually of one who is eighteen or older. (Additionally, this part of the act may reach any such visual depiction even if it is of no real or actual person at all, as would be true, for example, of a graphic artist's imaginative drawings of prepubescent minors engaged in sexually-explicit conduct or poses)].

the material is presented *so to suggest* it is (though it is not), the producer (including as a "producer" any distributor or exhibitor) is subject to conviction — *unless* in the case of a producer,[49k] the defendant can and does prove the following to be true, in which case only shall he or she have an affirmative defense:

> (1) the alleged child pornography was produced using an *actual* person or persons engaging in sexually explicit conduct; [*and*]
> (2) each such person was an adult at the time the material was produced; [*and*]
> (3) the defendant did not advertise, promote, present, describe, or distribute the material in such a manner as to convey the impression it is or contains a visual depiction of a minor engaging in sexually explicit conduct.

These 1996 additions to the federal act clearly carry quite far beyond the original, limited design of 18 U.S.C. §2252. Even so, can these provisions also be squared with the first amendment? If so, on what possible rationale(s), and to what extent?[491]

Casebook, p. 845
Add as a note following *Barnes v. Glen Theatre, Inc.*

49k. (But evidently *not* in the case of one who knowingly receives and has in their possession three or more such visual depictions, i.e., the "affirmative defense" as immediately described in the text (and as set forth in § 2252A(c) of the Act), is evidently *not* available to one who "knowingly possesses any book, magazine periodical, film, videotape, computer disk, or any other material that contains 3 or more images of child pornography that has been...transported in interstate or foreign commerce by any means...or that was produced using materials that have been [so transported]." (See 18 U.S.C. § 2256(8) (defining "child pornography"), and compare § 2252A(a) describing who is subject to criminal prosecution for producing, distributing, or possessing such material), and §2252A(c) (describing who may and may not present an affirmative defense, and describing the necessary elements of such defense).)

49l. For two recent — but far from conclusive — lower court opinions, *see The Free Speech Coalition v. Reno*, 1997 WL 487758 (N.D. Cal.) (sustaining the act against first amendment "overbreadth" objections); *United States v. Hilton*, 1999 F. Supp. 131 (D. Me. 1998) (voiding the act on first amendment "vagueness" grounds), *reversed*, 167 F.3d 61 (1st Cir. 1999), *petition for certiorari filed. See also American Booksellers Ass'n v. Hudnut* (casebook at 252); *Ginsberg v. United States* (casebook at 790); *Mishkin v. New York* (Casebook at 797). (Recall still again that there is, in respect to what is covered in these provisions, just as in *Ferber*, no requirement that the material be "obscene.")

For virtual reprise of *Barnes v. Glen Theatre, Inc., see City of Erie v. Pap's A.M.,* 530 U.S. ____ (March 29, 2000). (City ordinance banning "public nudity" including "nude erotic dancing," and requiring minimum "pasties" and "G-string" on adult performers; *sustained,* five-to-three). (Judgment of Court in an Opinion by O'Connor, J., joined by Rehnquist, C.J., Kennedy and Breyer, JJ., applying *O'Brien* to sustain the ordinance; separate opinion by Scalia, J., which Thomas, J. joined, finding no First Amendment question. Souter, J., dissented, finding *O'Brien* appropriate but faulting majority's application (and retracting parts of his *Barnes* concurrence); Stevens and Ginsburg, JJ., separately dissenting, finding *O'Brien* plainly inapplicable and concluding as had the state supreme court, that the ordinance was not sustainable under *Ward* (i.e., not sustainable as a content-neutral, "time, place, and manner" test).)

RENO v. AMERICAN CIVIL LIBERTIES UNION
521 U.S. 844 (1997)

JUSTICE STEVENS delivered the opinion of the Court.

At issue is the constitutionality of two statutory provisions enacted to protect minors from "indecent" and "patently offensive" communications on the Internet. Notwithstanding the legitimacy and importance of the congressional goal of protecting children from harmful materials, we agree with the three-judge District Court that the statute abridges "the freedom of speech" protected by the First Amendment.

I

The District Court made extensive findings of fact, most of which were based on a detailed stipulation by the parties. *** Because those findings provide the underpinning for the legal issues, we begin with a summary of the undisputed facts.

The Internet

The Internet *** is the outgrowth of what began in 1969 as a military program called "ARPANET," which was designed to enable computers operated by the military, defense contractors, and universities conducting defense-related research to communicate with one another by redundant channels even if some portions of the network were damaged in a war. While ARPANET no longer exists, it provided an example for the development of a number of civilian networks that, eventually linking with each other, now enable tens of millions of people to communicate with one another and to access vast amounts of information from around the world. The Internet is "a unique and wholly new medium of worldwide human communication."

The Internet has experienced "extraordinary growth." The number of "host" computers — those that store information and relay communications — increased from about 300 in 1981 to approximately 9,400,000 by the time of the trial in 1996. Roughly 60% of these hosts are located in the United States. About 40 million people used the Internet at the time of trial, a number that is expected to mushroom to 200 million by 1999.

Individuals can obtain access to the Internet from many different sources, generally hosts themselves or entities with a host affiliation. Most universities provide access for their students and faculty; many corporations provide their employees with access through an office network; many communities and local libraries provide free access; and an increasing number of storefront "computer coffee shops" provide access for a small hourly fee. Several major national "online services" offer access to their own extensive proprietary networks as well as a link to the much larger resources of the Internet. These commercial online services had almost 12 million individual subscribers at the time of trial.

Anyone with access to the Internet may take advantage of a wide variety of communication and information retrieval methods. [T]hose most relevant to this case are electronic mail ("e-mail"), automatic mailing list services ("mail exploders," sometimes referred to as "listservs"), "newsgroups," "chat rooms," and the "World Wide Web." *** A mail exploder is a sort of e-mail group. Subscribers can send messages to a common e-mail address, which then forwards the message to the group's other subscribers. Newsgroups also serve groups of regular participants, but these postings may be read by others as well. There are thousands of such groups, each serving to foster an exchange of information or opinion on a particular topic running the gamut from, say, the music of Wagner to Balkan politics to AIDS prevention to the Chicago Bulls. ***

The best known category of communication over the Internet is the World Wide Web, which allows users to search for and retrieve information stored in remote computers, as well as, in some cases, to communicate back to designated sites. In concrete terms, the Web consists of a vast number of documents stored in different computers all over the world. Some of these documents are simply files containing information. However, more elaborate documents, commonly known as Web pages, are also prevalent. *** The Web is comparable, from the readers' viewpoint, to both a vast library including millions of readily available and indexed publications and a sprawling mall offering goods and services.

From the publishers' point of view, it constitutes a vast platform from which to address and hear from a world-wide audience of millions of readers, viewers, researchers, and buyers. Any person or organization with a computer connected to the Internet can "publish" information. *** Publishers may either make their material available to the entire pool of Internet users, or confine access to a selected group, such as those willing to pay for the privilege. No single organization controls any membership in the Web, nor is there any centralized point from which individual Web sites or services can be blocked from the Web.

Sexually Explicit Material

Sexually explicit material on the Internet includes text, pictures, and chat and extends from the modestly titillating to the hardest-core. These files are created, named, and posted in the same manner as material that is not sexually explicit, and may be accessed either deliberately or unintentionally during the course of an imprecise search. Thus, for example,

> "when the UCR/California Museum of Photography posts to its Web site nudes by Edward Weston and Robert Mapplethorpe to announce that its new exhibit will travel to Baltimore and New York City, those images are available not only in Los Angeles, Baltimore, and New York City, but also in Cincinnati, Mobile, or Beijing — wherever Internet users live. Similarly, the safer sex instructions that Critical Path posts to its Web site, written in street language so that the teenage receiver can understand them, are available not just in Philadelphia, but also in Provo and Prague."

Systems have been developed to help parents control the material that may be available on a home computer with Internet access. *** Although parental control software currently can screen for certain suggestive words or for known sexually explicit sites, it cannot now screen for sexually explicit images." ***

Age Verification

The problem of age verification differs for different uses of the Internet. The District Court categorically determined that there "is no effective way to determine the identity or the age of a user who is accessing material through e-mail, mail exploders, newsgroups or chat rooms." The Government offered no evidence that there was a reliable way to screen recipients and participants in such fora for age. Moreover, even if it were technologically feasible to block minors' access to newsgroups and chat rooms containing discussions of art, politics or other subjects that potentially elicit "indecent" or "patently offensive" contributions, it would not be possible to block their access to that material and still allow them access to the remaining content, even if the overwhelming majority of that content was not indecent.

Technology exists by which an operator of a Web site may condition access on the verification of requested information such as a credit card number or an adult password. *** Using credit card possession as a surrogate for proof of age would impose costs on non-commercial Web sites that would require many of them to shut down. For that reason, at the time of the trial, credit card verification was "effectively unavailable to a substantial number of Internet content providers." Moreover, the imposition of such a requirement "would completely bar adults who do not have a credit card and lack the resources to obtain one from accessing any blocked material."

Commercial pornographic sites that charge their users for access have assigned them passwords as a method of age verification. The record does not contain any evidence concerning the reliability of these technologies. [T]he District Court found that an adult password requirement would impose significant burdens on noncommercial sites, both because they would discourage users from accessing their sites and because the cost of creating and maintaining such screening systems would be "beyond their reach." ***

II

The [primary purpose of the] Telecommunications Act of 1996 was to reduce regulation and encourage "the rapid deployment of new telecommunicationstechnologies." *** An amendment offered in the Senate was the source of the two statutory provisions challenged in this case. *** The first [§ 223(a)] prohibits the knowing transmission of obscene or indecent messages to any recipient under 18 years of age. It provides in pertinent part:

> (a) Whoever [by means of any telecommunications device] knowingly — ***

> (1) initiates the transmission of any comment, request, suggestion, proposal, image, or other communication which is obscene or indecent, knowing that the recipient of the communication is under 18 years of age, [or]

> (2) knowingly permits any telecommunications facility under his control to be used for any activity prohibited by paragraph (1) with the intent that it be used for such activity — shall be fined under Title 18, or imprisoned not more than two years, or both.

The second provision [§ 223(d)] prohibits the knowing sending or displaying of patently offensive messages in a manner that is available to a person under 18 years of age. It provides:

Whoever — ***

> (1) knowingly uses any interactive computer service to display in a manner available to a person under 18 years of age, any comment, request, suggestion, proposal, image, or other communication that, in context, depicts or describes, in terms patently offensive as measured by contemporary community standards, sexual or excretory activities or organs, [or]

(2) knowingly permits any telecommunications facility under such person's control to be used for an activity prohibited by paragraph (1) with the intent that it be used for such activity —

— shall be fined under Title 18, United States Code, or imprisoned not more than two years, or both.

The breadth of these prohibitions is qualified by two affirmative defenses. One covers those who take "good faith, reasonable, effective, and appropriate actions" to restrict access by minors to the prohibited communications. The other covers those who restrict access to covered material by requiring certain designated forms of age proof, such as a verified credit card or an adult identification number or code.

[III - XI]

[T]he Government contends that the CDA is plainly constitutional under three of our prior decisions: (1) *Ginsberg v. New York*; (2) *FCC v. Pacifica Foundation*; and (3) *Renton v. Playtime Theatres, Inc*. ***

In four important respects, the statute upheld in *Ginsberg* was narrower than the CDA. First, we noted in *Ginsberg* that "the prohibition against sales to minors does not bar parents who so desire from purchasing the magazines for their children." Under the CDA, by contrast, neither the parents' consent — nor even their participation — in the communication would avoid the application of the statute. Second, the New York statute applied only to commercial transactions, whereas the CDA contains no such limitation. Third, the New York statute cabined its definition of material that is harmful to minors with the requirement that it be "utterly without redeeming social importance for minors." The CDA fails to provide us with any definition of the term "indecent" as used in § 223(a)(1) and, importantly, omits any requirement that the "patently offensive" material covered by § 223(d) lack serious literary, artistic, political, or scientific value. Fourth, the New York statute defined a minor as a person under the age of 17, whereas the CDA, in applying to all those under 18 years, includes an additional year of those nearest majority. ***

*** [T]here are [likewise] significant differences between the order upheld in *Pacifica* and the CDA. First, the order in *Pacifica*, issued by an agency that had been regulating radio stations for decades, targeted a specific broadcast that represented a rather dramatic departure from traditional program content in order to designate when — rather than whether — it would be permissible to air such a program in that particular medium. The CDA's broad categorical prohibitions are not limited to particular times and are not dependent on any evaluation by an agency familiar with the unique characteristics of the Internet. Second, the Commission's declaratory order was not punitive; we expressly refused to decide whether the indecent broadcast "would justify a criminal prosecution." Finally, the Commission's order applied to a medium which as a matter of history had "received the most limited First Amendment protection," in large part because warnings could not adequately protect the listener from unexpected program content. The Internet, however, has no comparable history. Moreover, the District Court found that the risk of encountering indecent material by accident is remote because a series of affirmative steps is required to access specific material.

In *Renton*, we upheld a zoning ordinance that kept adult movie theatres out of residential neighborhoods. *** According to the Government, the CDA is constitutional because it constitutes a sort of "cyberzoning" on the Internet. But the CDA applies broadly to the entire universe of cyberspace. And the purpose of the CDA is to protect children from the primary effects of "indecent" and "patently offensive" speech, rather than any "secondary" effect of such speech. Thus, the CDA is a content-based blanket restriction on speech, and, as such, cannot be "properly analyzed as a form of time, place, and manner regulation." ***

Finally, unlike the conditions that prevailed when Congress first authorized regulation of the broadcast spectrum, the Internet can hardly be considered a "scarce" expressive commodity. *** [O]ur cases provide no basis for qualifying the level of First Amendment scrutiny that should be applied to this medium.

Regardless of whether the CDA is so vague that it violates the Fifth Amendment, the many ambiguities concerning the scope of its coverage render it problematic for purposes of the First Amendment. For instance, each of the two parts of the CDA uses a different linguistic form. The first uses the word "indecent," while the second speaks of material that "in context, depicts or describes, in terms patently offensive as measured by contemporary community standards, sexual or excretory activities or organs." Given the absence of a definition of either term, this difference in language will provoke uncertainty among speakers about how the two standards relate to each other and just what they mean.[37] ***

We are persuaded that the CDA lacks the precision that the First Amendment requires when a statute regulates the content of speech. In order to deny minors access to potentially harmful speech, the CDA effectively suppresses a large amount of speech that adults have a constitutional right to receive and to address to one another. *** It is true that we have repeatedly recognized the governmental interest in protecting children from harmful materials. But that interest does not justify an unnecessarily broad suppression of speech addressed to adults. [T]he Government may not "reduc[e] the adult population *** to *** only what is fit for children." ***

In arguing that the CDA does not so diminish adult communication, the Government relies on the incorrect factual premise that prohibiting a transmission whenever it is

---

37. The statute does not indicate whether the "patently offensive" and "indecent" determinations should be made with respect to minors or the population as a whole.

known that one of its recipients is a minor would not interfere with adult-to-adult communication. [T]his premise is untenable. *** Knowledge that, for instance, one or more members of a 100-person chat group will be minor — and therefore that it would be a crime to send the group an indecent message — would surely burden communication among adults.[42]

The breadth of the CDA's coverage is wholly unprecedented. Unlike the regulations upheld in *Ginsberg* and *Pacifica*, the scope of the CDA is not limited to commercial speech or commercial entities. Its open-ended prohibitions embrace all nonprofit entities and individuals posting indecent messages or displaying them on their own computers in the presence of minors. The general, undefined terms "indecent" and "patently offensive" cover large amounts of nonpornographic material with serious educational or other value.[44] Moreover, the "community standards" criterion as applied to the Internet means that any communication available to a nation-wide audience will be judged by the standards of the community most likely to be offended by the message. The regulated subject matter includes any of the seven "dirty words" used in the *Pacifica* monologue, the use of which the Government's expert acknowledged could constitute a felony. It may also extend to discussions about prison rape or safe sexual practices, artistic images that include nude subjects, and arguably the card catalogue of the Carnegie Library.

In an attempt to curtail the CDA's facial overbreadth, the Government advances three additional arguments for sustaining the Act's affirmative prohibitions: *** The Government first contends that, even though the CDA effectively censors discourse on many of the Internet's modalities-such as chat groups, newsgroups, and mail exploders — it is nonetheless constitutional because it provides a "reasonable opportunity" for speakers to engage in the restricted speech on the World Wide Web. This argument is unpersuasive because the CDA regulates speech on the basis of its content. A "time, place, and manner" analysis is therefore inapplicable. *** The Government's position is equivalent to arguing that a statute could ban leaflets on certain subjects as long as individuals are free to publish books.

The Government also asserts that the "knowledge" requirement of both §§ 223(a) and (d), especially when coupled with the "specific child" element found in § 223(d), saves the CDA from overbreadth. This argument ignores the fact that most Internet fora — including chat rooms, newsgroups, mail exploders, and the Web — are open to all

---

42. The Government agrees that these provisions are applicable whenever "a sender transmits a message to more than one recipient, knowing that at least one of the specific persons receiving the message is a minor."

44. Transmitting obscenity and child pornography, whether via the Internet or other means, is already illegal under federal law for both adults and juveniles. See 18 U.S.C. §§ 1464-1465 (criminalizing obscenity); § 2251 (criminalizing child pornography).

comers. *** Even the strongest reading of the "specific person" requirement of § 223(d) cannot save the statute. It would confer broad powers of censorship, in the form of a "heckler's veto," upon any opponent of indecent speech who might simply log on and inform the would-be discoursers that his 17-year-old child — a "specific person under 18 years of age," — would be present. ***

The Government's three remaining arguments focus on the defenses provided in § 223(e)(5). First, relying on the "good faith, reasonable, effective, and appropriate actions" provision, the Government suggests that "tagging" provides a defense that saves the constitutionality of the Act. *** The Government recognizes that its proposed screening software does not currently exist. Even if it did, there is no way to know whether a potential recipient will actually block the encoded material. Without the impossible knowledge that every guardian in America is screening for the "tag," the transmitter could not reasonably rely on its action to be "effective."

For its second and third arguments concerning defenses — which we can consider together — the Government relies on the latter half of § 223(e)(5), which applies when the transmitter has restricted access by requiring use of a verified credit card or adult identification. *** [T]his defense would not significantly narrow the statute's burden on noncommercial speech. Even with respect to the commercial pornographers that would be protected by the defense, the Government failed to adduce any evidence that these verification techniques actually preclude minors from posing as adults.[47] ***

For the foregoing reasons, the judgment of the district court is affirmed.***

JUSTICE O'CONNOR, with whom THE CHIEF JUSTICE joins, concurring in the judgment in part and dissenting in part.

I write separately to explain why I view the *** CDA as little more than an attempt by Congress to create "adult zones" on the Internet. *** The Court has previously sustained such zoning laws, but only if they respect the First Amendment rights of adults and minors. That is to say, a zoning law is valid if (I) it does not unduly restrict adult access to the material; and (ii) minors have no First Amendment right to read or view the banned material. ***

The Court in *Ginsberg* did not question — and therefore necessarily assumed — that an adult zone, once created, would succeed in preserving adults' access while denying minors' access to the regulated speech. Before today, there was no reason to question this assumption, for the Court has previously only considered laws that operated in the

---

47. Thus, ironically, this defense may significantly protect commercial purveyors of obscene postings while providing little (or no) benefit for transmitters of indecent messages that have significant social or artistic value.

physical world, a world that with two characteristics that make it possible to create "adult zones": geography and identity. A minor can see an adult dance show only if he enters an establishment that provides such entertainment. And should he attempt to do so, the minor will not be able to conceal completely his identity (or, consequently, his age). ***

Although the prospects for the eventual zoning of the Internet appear promising, I agree with the Court that we must evaluate the constitutionality of the CDA as it applies to the Internet as it exists today. Given the present state of cyberspace, I agree with the Court that the "display" provision cannot pass muster. Until gateway technology is available throughout cyberspace, and it is not in 1997, a speaker cannot be reasonably assured that the speech he displays will reach only adults because it is impossible to confine speech to an "adult zone." *** As a result, the "display" provision cannot withstand scrutiny.

The "indecency transmission" and "specific person" provisions present a closer issue, for they are not unconstitutional in all of their applications. [T]he "indecency transmission" provision makes it a crime to transmit knowingly an indecent message to a person the sender knows is under 18 years of age. The "specific person" provision proscribes the same conduct, although it does not as explicitly require the sender to know that the intended recipient of his indecent message is a minor. Appellant urges the Court to construe the provision to impose such a knowledge requirement, and I would do so. ***

*** Because the rights of adults are infringed only by the "display" provision and by the "indecency transmission" and "specific person" provisions as applied to communications involving more than one adult, I would invalidate the CDA only to that extent. Insofar as the "indecency transmission" and "specific person" provisions prohibit the use of indecent speech in communications between an adult and one or more minors, however, they can and should be sustained. The Court reaches a contrary conclusion, and from that holding that I respectfully dissent.

––––––

NOTES AND RECENT DEVELOPMENTS PERTINENT TO *RENO* AND THE INTERNET

1. After the Court decided *Reno v. ACLU*, Congress enacted the Child Online Protection Act ("COPA"), 47 U.S.C. § 231. The statute provides that whoever "knowingly and with knowledge of the character of the material, in interstate or foreign commerce by means of the World Wide Web, makes any communication for commercial purposes that is available to any minor and that includes any material that is harmful to minors shall be fined not more than $50,000 . . . ." Section 431(e)(6) defines material that is "harmful to minors" as material

— that is obscene *or* that

(A) the average person, applying contemporary community standards, would find, taking the material as a whole and with respect to minors, is designed to appear to, or is designed to pander to, the prurient interest;

(B) depicts, describes, or represents, in a manner patently offensive with respect to minors, an actual or simulated sexual act or sexual contact, an actual or simulated normal or perverted sexual act, or a lewd exhibition of the genitals or post-pubescent female breast; and

(C) taken as a whole, lacks serious literary, artistic, political, or scientific value for minors.

Has Congress remedied the problem(s), or is this susceptible to the same sort of challenge as that brought by plaintiffs in *Reno v. ACLU*? See *ACLU v. Reno*, 31 F. Supp.2d 473 (E.D. Pa. 1999).

2. A different section of the Communications Decency Act, not involved in *Reno*, relieves providers or users of any "interactive computer service"[61] of liability for declining to carry any material the provider or user of such a service finds objectionable. 47 U.S.C.§ 230(c) is captioned: "Protection for "good samaritan" blocking and screening of offensive material."

Subsection (2) of § 230(c) provides:

Civil Liability. No provider or user of an interactive computer service shall be held liable on account of —

(A) Any action voluntarily in good faith to restrict access to or availability of material that the provider or user considers to be obscene, lewd, lascivious, filthy, excessively violent, harassing, or otherwise objectionable, whether or not such material is constitutionally protected...

---

61. The phrase "interactive computer service" is defined in the same section (§ 230(e)) as follows: "any information service, system, or access software provider that provides or enables computer access by multiple users to a computer server, including specifically a service or system that provides access to the Internet and such systems operated or services offered by libraries or educational institutions."

On its face this section would appear to apply to *any* provider or to any user of such a service, including "providers" or "users" operating under state and local government authority. Even so, it probably does not do so.[62] Section 230 is captioned: "Protection for *private* blocking and screening of offensive material," and the few courts thus far addressing the section have construed it to reflect a policy by Congress merely (if significantly) to insulate private parties and companies from possible tort or other state-law based suits by persons seeking legal recourse against them for blocking access to material they wish to receive.[63]

---

62. Were it to do so, the first amendment issues confronted in *Reno* would be obvious (i.e., to grant a virtual censorship power to units of state and local government in the sweeping terms of this section, is a near-certain formula to insure the act would not be sustained).

63. *See, e.g., Zeran v. America Online Inc.*, 129 F.3d 327 (4th Cir. 1997), *cert. denied*, 118 S. Ct. 2341 (1998); *Mainstream Loudoun v. Bd. Of Trustees of Loudoun Cty Library*, 2 F. Supp.2d 783 (E.D. Va. 1998) (both cases construing § 230(c)(2) this way). Section 230(d) lends some support to this interpretation. [Section] 230(d)(3) is captioned "Effect on ... State law," and provides that "No cause of action may be brought and no liability may be imposed under any State or local law that is inconsistent with this section." A "state or local law" would presumably be "inconsistent" with § 230(c)(2) insofar as it would provide a cause of action against a provider or user of an interactive computer service screening, or blocking, or refusing access in any manner § 230 expressly permits them "voluntarily" so to choose to do. (Given this understanding of the act, note its similarly to the provisions of the cablevision act reviewed in *Denver Area*, p. 19 of this Supplement, which expressly permit cable companies to block access to "indecent" material on leased access and public access channels, sustained in part, held unconstitutional in part.) (Recall from *PruneYard Shopping Center*, casebook at p. 599, that some states, e.g., California, have constitutional provisions protecting freedom of speech from private abridgment and not merely from abridgment by government. Section 230(d)(3) would appear to preclude the California Supreme Court from applying any such provision against any private party acting within the scope of § 230(c)(2)(A)).

The legislative history accompanying § 230(c) also suggests it is meant to protect interactive computer service providers, such as AOL and Compuserve, from becoming liable, as publishers, to persons suing for defamation, for digitalized statements sent over the service provider's system, merely because they presume to screen some of the material accessed through their systems, but do not presume to act as "editors" in any general sense. Generally, commercial information service providers who merely provide the interactive connecting and transmission service for paying users are not regarded as "publishers" of the information carried by means of their service (and thus are not liable themselves for libelous statements other originate and send or retransmit through their system). *See* discussion in *Cubby, Inc. v. Compuserve, Inc.*, 776 F. Supp. 135 (S.D.N.Y. 1991); *see also* Michael Hadley, Note, *The Gertz Doctrine and Internet Defamation,* 84 Va. L. Rev. 477 (1998). Where such a company assumes responsibility for "editing" what comes through its system, however, it may be sued as a (re)publisher of a libelous statement. *See, e.g., Stratton Oakmont, Inc. v. Prodigy Services Co.*, 1995 WL 323710 (N.Y.S.Ct.). What § 230(d)(3) does is to make clear that a commercial private service provider shall not become liable in libel for acting as an "editor"

Even so, some government entities *have* mandated the installation of software blocking programs on their own government initiative, on computer terminals maintained under their authority, limiting what adults as well as "children" (minors) are able to access. And some have done so, even in a manner as broad (or broader) than the restriction imposed by Congress held void for overbreadth, in *Reno*. For example, pursuant to a general Virginia statute authorizing local public library boards to adopt regulations for "the government of the free public library system as may be expedient," a county library board in Virginia directed that site-blocking software be installed in each branch library on computers, effective to block material deemed harmful to juveniles. To implement the policy, the county library board chose "X-Stop," a commercial software product which, as installed, blocked access to sites local library patrons would otherwise be able to access from computer terminals at the public library, but were no longer able so to do because of the X-Stop screening. Local resident adult library users finding Internet access sites blocked by the X-Stop software, when they came to the library and attempted to use the public library computer terminals, filed suit in federal district court to have the board enjoined from maintaining the system.[64] Considering the case in light of *Reno*, how might one expect the court to rule?[65]

———

UNITED STATES v. PLAYBOY ENTERTAINMENT GROUP
530 U.S.____ May 22, 2000

KENNEDY, J., delivered the opinion of the Court, in which STEVENS, SOUTER, THOMAS, and GINSBURG, JJ., joined. *

This case presents a challenge to § 505 of the Telecommunications Act of 1996. Section 505 requires cable television operators who provide channels "primarily dedicated to sexually-oriented programming" either to "fully scramble or otherwise fully block" those channels or to limit their transmission to hours when children are

---

in the manner Congress expressly authorizes in § 230(c).

64. The case in this respect is similar to *Board of Educ. v. Pico*, casebook at p. 383 (suit by students to enjoin removal of books from public school library), and to *Lamont v. Postmaster General*, 381 U.S. 301 (1965) (noted in casebook at p. 428, n. 65) (suit by postal addressee of intercepted mail).

65. *See Mainstream Loudoun v. Bd. of Trustees of Loudoun Cty. Library*, 2 F. Supp.2d 783 (E.D. Va. 1998).

* [Separate concurring opinions by Stevens, J. and by Thomas, J., and a separate dissenting opinion by Scalia, J., are omitted. The dissenting opinion by Breyer, J., joined by Scalia and O'Connor, J.J., and by Rehnquist, C.J., appears at p. 106 *infra*.]

unlikely to be viewing, set by administrative regulation as the time between 10 p.m. and 6 a.m.* Appellee Playboy Entertainment Group, Inc., challenged the statute as unnecessarily restrictive content-based legislation violative of the First Amendment. After a trial, a three-judge District Court concluded that a regime in which viewers could order signal blocking on a household-by-household basis presented an effective, less restrictive alternative to § 505. [W]e affirm.

I

Playboy transmits its programming to cable television operators, who retransmit it to their subscribers, either through monthly subscriptions to premium channels or on a so-called "pay-per-view" basis. Cable operators transmit Playboy's signal, like other premium channel signals, in scrambled form. The operators then provide paying subscribers with an "addressable converter," a box placed on the home television set. The converter permits the viewer to see and hear the descrambled signal. It is conceded that almost all of Playboy's programming consists of sexually explicit material as defined by the statute.

The statute was enacted because not all scrambling technology is perfect. With imperfect scrambling, viewers who have not paid to receive Playboy's channels may happen across discernible images of a sexually explicit nature. How many viewers, how discernible the scene or sound, and how often this may occur are at issue in this case. ***

[T]he District Court held a full trial and concluded that § 505 violates the First Amendment. It agreed that the interests the statute advanced were compelling but concluded the Government might further those interests in less restrictive ways. One plausible, less restrictive alternative could be found in another section of the Act: § 504, which requires a cable operator, "upon request by a cable service subscriber … without charge, [to] fully scramble or otherwise fully block" any channel the subscriber does not wish to receive. As long as subscribers knew about this opportunity, the court reasoned, § 504 would provide as much protection against unwanted programming as would § 505. At the same time, 504 was content neutral and would be less restrictive of Playboy's First Amendment rights. The court described what "adequate notice" would include, suggesting "[operators] should communicate to their subscribers the information that certain channels broadcast sexually-oriented programming; that signal bleed... may appear; that children may view signal bleed without their parents' knowledge or permission; that channel blocking devices are available free of charge and that a request for a free device can be made by a telephone call to the [operator]."*** The District Court concluded that § 504 so supplemented would be an effective, less restrictive alternative to § 505, and consequently declared § 505 unconstitutional and enjoined its enforcement. The court also required Playboy to insist on these notice provisions in its contracts with cable operators.

II

Two essential points should be understood concerning the speech at issue here. First, we shall assume that many adults themselves would find the material highly offensive; and when we consider the further circumstance that the material comes unwanted into homes where children might see or hear it against parental wishes or consent, there are legitimate reasons for regulating it. Second, all parties bring the case to us on the premise that Playboy's programming has First Amendment protection. As this case has been litigated, it is not alleged to be obscene; adults have a constitutional right to view it; the Government disclaims any interest in preventing children from seeing or hearing it with the consent of their parents... These points are undisputed.

The speech in question is defined by its content; and the statute which seeks to restrict it is content based. Section 505 is not "'justified without reference to the content of the regulated speech.'" *Ward v. Rock Against Racism*, 491 U.S. 781, 791 (1989). It "focuses only on the content of the speech and the direct impact that speech has on its listeners." *Boos v. Barry*, 485 U.S. 312, 321(1988). This is the essence of content-based regulation. Not only does § 505 single out particular programming content for regulation, it also singles out particular programmers. The speech in question was not thought by Congress to be so harmful that all channels were subject to restriction.***Section 505 limited Playboy's market as a penalty for its programming choice, though other channels capable of transmitting like material are altogether exempt.

The effect of the federal statute on the protected speech is [sustained]. According to the District Court, "30 to 50% of all adult programming is viewed by households prior to 10 p.m.," when the safe-harbor period begins. To prohibit this much speech is a significant restriction of communication between speakers and willing adult listeners, communication which enjoys First Amendment protection. It is of no moment that the statute does not impose a complete prohibition. The distinction between laws burdening and laws banning speech is but a matter of degree.*** If a statute regulates speech based on its content, it must be narrowly tailored to promote a compelling Government interest. If a less restrictive alternative would serve the Government's purpose, the legislature must use that alternative. *Reno,* 521 U.S. at 874. ("[The CDA's Internet indecency provisions'] burden on adult speech is unacceptable if less restrictive alternatives would be at least as effective in achieving the legitimate purpose that the statute was enacted to serve").

Our precedents teach these principles. Where the designed benefit of a content-based speech restriction is to shield the sensibilities of listeners, the general rule is that the right of expression prevails, even where no less restrictive alternative exists. We are expected to protect our own sensibilities "simply by averting [our] eyes." *Cohen v. California*, 403 U.S. 15, 21 (1971). [E]ven where speech is indecent and enters the home, the objective of shielding children does not suffice to support a blanket ban if the protection can be accomplished by a less restrictive alternative.

There is, moreover, a key difference between cable television and the broadcasting media, which is the point on which this case turns: Cable systems have the capacity to block unwanted channels on a household-by-household basis. The option to block reduces the likelihood, so concerning to the Court *in Pacifica,* that traditional First Amendment scrutiny would deprive the Government of all authority to address this sort of problem. The corollary, of course, is that targeted blocking enables the Government to support parental authority without affecting the First Amendment interests of speakers and willing listeners. *** This is not to say that the absence of an effective blocking mechanism will in all cases suffice to support a law restricting the speech in question; but if a less restrictive means is available for the Government to achieve its goals, the Government must use it.

III

When a plausible, less restrictive alternative is offered to a content-based speech restriction, it is the Government's obligation to prove that the alternative will be ineffective to achieve its goals.

The Government has not met that burden here. In support of its position, the Government cites empirical evidence showing that § 504, as promulgated and implemented before trial, generated few requests for household-by-household blocking. A survey of cable operators determined that fewer than 0.5% of cable subscribers requested full blocking during that time. The uncomfortable fact is that § 504 was the sole blocking regulation in effect for over a year; and the public greeted it with a collective yawn. The District Court was correct to direct its attention to the import of this tepid response. Placing the burden of proof upon the Government, the District Court examined whether § 504 was capable of serving as an effective, less restrictive means of reaching the Government's goals. It concluded that § 504, if publicized in an adequate manner, could be.

*** There is no evidence that a well-promoted voluntary blocking provision would not be capable at least of informing parents about signal bleed (if they are not yet aware of it) and about their rights to have the bleed blocked (if they consider it a problem and have not yet controlled it themselves).

The Government finds at least two problems with the conclusion of the three-judge District Court. First, the Government takes issue with the District Court's reliance, without proof, on a "hypothetical, enhanced version of Section 504." It was not the District Court's obligation, however, to predict the extent to which an improved notice scheme would improve § 504. It was for the Government, presented with a plausible, less restrictive alternative, to prove the alternative to be ineffective, and § 505 to be the least restrictive available means.

Having adduced no evidence in the District Court showing that an adequately advertised § 504 would not be effective to aid desirous parents in keeping signal bleed out of their own households, the Government can now cite nothing in the record to support the point. The Government instead takes quite a different approach.

After only an offhand suggestion that the success of a well-communicated § 504 is "highly unlikely," the Government sets the point aside, arguing instead that society's independent interests will be unserved if parents fail to act on that information. [But even] on the assumption that the Government has an interest in substituting itself for informed and empowered parents, its interest is not sufficiently compelling to justify this widespread restriction on speech. The Government's argument stems from the idea that parents do not know their children are viewing the material on a scale or frequency to cause concern, or if so, that parents do not want to take affirmative steps to block it and their decisions are to be superseded. The assumptions have not been established; and in any event the assumptions apply only in a regime where the option of blocking has not been explained. The whole point of a publicized § 504 would be to advise parents that indecent material may be shown and to afford them an opportunity to block it at all times, even when they are not at home and even after 10 p.m.***

The history of the law of free expression is one of vindication in cases involving speech that many citizens may find shabby, offensive, or even ugly. It follows that all content-based restrictions on speech must give us more than a moment's pause. If television broadcasts can expose children to the real risk of harmful exposure to indecent materials, even in their own home and without parental consent, there is a problem the Government can address. It must do so, however, in a way consistent with First Amendment principles. Here the Government has not met the burden the First Amendment imposes.

The judgment of the District Court is affirmed.

JUSTICE BREYER, with whom THE CHIEF JUSTICE, JUSTICE O'CONNOR, and JUSTICE SCALIA join, dissenting.

The basic, applicable First Amendment principles are not at issue. The Court must examine the statute before us with great care to determine whether its speech-related restrictions are justified by a "compelling interest," namely an interest in limiting children's access to sexually explicit material. In doing so, it recognizes that the legislature must respect adults' viewing freedom by "narrowly tailoring" the statute so that it restricts no more speech than necessary, and choosing instead any alternative that would further the compelling interest in a "less restrictive" but "at least as effective" way. See *Reno v. American Civil Liberties Union*, 521 U.S. 844, 874 (1997).

I turn then to the major point of disagreement. Section 504 gives parents the power to tell cable operators to keep any channel out of their home. Section 505 does more. Unless parents explicitly consent, it inhibits the transmission of adult cable channels to children whose parents may be unaware of what they are watching, whose parents cannot easily supervise television viewing habits, whose parents do not know of their § 504 "opt-out" rights, or whose parents are simply unavailable at critical times. In this respect, § 505 serves the same interests as the laws that deny children access to adult cabarets or X-rated movies.

Section 505 raises the cost of adult channel broadcasting. In doing so, it restricts, but does not ban adult speech. Adults may continue to watch adult channels, though less conveniently, by watching at night, recording programs with a VCR, or by subscribing to digital cable with better blocking systems. *Cf. Renton,* 475 U.S. at 53-55 (upholding zoning rules that force potential adult theatre patrons to travel to less convenient locations). The Government's justification for imposing this restriction -- limiting the access of children to channels that broadcast virtually 100% "sexually explicit" material -- is "compelling." The record shows no similarly effective, less restrictive alternative. Consequently § 505's restriction, viewed in light of the proposed alternative, is proportionate to need. That is to say, it restricts speech no more than necessary to further that compelling need. Taken together, these considerations lead to the conclusion that § 505 is lawful.

I respectfully dissent.

NATIONAL ENDOWMENT FOR THE ARTS v.FINLEY
524 U.S. 569 (1998)

JUSTICE O'CONNOR delivered the opinion of the Court.

I
A

[In 1965, an] enabling statute vest[ed] the NEA with substantial discretion to award grants; it identifie[d] only the broadest funding priorities, including "artistic and cultural significance, giving emphasis to American creativity and cultural diversity," "professional excellence," and the encouragement of "public knowledge, education, understanding, and appreciation of the arts." *** Since 1965, the NEA has distributed over three billion dollars in grants to individuals and organizations, funding that has served as a catalyst for increased state, corporate, and foundation support for the arts.

Throughout the NEA's history, only a handful of the agency's roughly 100,000 awards have generated formal complaints about misapplied funds or abuse of the public's trust. Two provocative works, however, prompted public controversy. The Institute of Contemporary Art at the University of Pennsylvania had used $30,000 of a visual arts grant it received from the NEA to fund a 1989 retrospective of photographer Robert Mapplethorpe's work. The exhibit included homoerotic photographs that several Members of Congress condemned as pornographic. Members also denounced artist Andres Serrano's work Piss Christ, a photograph of a crucifix immersed in urine.***

In the 1990 appropriations bill, Congress *** adopted *** a bipartisan compromise between Members opposing any funding restrictions and those favoring some guidance to the agency. The Amendment became § 954(d)(1), which directs the Chairperson, in establishing procedures to judge the artistic merit of grant applications, to "take into consideration general standards of decency and respect for the diverse beliefs and values of the American public."*

The NEA has not promulgated any official interpretation of the provision, but in December 1990, the Council unanimously adopted a resolution to implement § 954(d)(1) merely by ensuring that the members of the advisory panels that conduct the initial review of grant applications represent geographic, ethnic, and aesthetic diversity. John Frohnmayer, then Chairperson of the NEA, also declared that he would "count on [the] procedures" ensuring diverse membership on the peer review panels to fulfill Congress' mandate.

B

The four individual respondents in this case, Karen Finley, John Fleck, Holly Hughes, and Tim Miller, are performance artists who applied for NEA grants before § 954(d)(1) was enacted. *** When Congress enacted § 954(d)(1), respondents, now joined by the National Association of Artists' Organizations (NAAO), amended their complaint to challenge the provision as void for vagueness and impermissibly viewpoint based.*** The District Court denied the NEA's motion for judgment on the pleadings, and, after discovery, the NEA agreed to settle the individual respondents' statutory and as-applied constitutional claims by paying the artists.*** The District Court then granted summary judgment in favor of respondents on their facial constitutional challenge to § 954(d)(1) and enjoined enforcement of the provision.*** A divided panel of the Court of Appeals affirmed the District Court's ruling. ***Respondents raise a facial constitutional challenge to § 954(d)(1), and consequently they confront "a heavy burden" in advancing their claim. Facial invalidation "is, manifestly, strong medicine" that "has been employed by the Court sparingly and only as a last resort." *Broadrick v. Oklahoma*, 413 U.S. 601, 613 (1973). To prevail, respondents must

---

* [Title 20 U.S.C.§ 954 (d) provides that:

"No payment shall be made under this section except upon application therefor which is submitted to the National Endowment for the Arts in accordance with regulations issued and procedures established by the Chairperson. In establishing such regulations and procedures, the Chairperson shall ensure that

(1) artistic excellence and artistic merit are the criteria by which applications are judged, taking into consideration general standards of decency and respect for the diverse beliefs and values of the American public; and

(2) applications are consistent with the purposes of this section. Such regulations and procedures shall clearly indicate that obscenity is without artistic merit, is not protected speech, and shall not be funded."]

demonstrate a substantial risk that application of the provision will lead to the suppression of speech.

Respondents argue that the provision is a paradigmatic example of viewpoint discrimination because it rejects any artistic speech that either fails to respect mainstream values or offends standards of decency. The NEA, however, reads the provision as merely hortatory, and contends that it stops well short of an absolute restriction. *** We do not decide whether the NEA's view — that the formulation of diverse advisory panels is sufficient to comply with Congress' command — is in fact a reasonable reading of the statute. It is clear, however, that the text of § 954(d)(1) imposes no categorical requirement. The advisory language stands in sharp contrast to congressional efforts to prohibit the funding of certain classes of speech. See § 954(d)(2) ("Obscenity is without artistic merit, is not protected speech, and shall not be funded").

That § 954(d)(1) admonishes the NEA merely to take "decency and respect" into consideration, and that the legislation was aimed at reforming procedures rather than precluding speech, undercut respondents' argument that the provision inevitably will be utilized as a tool for invidious viewpoint discrimination. In cases where we have struck down legislation as facially unconstitutional, the dangers were both more evident and more substantial. In *R.A.V. v. St. Paul*, 505 U.S. 377 (1992), for example, we invalidated on its face a municipal ordinance that defined as a criminal offense the placement of a symbol on public or private property "'which one knows or has reasonable grounds to know arouses anger, alarm, or resentment in others on the basis of race, color, creed, religion, or gender.'" That provision set forth a clear penalty, proscribed views on particular "disfavored subjects," and suppressed "distinctive ideas, conveyed by a distinctive message." ***

The NEA's enabling statute contemplates a number of indisputably constitutional applications for both the "decency" prong of § 954(d)(1) and its reference to "respect for the diverse beliefs and values of the American public." Educational programs are central to the NEA's mission. And it is well established that "decency" is a permissible factor where "educational suitability" motivates its consideration. *Board of Ed., Island Trees Union Free School Dist. No. 26 v. Pico*, 457 U.S. 853, 871 (1982); see also *Bethel School Dist. No. 403 v. Fraser*, 478 U.S. 675, 683 (1986) ("Surely it is a highly appropriate function of public school education to prohibit the use of vulgar and offensive terms in public discourse").

Permissible applications of the mandate to consider "respect for the diverse beliefs and values of the American public" are also apparent. The agency expressly takes diversity into account, giving special consideration to "projects and productions ... that reach, or reflect the culture of, a minority, inner city, rural, or tribal community." ***

We recognize, of course, that reference to these permissible applications would not alone be sufficient to sustain the statute against respondents' First Amendment

challenge. But neither are we persuaded that, in other applications, the language of §
954(d)(1) itself will give rise to the suppression of protected expression. The agency
may decide to fund particular projects for a wide variety of reasons, "such as the
technical proficiency of the artist, the creativity of the work, the anticipated public
interest in or appreciation of the work, the work's contemporary relevance, its
educational value, its suitability for or appeal to special audiences (such as children or
the disabled), its service to a rural or isolated community, or even simply that the work
could increase public knowledge of an art form." Brief for Petitioners 32.

Respondents do not allege discrimination in any particular funding decision. (In fact,
after filing suit to challenge § 954(d)(1), two of the individual respondents received
NEA grants.) If the NEA were to leverage its power to award subsidies on the basis of
subjective criteria into a penalty on disfavored viewpoints, then we would confront a
different case. *** Unless and until § 954(d)(1) is applied in a manner that raises
concern about the suppression of disfavored viewpoints, however, we uphold the
constitutionality of the provision.

B*

Finally, although the First Amendment certainly has application in the subsidy
context, we note that the Government may allocate competitive funding according to
criteria that would be impermissible were direct regulation of speech or a criminal
penalty at stake. So long as legislation does not infringe on other constitutionally
protected rights, Congress has wide latitude to set spending priorities. In the 1990
Amendments that incorporated § 954(d)(1), Congress modified the declaration of
purpose in the NEA's enabling act to provide that arts funding should "contribute to
public support and confidence in the use of taxpayer funds," and that "public funds ...
must ultimately serve public purposes the Congress defines." § 951(5). And as we held
in *Rust*, Congress may "selectively fund a program to encourage certain activities it
believes to be in the public interest, without at the same time funding an alternative
program which seeks to deal with the problem in another way."

III

The lower courts also erred in invalidating § 954(d)(1) as unconstitutionally vague.
The terms of the provision are undeniably opaque, and if they appeared in a criminal
statute or regulatory scheme, they could raise substantial vagueness concerns. It is
unlikely, however, that speakers will be compelled to steer too far clear of any
"forbidden area" in the context of grants of this nature. We recognize, as a practical
matter, that artists may conform their speech to what they believe to be the decisionmaking criteria in order to acquire funding. But when the Government is acting as
patron rather than as sovereign, the consequences of imprecision are not
constitutionally severe.

---

* [Ginsburg, J., did not join this portion of the opinion.]

In the context of selective subsidies, it is not always feasible for Congress to legislate with clarity. Indeed, if this statute is unconstitutionally vague, then so too are all government programs awarding scholarships and grants on the basis of subjective criteria such as "excellence." See, e.g., 2 U.S.C. § 802 (establishing the Congressional Award Program to "promote initiative, achievement, and excellence among youths in the areas of public service, personal development, and physical *** fitness"); 20 U.S.C. § 956(c)(1) (providing funding to the National Endowment for the Humanities to promote "progress and scholarship in the humanities"). *** To accept respondents' vagueness argument would be to call into question the constitutionality of these valuable government programs and countless others like them.***

Section 954(d)(1) merely adds some imprecise considerations to an already subjective selection process. It does not, on its face, impermissibly infringe on First or Fifth Amendment rights. Accordingly, the judgment of the Court of Appeals is reversed and the case is remanded for further proceedings consistent with this opinion.

JUSTICE SCALIA, with whom JUSTICE THOMAS joins, concurring in the judgment.

"The operation was a success, but the patient died." What such a procedure is to medicine, the Court's opinion in this case is to law. It sustains the constitutionality of 20 U.S.C. § 954(d)(1) by gutting it. *** I write separately because, unlike the Court, I think that § 954(d)(1) must be evaluated as written, rather than as distorted by the agency it was meant to control. By its terms, it establishes content- and viewpoint-based criteria upon which grant applications are to be evaluated. And that is perfectly constitutional.

I

I agree with the Court that § 954(d)(1) "imposes no categorical requirement," in the sense that it does not require the denial of all applications that violate general standards of decency or exhibit disrespect for the diverse beliefs and values of Americans. Compare § 954(d)(2) ("Obscenity ... shall not be funded"). But the factors need not be conclusive to be discriminatory. To the extent a particular applicant exhibits disrespect for the diverse beliefs and values of the American public or fails to comport with general standards of decency, the likelihood that he will receive a grant diminishes. ***

This unquestionably constitutes viewpoint discrimination.[1] That conclusion is not altered by the fact that the statute does not "compel" the denial of funding, any more

---

1. If there is any uncertainty on the point, it relates to the adjective, which is not at issue in the current discussion. That is, one might argue that the decency and respect factors constitute content discrimination rather than viewpoint discrimination, which would render them easier to uphold. Since I believe this statute must be upheld in either event, I pass over this conundrum and assume the worst.

than a provision imposing a five-point handicap on all black applicants for civil service jobs is saved from being race discrimination by the fact that it does not compel the rejection of black applicants. If viewpoint discrimination in this context is unconstitutional (a point I shall address anon), the law is invalid unless there are some situations in which the decency and respect factors do not constitute viewpoint discrimination. And there is none. The applicant who displays "decency," that is, "conformity to prevailing standards of propriety or modesty," American Heritage Dictionary 483 (3d ed.1992), and the applicant who displays "respect," that is, "deferential regard," for the diverse beliefs and values of the American people, id., at 1536 will always have an edge over an applicant who displays the opposite. And the conclusion of viewpoint discrimination is not affected by the fact that what constitutes "decency" or "the diverse beliefs and values of the American people" is difficult to pin down, any more than a civil-service preference in favor of those who display "Republican-party values" would be rendered nondiscriminatory by the fact that there is plenty of room for argument as to what Republican-party values might be.

III

The Court devotes so much of its opinion to explaining why this statute means something other than what it says that it neglects to cite the constitutional text governing our analysis. The First Amendment reads: "Congress shall make no law ... *abridging* the freedom of speech." To abridge is "to contract, to diminish; to deprive of." T. Sheridan, A Complete Dictionary of the English Language (6th ed. 1796). With the enactment of § 954(d)(1), Congress did not abridge the speech of those who disdain the beliefs and values of the American public, nor did it abridge indecent speech. Those who wish to create indecent and disrespectful art are as unconstrained now as they were before the enactment of this statute. Avant-garde artistes such as respondents remain entirely free to epater les bourgeois;[2]   they are merely deprived of the additional satisfaction of having the bourgeoisie taxed to pay for it.***

Respondents, relying on *Rosenberger v. Rector and Visitors of Univ. of Va.*, argue that viewpoint-based discrimination is impermissible unless the government is the speaker or the government is "disburs[ing] public funds to private entities to convey a governmental message." It is impossible to imagine why that should be so; one would think that directly involving the government itself in the viewpoint discrimination (if it is unconstitutional) would make the situation even worse. Respondents are mistaken.

---

2. Which they do quite well. The oeuvres d'art for which the four individual plaintiffs in this case sought funding have been described as follows:

"Finley's controversial show, 'We Keep Our victims Ready,' contains three segments. In the second segment, Finley visually recounts a sexual assault by stripping to the waist and smearing chocolate on her breasts and by using profanity to describe the assault. Fleck appears dressed as a mermaid, urinates on the stage and creates an altar out of a toilet by putting a photograph of Jesus Christ on the lid."

It is the very business of government to favor and disfavor points of view on (in modern times, at least) innumerable subjects — which is the main reason we have decided to elect those who run the government, rather than save money by making their posts hereditary. And it makes not a bit of difference, insofar as either common sense or the Constitution ·s concerned, whether these officials further their (and, in a democracy, our) favored point of view by achieving it directly (having government-employed artists paint pictures, for example, or government-employed doctors perform abortions); or by advocating it officially (establishing an Office of Art Appreciation, for example, or an Office of Voluntary Population Control); or by giving money to others who achieve or advocate it (funding private art classes, for example, or Planned Parenthood).[3]

The nub of the difference between me and the Court is that I regard the distinction between "abridging" speech and funding it as a fundamental divide, on this side of which the First Amendment is inapplicable. The Court, by contrast, seems to believe that the First Amendment, despite its words, has some ineffable effect upon funding, imposing constraints of an indeterminate nature which it announces (without troubling to enunciate any particular test) are not violated by the statute here — or, more accurately, are not violated by the quite different, emasculated statute that it imagines.*** It is no secret that the provision was prompted by, and directed at, the funding of such offensive productions. Instead of banning the funding of such productions absolutely, which I think would have been entirely constitutional, Congress took the lesser step of requiring them to be disfavored in the evaluation of grant applications. The Court's opinion today renders even that lesser step a nullity. For that reason, I concur only in the judgment.

JUSTICE SOUTER, dissenting

The question here is whether the italicized segment of this statute is unconstitutional on its face: "artistic excellence and artistic merit are the criteria by which applications [for grants from the National Endowment for the Arts] are judged, *taking into consideration general standards of decency and respect for the diverse beliefs and values of the American public.*" It is.

The decency and respect proviso mandates viewpoint-based decisions in the disbursement of government subsidies, and the Government has wholly failed to explain

---

3. I suppose it would be unconstitutional for the government to give money to an organization devoted to the promotion of candidates nominated by the Republican party   — but it be would just as unconstitutional for the government itself to promote candidates nominated by the Republican party, and I do not think that that unconstitutionality has anything to do with the First Amendment.

why the statute should be afforded an exemption from the fundamental rule of the First Amendment that viewpoint discrimination in the exercise of public authority over expressive activity is unconstitutional. *** Nor may the question raised be answered in the Government's favor on the assumption that some constitutional applications of the statute are enough to satisfy the demand of facial constitutionality[.] This assumption is irreconcilable with our long standing and sensible doctrine of facial overbreadth, applicable to claims brought under the First Amendment's speech clause. I respectfully dissent.

I

"If there is a bedrock principle underlying the First Amendment, it is that the government may not prohibit the expression of an idea simply because society finds the idea itself offensive or disagreeable." *Texas v. Johnson*, 491 U.S. 397, 414 (1989). *** Because this principle applies not only to affirmative suppression of speech, but also to disqualification for government favors, Congress is generally not permitted to pivot discrimination against otherwise protected speech on the offensiveness or unacceptability of the views it expresses.

It goes without saying that artistic expression lies within this First Amendment protection. The constitutional protection of artistic works turns not on the political significance that may be attributable to such productions, though they may indeed comment on the political,[1] but simply on their expressive character, which falls within a spectrum of protected "speech" extending outward from the core of overtly political declarations. Put differently, art is entitled to full protection because our "cultural life," just like our native politics, "rests upon [the] ideal" of governmental viewpoint neutrality. *Turner Broadcasting System, Inc. v. FCC*, 512 U.S. 622, 641 (1994).

When called upon to vindicate this ideal, we characteristically begin by asking "whether the government has adopted a regulation of speech because of disagreement with the message it conveys. The government's purpose is the controlling consideration." *Ward v. Rock Against Racism.* The answer in this case is damning. One need do nothing more than read the text of the statute to conclude that Congress's purpose in imposing the decency and respect criteria was to prevent the funding of art that conveys an offensive message; the decency and respect provision on its face is quintessentially viewpoint based, and quotations from the Congressional Record merely confirm the obvious legislative purpose. In the words of the cosponsor of the bill

---

1. Art "may affect public attitudes and behavior in a variety of ways, ranging from direct espousal of a political or social doctrine to the subtle shaping of thought which characterizes all artistic expression." *Joseph Burstyn, Inc. v. Wilson*, 343 U.S. 495, 501 (1952).

enacted the proviso, "works which deeply offend the sensibilities of significant portions of the public ought not to be supported with public funds."[2]

II

In the face of such clear legislative purpose, so plainly expressed, the Court has its work cut out for it in seeking a constitutional reading of the statute.

A

The Court says, first, that because the phrase "general standards of decency and respect for the diverse beliefs and values of the American public" is imprecise and capable of multiple interpretations, "the considerations that the provision introduces, by their nature, do not engender the kind of directed viewpoint discrimination that would prompt this Court to invalidate a statute on its face." Unquestioned case law, however, is clearly to the contrary. *** Except when protecting children from exposure to indecent material, see *FCC v. Pacifica Foundation*, 438 U.S. 726 (1978), the First Amendment has never been read to allow the government to rove around imposing general standards of decency, see, e.g., *Reno v. American Civil Liberties Union*, 521 U.S. ___ (1997) (striking down on its face a statute that regulated "indecency" on the Internet). Because "the normal definition of 'indecent' ... refers to nonconformance with accepted standards of morality," *FCC v. Pacifica Foundation*, *supra*, at 740, restrictions turning on decency, especially those couched in terms of "general standards of decency," are quintessentially viewpoint based: they require discrimination on the basis of conformity with mainstream mores. ***

Just as self-evidently, a statute disfavoring speech that fails to respect America's "diverse beliefs and values" is the very model of viewpoint discrimination; it penalizes any view disrespectful to any belief or value espoused by someone in the American populace. Boiled down to its practical essence, the limitation obviously means that art that disrespects the ideology, opinions, or convictions of a significant segment of the American public is to be disfavored, whereas art that reinforces those values is not. After all, the whole point of the proviso was to make sure that works like Serrano's ostensibly blasphemous portrayal of Jesus would not be funded, while a reverent treatment, conventionally respectful of Christian sensibilities, would not run afoul of the law. Nothing could be more viewpoint based than that. ***

III

---

2. There is, of course, nothing whatsoever unconstitutional about this view as a general matter. Congress has no obligation to support artistic enterprises that many people detest. The First Amendment speaks up only when Congress decides to participate in the Nation's artistic life by legal regulation, as it does through a subsidy scheme like the NEA. If Congress does choose to spend public funds in this manner, it may not discriminate by viewpoint in deciding who gets the money.

*** Our most thorough statement of these principles is found in the recent case of *Rosenberger v. Rector and Visitors of Univ. of Va.*, 515 U.S. 819,(1995), which held that the University of Virginia could not discriminate on viewpoint in underwriting the speech of student-run publications. *** *Rosenberger* controls here. The NEA, like the student activities fund in *Rosenberger*, is a subsidy scheme created to encourage expression of a diversity of views from private speakers. *** The NEA's purpose is to "support new ideas" and "to help create and sustain ... a climate encouraging freedom of thought, imagination, and inquiry." §§ 951(10),(7). Given this congressional choice to sustain freedom of expression, *Rosenberger* teaches that the First Amendment forbids decisions based on viewpoint popularity. So long as Congress chooses to subsidize expressive endeavors at large, it has no business requiring the NEA to turn down funding applications of artists and exhibitors who devote their "freedom of thought, imagination, and inquiry" to defying our tastes, our beliefs, or our values.

The Court says otherwise, claiming to distinguish *Rosenberger* on the ground that the student activities funds in that case were generally available to most applicants, whereas NEA funds are disbursed selectively and competitively to a choice few. But the Court in *Rosenberger* anticipated and specifically rejected just this distinction when it held in no uncertain terms that "the government cannot justify viewpoint discrimination among private speakers on the economic fact of scarcity." Scarce money demands choices, of course, but choices "on some acceptable [viewpoint] neutral principle," like artistic excellence and artistic merit;[9] "nothing in our decision[s] indicate[s] that scarcity would give the State the right to exercise viewpoint discrimination that is otherwise impermissible." ***

IV

Although I, like the Court, recognize that "facial challenges to legislation are generally disfavored," the proviso is the type of statute that most obviously lends itself to such an attack. The NEA does not offer a list of reasons when it denies a grant application, and an artist or exhibitor whose subject raises a hint of controversy can never know for sure whether the decency and respect criteria played a part in any decision by the NEA to deny funding. *** In the world of NEA funding, this is so because the makers or exhibitors of potentially controversial art will either trim their work to avoid anything likely to offend, or refrain from seeking NEA funding altogether. Either way, to whatever extent NEA eligibility defines a national mainstream, the proviso will tend to create a timid esthetic. *** The Court does not strike down the proviso, however. Instead, it preserves the irony of a statutory mandate to deny recognition to virtually any expression capable of causing offense in any

---

9. While criteria of "artistic excellence and artistic merit" may raise intractable issues about the identification of artistic worth, and could no doubt be used covertly to filter out unwanted ideas, there is nothing inherently viewpoint discriminatory about such merit-based criteria.

quarter as the most recent manifestation of a scheme enacted to "create and sustain …
a climate encouraging freedom of thought, imagination, and inquiry." § 951(7).

————

Chapter 5

AN INTRODUCTION TO THE CHURCH-STATE
CLAUSES OF THE FIRST AMENDMENT

Casebook, p. 855
Add citation to footnote 19

For another discussion of the strong separationist approach, see Edward J. Eberle, *Roger Williams' Gift: Religious Freedom in America*, 4 Roger Williams Univ. L. Rev. 425 (1999).

Casebook, p. 859
Add a footnote 32a, right after footnote 32

32a. For a recent effort to work through the incorporation issue discussed in these pages, see Kurt T. Lash, *The Second Adoption of the Establishment Clause: The Rise of the Nonestablishment Principle*, 27 Ariz. St. L. J. 1085 (1995).

Casebook, p. 860
Add to bibliography

Greenwalt, Kent, Private Conscience and Public Reasons (1995)

Hall, Timothy J., Separating Church and State: Roger Williams and Religious Liberty (1998)

Smith, Steven, Foreordained Failure: The Quest for a Constitutional Principle of Religious Freedom (1995)

Thiemann, Ronald, Religion in Public Life: A Dilemma for Democracy (1996)

Chapter 6

"CONGRESS SHALL MAKE NO LAW RESPECTING AN ESTABLISHMENT OF RELIGION"

B. The General Test Refined

Casebook, p. 926
Add as a NOTE following *Wolman v. Walter*

NOTE

See pp.136-150 *infra*, this supplement (*Mitchell v. Helms*, 530 U.S. ____ (June 28, 2000) overrules *Wolman v. Walter*).

C. The General Test Modified and In Dispute

Casebook, p. 939
Add as a new case, following *Zobrest v. Catalina Foothills School District*

ROSENBERGER V. RECTOR AND VISITORS OF
THE UNIVERSITY OF VIRGINIA
515 U.S. 819 (1995)

Justice KENNEDY delivered the opinion of the Court.* ***

III

Before its brief on the merits in this Court, the University had argued at all stages of the litigation that inclusion of WAP's contractors in SAF funding authorization would violate the Establishment Clause.** ***

A central lesson of our decisions is that a significant factor in upholding governmental programs in the face of Establishment Clause attack is their neutrality towards religion. *** The first case in our modern Establishment Clause jurisprudence was *Everson v. Board of Ed. of Ewing*, 330 U.S. 1 (1947). There we cautioned that

------

* [**Ed. Note**: For a reminder of the parties, facts, and issues addressed in Parts I and II of this case, *see* p. 7 *supra*, this Supplement.]

** [**Ed. Note.** In brief, the university sought to defend its refusal to use student fees to pay for publications sponsored by Wide Awake Productions (WAP) partly on the basis that it was constrained by the Establishment Clause not to do so — that any use it might make of mandatory student fees to subsidize religious organizations *by underwriting the costs of their religious publications*, was forbidden by the Establishment Clause — the university so understood the decisions of the Supreme Court.]

in enforcing the prohibition against laws respecting establishment of religion, we must "be sure that we do not inadvertently prohibit [the government] from extending its general state law benefits to all its citizens without regard to their religious belief." ***

The governmental program here is neutral toward religion. There is no suggestion that the University created it to advance religion or adopted some ingenious device with the purpose of aiding a religious cause. The object of the SAF is to open a forum for speech and to support various student enterprises, including the publication of newspapers, in recognition of the diversity and creativity of student life. The University's SAF Guidelines have a separate classification for, and do not make third-party payments on behalf of, "religious organizations," which are those "whose purpose is to practice a devotion to an acknowledged ultimate reality or deity." The category of support here is for "student news, information, opinion, entertainment, or academic communications media groups," of which Wide Awake was 1 of 15 in the 1990 school year. WAP did not seek a subsidy because of its Christian editorial viewpoint; it sought funding as a student journal, which it was.

The neutrality of the program distinguishes the student fees from a tax levied for the direct support of a church or group of churches. A tax of that sort, of course, would run contrary to Establishment Clause concerns dating from the earliest days of the Republic. The apprehensions of our predecessors involved the levying of taxes upon the public for the sole and exclusive purpose of establishing and supporting specific sects. The exaction here, by contrast, is a student activity fee designed to reflect the reality that student life in its many dimensions includes the necessity of wide-ranging speech and inquiry and that student expression is an integral part of the University's educational mission. The fee is mandatory, and we do not have before us the question whether an objecting student has the First Amendment right to demand a pro rata return to the extent the fee is expended for speech to which he or she does not subscribe. See *Keller v. State Bar of Cal.*, 496 U.S. 1, 15-16 (1990); *Abood v. Detroit Bd. of Ed.*, 431 U.S. 209, 235-236 (1977). We must treat it, then, as an exaction upon the students. But the $14 paid each semester by the students is not a general tax designed to raise revenue for the University. The SAF cannot be used for unlimited purposes, much less the illegitimate purpose of supporting one religion. Much like the arrangement in *Widmar*, the money goes to a special fund from which any group of students with CIO status can draw for purposes consistent with the University's educational mission; and to the extent the student is interested in speech, withdrawal is permitted to cover the whole spectrum of speech, whether it manifests a religious view, an antireligious view, or neither. Our decision, then, cannot be read as addressing an expenditure from a general tax fund. Here, the disbursements from the fund go to private contractors for the cost of printing that which is protected under the Speech Clause of the First Amendment. This is a far cry from a general public assessment designed and effected to provide financial support for a church.

Government neutrality is apparent in the State's overall scheme in a further meaningful respect. "*** [T]he government has not fostered or encouraged" any mistaken impression that the student newspapers speak for the University. *Capitol Square Review and Advisory Bd. v. Pinette*, 515 U.S. 753, 766. ***

The Court of Appeals (and the dissent) are correct to extract from our decisions the principle that we have recognized special Establishment Clause dangers where the government makes direct money payments to sectarian institutions. The error is not in identifying the principle, but in believing that it controls this case. Even assuming that WAP is no different from a church and that its speech is the same as the religious exercises conducted in *Widmar* (two points much in doubt), the Court of Appeals decided a case that was, in essence, not before it, and the dissent would have us do the same. We do not confront a case where, even under a neutral program that includes nonsectarian recipients, the government is making direct money payments to an institution or group that is engaged in religious activity. Neither the Court of Appeals nor the dissent, we believe, takes sufficient cognizance of the undisputed fact that no public funds flow directly to WAP's coffers.

It does not violate the Establishment Clause for a public university to grant access to its facilities on a religion-neutral basis to a wide spectrum of student groups, including groups that use meeting rooms for sectarian activities, accompanied by some devotional exercises. This is so even where the upkeep, maintenance, and repair of the facilities attributed to those uses are paid from a student activities fund to which students are required to contribute. The government usually acts by spending money. Even the provision of a meeting room involve[s] governmental expenditure, if only in the form of electricity and heating or cooling costs. The error made by the Court of Appeals, as well as by the dissent, lies in focusing on the money that is undoubtedly expended by the government, rather than on the nature of the benefit received by the recipient. If the expenditure of governmental funds is prohibited whenever those funds pay for a service that is, pursuant to a religion-neutral program, used by a group for sectarian purposes, then *Widmar*, *Mergens*, and *Lamb's Chapel* would have to be overruled. Given our holdings in these cases, it follows that a public university may maintain its own computer facility and give student groups access to that facility, including the use of the printers, on a religion neutral, say first-come-first-served, basis. If a religious student organization obtained access on that religion-neutral basis and used a computer to compose or a printer or copy machine to print speech with a religious content or viewpoint, the State's action in providing the group with access would no more violate the Establishment Clause than would giving those groups access to an assembly hall. There is no difference in logic or principle, and no difference of constitutional significance, between a school using its funds to operate a facility to which students have access, and a school paying a third-party contractor to operate the facility on its behalf. ***

By paying outside printers, the University in fact attains a further degree of separation from the student publication, for it avoids the duties of supervision, escapes the costs of upkeep, repair, and replacement attributable to student use, and has a clear record of costs. ***

Were the dissent's view to become law, it would require the University, in order to avoid a constitutional violation, to scrutinize the content of student speech, lest the expression in question — speech otherwise protected by the Constitution — contain too great a religious content. The dissent, in fact, anticipates such censorship as "crucial" in distinguishing between "works characterized by the evangelism of Wide Awake and writing that merely happens to express views that a given religion might approve." That eventuality raises the specter of governmental censorship, to ensure that all student writings and publications meet some baseline standard of secular orthodoxy. To impose that standard on student speech at a university is to imperil the very sources of free speech and expression. ***

To obey the Establishment Clause, it was not necessary for the University to deny eligibility to student publications because of their viewpoint. The neutrality commanded of the State by the separate Clauses of the First Amendment was compromised by the University's course of action. The viewpoint discrimination inherent in the University's regulation required public officials to scan and interpret student publications to discern their underlying philosophic assumptions respecting religious theory and belief. That course of action was a denial of the right of free speech and would risk fostering a pervasive bias or hostility to religion, which could undermine the very neutrality the Establishment Clause requires. There is no Establishment Clause violation in the University's honoring its duties under the Free Speech Clause.

The judgment of the Court of Appeals must be, and is, reversed.

Justice O'CONNOR, concurring. [omitted]

Justice THOMAS, concurring. [omitted]*

Justice SOUTER, with whom Justice STEVENS, Justice GINSBURG, and Justice BREYER join, dissenting.

*** The masthead of every issue bears St. Paul's exhortation, that "[t]he hour has come for you to awake from your slumber, because our salvation is nearer now than

---

* [**Ed. Note.** Justice Thomas expressly joins "the Court's Opinion," but goes further; he aggressively takes issue with the "no direct financial aid" to religious organizations and proposes that cash subsidies, inclusive of religious organizations as a subset of a larger class, should not be deemed forbidden by the Establishment clause...]

when we first believed. Romans 13:11." Each issue of Wide Awake contained in the record makes good on the editor's promise and echoes the Apostle's call to accept salvation:

"The only way to salvation through Him is by confessing and repenting of sin. It is the Christian's duty to make sinners aware of their need for salvation. Thus, Christians must confront and condemn sin, or else they fail in their duty of love."

Using public funds for the direct subsidization of preaching the word is categorically forbidden under the Establishment Clause, and if the Clause was meant to accomplish nothing else, it was meant to bar this use of public money. *** Four years before the First Congress proposed the First Amendment, Madison gave his opinion on the legitimacy of using public funds for religious purposes, in the Memorial and Remonstrance Against Religious Assessments, which played the central role in ensuring the defeat of the Virginia tax assessment bill in 1786 and framed the debate upon which the Religion Clauses stand:

> "Who does not see that ... the same authority which
> can force a citizen to contribute three pence only of
> his property for the support of any one establishment,
> may force him to conform to any other establishment
> in all cases whatsoever?"

Madison wrote against a background in which nearly every Colony had exacted a tax for church support, *Everson*, at 10, n. 8, the practice having become "so commonplace as to shock the freedom-loving colonials into a feeling of abhorrence." Madison's Remonstrance captured the colonists' "conviction that individual religious liberty could be achieved best under a government which was stripped of all power to tax, to support, or otherwise to assist any or all religions, or to interfere with the beliefs of any religious individual or group."[1]

---

1. Justice THOMAS suggests that Madison would have approved of the assessment bill if only it had satisfied the principle of evenhandedness. Nowhere in the Remonstrance, however, did Madison advance the view that Virginia should be able to provide financial support for religion as part of a generally available subsidy program. Indeed, while Justice THOMAS claims that the "funding provided by the Virginia assessment was to be extended only to Christian sects," it is clear that the bill was more general in scope than this. While the bill, ***, provided that each taxpayer could designate a religious society to which he wanted his levy paid, it would also have allowed a taxpayer to refuse to appropriate his levy to any religious society, in which case the legislature was to use these unappropriated sums to fund "seminaries of learning" (contrary to Justice THOMAS's unsupported assertion, this portion of the bill was no less obligatory than any other). While some of these seminaries undoubtedly would have been religious in character, others would not have been, as a seminary was generally understood at the time to be "any school, academy, college or university, in which young persons are

The principle against direct funding with public money is patently violated by the contested use of today's student activity fee.[3] Like today's taxes generally, the fee is Madison's threepence. The University exercises the power of the State to compel a student to pay it, and the use of any part of it for the direct support of religious activity thus strikes at what we have repeatedly held to be the heart of the prohibition on establishment. *** The Court, accordingly, has never before upheld direct state funding of the sort of proselytizing published in Wide Awake and, in fact, has categorically condemned state programs directly aiding religious activity. ***

II

There is no viewpoint discrimination in the University's application of its Guidelines to deny funding to Wide Awake. Under those Guidelines, a "religious activit[y]," which is not eligible for funding, is "an activity which primarily promotes or manifests a particular belief(s) in or about a deity or an ultimate reality." It is clear that this is the basis on which Wide Awake Productions was denied funding. *** If the Guidelines were written or applied so as to limit only such Christian advocacy and no other evangelical efforts that might compete with it, the discrimination would be based on viewpoint. But that is not what the regulation authorizes; it applies to Muslim and Jewish and Buddhist advocacy as well as to Christian. And since it limits funding to activities promoting or manifesting a particular belief not only "in" but "about" a deity or ultimate reality, it applies to agnostics and atheists as well as it does to deists and theists as the University maintained at oral argument, and as the Court recognizes. ***

The Guidelines are thus substantially different from the access restriction considered in *Lamb's Chapel*, the case upon which the Court heavily relies in finding a viewpoint distinction here. *Lamb's Chapel* addressed a school board's regulation prohibiting the after-hours use of school premises "by any group for religious purposes," even though the forum otherwise was open for a variety of social, civic, and recreational purposes. "Religious" was understood to refer to the viewpoint of a believer, and the regulation did not purport to deny access to any speaker wishing to express a non-religious or expressly antireligious point of view on any subject. *** With this understanding, it

---

instructed in the several branches of learning which may qualify them for their future employments." N. Webster, An American Dictionary of the English Language (1st ed. 1828); *see also* 14 The Oxford English Dictionary 956 (2d ed.1989). Not surprisingly, then, scholars have generally agreed that the bill would have provided funding for nonreligious schools. ***

3. In the District Court, the parties agreed to the following facts: "The University of Virginia has charged at all times relevant herein and currently charges each full-time student a compulsory student activity fee of $14.00 per semester. There is no procedural or other mechanism by which a student may decline to pay the fee."

was unremarkable that in *Lamb's Chapel* we unanimously determined that the access restriction, as applied to a speaker wishing to discuss family values from a Christian perspective, impermissibly distinguished between speakers on the basis of viewpoint. Equally obvious is the distinction between that case and this one, where the regulation is being applied, not to deny funding for those who discuss issues in general from a religious viewpoint, but to those engaged in promoting or opposing religious conversion and religious observances as such. If this amounts to viewpoint discrimination, the Court has all but eviscerated the line between viewpoint and content. ***

I respectfully dissent.

———

Casebook, p. 951
Add as new material following *Board of Education of Kiryas Joel v. Grumet*

In *Kiryas Joel*, as the Court noted in its Opinion, special education services were required by a federal spending measure designating how certain federal funds were to be spent in aid of certain "at-risk" elementary and secondary school children (Title I of the Elementary and Secondary Education Act of 1965, 20 U.S.C. § 6301 et seq). The act required special (remedial) services to be provided through the state to eligible students identified as students: (a) residing in a low-income area; and (b) disadvantaged in being at risk of failing, educationally, because of impaired hearing, mental retardation, or other physical, mental, or emotional disorders, whether attending a private school or a public school.

As noted in *Kiryas Joel*, these required services were first provided by the Monroe-Woodbury Central School District on site of the Satmar religious school, integrated in the daily operation of the school. As also noted, however, that arrangement had been discontinued because the Supreme Court had held that the direct, ongoing engagement of public school personnel in furnishing tax-supported educational services administratively integrated on parochial school premises was not permissible under the first or fourteenth amendments. Specifically, in *Aguilar v. Felton*, 473 U.S. 402 (1985), and *School Dist. of Grand Rapids v. Ball*, 473 U.S. 383 (1984) (a case involving "enrichment" programs rather than merely "remedial" programs as in *Aguilar*), the Court had held that such arrangements were inconsistent with the "primary effect" and "no entanglement" requirements of the three-part *Lemon* test.

After *Aguilar*, as also noted by the Court, the public school district had sought to supply such services by making arrangements for eligible children in the Satmar religious schools to receive the same services in nearby public schools of the Monroe-Woodbury Central School District.[3a] This provision was satisfactory under the federal

———

3a. In other instances, in New York and elsewhere, immediately following the Court's decisions in *Aguilar* and in *Ball*, suitably equipped mobile vans were utilized, parking nearby

statute, but not satisfactory to the parents of the handicapped Hasidic children who, held out from the public school, now only "received privately funded special services or went without," until the New York legislature adopted the special legislation facilitating the "public school district" precisely tailored to the exact 320 acres "owned and inhabited entirely by Satmars." The New York law, in turn, was held invalid (albeit by a sharply divided Court), as we have just seen, as a religious gerrymander — an impermissible act in aid of a religious establishment in *Kiryas Joel*.[3b]

In *Kiryas Joel* itself, however, the Court also noted the case had come to the Court only one year after the Court's then-recent (5/4) decision in *Zobrest v. Catalina Foothills School Dist.*, 509 U.S. 1 (1993) (casebook at p. 933) — a case sustaining the use of an assigned public employee to serve as sign-language interpreter to a hearing impaired student in all of his classes inside a Catholic school. And in light of the Court's decision in *Zobrest*, five Justices openly expressed doubts in the *Kiryas Joel* case as to whether the Court's own prior decisions in *Aguilar* and *Ball* were reconcilable with the Court's (new?) view as reflected in *Zobrest*.

---

parochial schools, with arrangements made with the parochial schools to schedule eligible students to receive the special education services immediately adjacent to the parochial school.

3b. In an editor's note to Justice O'Connor's concurring opinion in *Kiryas Joel*, the question was raised whether a less targeted (i.e. "less targeted" solely to the village of Kiryas Joel) act of the New York legislature could be adopted, and whether, were such legislation to be adopted, pursuant to which the village were once again to form the same de facto wholly Satmar separate school district, it might now be sustained (i.e. as not void under the Establishment Clause). (See casebook at p. 946 for discussion and reference.) As further indicated in that footnote (noting this subsequent development and the nature of the law), in fact the New York legislature did adopt such a law within two weeks. The "neutral criteria" were framed to ensure that the village of Kiryas Joel would qualify, and the village once again opted out of the Monroe-Woodbury school district. In the end, however, the New York Court of Appeals held the new state law invalid. The "neutral criteria" were such that few (if any) other municipalities within an existing school district could qualify; and the defendants in litigation acknowledged the law was enacted in direct response to the Supreme Court's decision in *Kiryas Joel*, and was designed explicitly to provide the Satmar village with a mechanism to secure their own school district. The New York Court of Appeals reasoned that chapter 241 was not a "religion-neutral law of general applicability" that Kiryas Joel happened to have invoked just as others might have. Chapter 241, the court concluded, simply replicated the prior unconstitutional law. See 90 N.Y.2d 57 (1997). The New York legislature did attempt a third time, using "neutral" criteria such that two municipalities (Kiryas Joel and one other) qualified, but the New York Supreme Court again found the scheme unconstitutional. See *Grumet v. Pataki*, 19999 WL 289458 (N.Y. 1999), *cert. pending*. The Court's subsequent decision in *Agostini* (see below, supplement at __) may offer the Satmar Hasidim in question another alternative.

But if these cases (i.e. *Aguilar* and *Ball*) were to be overruled, very possibly the decision in *Kiryas Joel* might also become essentially a moot point; there would be no need for the "off premises" arrangements for the assistance of eligible Satmar children enrolled in Hasidic schools. Rather, once again, public personnel could be provided, to co-operate with the Hasidic schools, to supply the remedial education courses directly on Hasidic school premises, integrated with the Hasidic school day (and so, too, equally, of course, at Catholic schools or other religiously affiliated, nonpublic schools). Nearly at once, proceedings were reopened in federal district court in New York by those who had lost in *Aguilar*, seeking lifting of the injunction that had previously issued in *Aguilar*.

The case proceeded through the two lower federal courts both of which refused the request to lift the injunction, essentially on the ground that until the Supreme Court expressly addressed the issue and declared otherwise, they were bound by the decision in *Aguilar* as the "law of the case." Following grant of certiorari by the Supreme Court, however, on May 23, 1997, the Court did overrule both *Aguilar* and a portion of *Ball*. Excerpts from the principal Opinions by O'Connor, J. for the Court and in dissent by Souter, J. (joined by Stevens and Ginsburg, J.J., and by Breyer, J., as to Part II), immediately follow.

Casebook, p. 951
Add as new case following *Board of Education of Kiryas Joel v. Grumet*

AGOSTINI v. FELTON
117 U.S. 771 (1997)

JUSTICE O'CONNOR delivered the opinion of the Court. ***

III

A

In order to evaluate whether *Aguilar* has been eroded by our subsequent Establishment Clause cases, it is necessary to understand the rationale upon which *Aguilar*, as well as its companion case, *School Dist. of Grand Rapids v. Ball*, 473 U.S. 373 (1985), rested.

In *Ball*, the Court evaluated two programs implemented by the School District of Grand Rapids, Michigan. The district's Shared Time program, the one most analogous to Title I, provided remedial and "enrichment" classes, at public expense, to students attending nonpublic schools. The classes were taught during regular school hours by publicly employed teachers, using materials purchased with public funds, on the premises of nonpublic schools. *** The Court conducted its analysis by applying the three-part test set forth in *Lemon v. Kurtzman*. ***

The Court found that the program violated the Establishment Clause's prohibition against "government-financed or government-sponsored indoctrination into the beliefs of a particular religious faith" in at least three ways. First, *** the Court observed that "the teachers participating in the programs may become involved in intentionally or inadvertently inculcating particular religious tenets or beliefs." *** [T]he Court disregarded the lack of evidence of any specific incidents of religious indoctrination as largely irrelevant, reasoning that potential witnesses to any indoctrination — the parochial school students, their parents, or parochial school officials — might be unable to detect or have little incentive to report the incidents.

The presence of public teachers on parochial school grounds had a second, related impermissible effect: It created a "graphic symbol of the 'concert or union or dependency' of church and state." *** The Court feared that this perception of a symbolic union between church and state would "conve[y] a message of government endorsement *** of religion" and thereby violate a "core purpose" of the Establishment Clause.

Third, the Court found that the Shared Time program impermissibly financed religious indoctrination by subsidizing "the primary religious mission of the institutions affected." ***

The New York City Title I program challenged in *Aguilar* closely resembled the Shared Time program struck down in Ball, but the Court found fault with an aspect of the Title I program not present in Ball: The Board had "adopted a system for monitoring the religious content of publicly funded Title I classes in the religious schools." Even though this monitoring system might prevent the Title I program from being used to inculcate religion, the Court concluded, as it had in Lemon and Meek, that the level of monitoring necessary to be "certain" that the program had an exclusively secular effect would "inevitably resul[t] in the excessive entanglement of church and state," thereby running afoul of *Lemon*'s third prong. ***

B

Our more recent cases have undermined the assumptions upon which *Ball* and *Aguilar* relied. To be sure, the general principles we use to evaluate whether government aid violates the Establishment Clause have not changed since *Aguilar* was decided. For example, we continue to ask whether the government acted with the purpose of advancing or inhibiting religion, and the nature of that inquiry has remained largely unchanged. *** Likewise, we continue to explore whether the aid has the "effect" of advancing or inhibiting religion. What has changed since we decided *Ball* and *Aguilar* is our understanding of the criteria used to assess whether aid to religion has an impermissible effect.

1

As we have repeatedly recognized, government inculcation of religious beliefs has the impermissible effect of advancing religion. Our cases subsequent to *Aguilar* have, however, modified in two significant respects the approach we use to assess indoctrination. First, we have abandoned the presumption *** that the placement of public employees on parochial school grounds inevitably results in the impermissible effect of state-sponsored indoctrination or constitutes a symbolic union between government and religion. In *Zobrest v. Catalina Foothills School Dist.*, we examined whether the IDEA, 20 U.S.C. § 1400 et seq., was constitutional as applied to a deaf student who sought to bring his state-employed sign-language interpreter with him to his Roman Catholic high school. *** Because the only government aid in *Zobrest* was the interpreter, who was herself not inculcating any religious messages, no government indoctrination took place and we were able to conclude that "the provision of such assistance [was] not barred by the Establishment Clause." *Zobrest* therefore expressly rejected the notion — relied on in *Ball* and *Aguilar* — that, solely because of her presence on private school property, a public employee will be presumed to inculcate religion in the students. *Zobrest* also implicitly repudiated another assumption on which *Ball* and *Aguilar* turned: that the presence of a public employee on private school property creates an impermissible "symbolic link" between government and religion. ***

Second, we have departed from the rule relied on in *Ball* that all government aid that directly aids the educational function of religious schools is invalid. In *Witters v. Washington Dept. of Servs. for Blind*, 474 U.S. 481 (1986), we held that the Establishment Clause did not bar a State from issuing a vocational tuition grant to a blind person who wished to use the grant to attend a Christian college and become a pastor, missionary, or youth director. *** The grants were disbursed directly to students, who then used the money to pay for tuition at the educational institution of their choice. ***

Zobrest and *Witters* make clear that, under current law, the Shared Time program in *Ball* and New York City's Title I program in *Aguilar* will not, as a matter of law, be deemed to have the effect of advancing religion through indoctrination. *** In all relevant respects, the provision of instructional services under Title I is indistinguishable from the provision of sign-language interpreters under the IDEA. Both programs make aid available only to eligible recipients. That aid is provided to students at whatever school they choose to attend. Although Title I instruction is provided to several students at once, whereas an interpreter provides translation to a single student, this distinction is not constitutionally significant. Moreover, as in *Zobrest*, Title I services are by law supplemental to the regular curricula. These services do not, therefore, "reliev[e] sectarian schools of costs they otherwise would have borne in educating their students." *** No Title I funds ever reach the coffers of religious schools, compare *Committee for Public Ed. & Religious Liberty v. Regan*, (involving a program giving "direct cash reimbursement" to religious schools for performing certain state- mandated tasks), and Title I services may not be provided to religious schools on a school-wide basis, 34 CFR § 200.12(b) (1996). Title I funds are instead distributed to a public agency (an LEA) that dispenses services directly to the eligible students within its boundaries, no matter where they choose to attend school. ***

What is most fatal to the argument that New York City's Title I program directly subsidizes religion is that it applies with equal force when those services are provided off-campus, and *Aguilar* implied that providing the services off-campus is entirely consistent with the Establishment Clause. JUSTICE SOUTER resists the impulse to upset this implication, contending that it can be justified on the ground that Title I services are "less likely to supplant some of what would otherwise go on inside [the sectarian schools] and to subsidize what remains" when those services are offered off-campus. But JUSTICE SOUTER does not explain why a sectarian school would not have the same incentive to "make patently significant cut-backs" in its curriculum no matter where Title I services are offered, since the school would ostensibly be excused from having to provide the Title I-type services itself. Because the incentive is the same either way, we find no logical basis upon which to conclude that Title I services are an impermissible subsidy of religion when offered on-campus, but not when offered off-campus. ***

2

Although we examined in *Witters* and *Zobrest* the criteria by which an aid program identifies its beneficiaries, we did so solely to assess whether any use of that aid to indoctrinate religion could be attributed to the State. A number of our Establishment Clause cases have found that the criteria used for identifying beneficiaries are relevant in a second respect, apart from enabling a court to evaluate whether the program subsidizes religion. Specifically, the criteria might themselves have the effect of advancing religion by creating a financial incentive to undertake religious indoctrination. *** This incentive is not present, however, where the aid is allocated on the basis of neutral, secular criteria that neither favor nor disfavor religion, and is made available to both religious and secular beneficiaries on a nondiscriminatory basis. ***

3

We turn now to *Aguilar*'s conclusion that New York City's Title I program resulted in an excessive entanglement between church and state. Whether a government aid program results in such an entanglement has consistently been an aspect of our Establishment Clause analysis. *** [T]he Court's finding of "excessive" entanglement in *Aguilar* rested on three grounds: (I) the program would require "pervasive monitoring by public authorities" to ensure that Title I employees did not inculcate religion; (ii) the program required "administrative cooperation" between the Board and parochial schools; and (iii) the program might increase the dangers of "political divisiveness." Under our current understanding of the Establishment Clause, the last two considerations are insufficient by themselves to create an "excessive" entanglement. They are present no matter where Title I services are offered, and no court has held that Title I services cannot be offered off-campus. Further, the assumption underlying the first consideration has been undermined. *** [A]fter *Zobrest* we no longer presume that public employees will inculcate religion simply because they happen to be in a sectarian environment. ***

To summarize, New York City's Title I program does not run afoul of any of three primary criteria we currently use to evaluate whether government aid has the effect of advancing religion: it does not result in governmental indoctrination; define its recipients by reference to religion; or create an excessive entanglement. *** Accordingly, we must acknowledge that *Aguilar*, as well as the portion of *Ball* addressing Grand Rapids' Shared Time program, are no longer good law. ***

For these reasons, we reverse the judgment of the Court of Appeals and remand to the District Court with instructions to vacate its September 26, 1985, order.

It is so ordered.

JUSTICE SOUTER, with whom JUSTICE STEVENS and JUSTICE GINSBURG join, and with whom JUSTICE BREYER joins as to Part II, dissenting.

I

*** I believe *Aguilar* was a correct and sensible decision, and my only reservation about its opinion is that the emphasis on the excessive entanglement produced by monitoring religious instructional content obscured those facts that independently called for the application of two central tenets of Establishment Clause jurisprudence. The State is forbidden to subsidize religion directly and is just as surely forbidden to act in any way that could reasonably be viewed as religious endorsement. ***

These principles were violated by the programs at issue in *Aguilar* and *Ball*, as a consequence of several significant features common to both Title I, as implemented in New York City before *Aguilar*, and the Grand Rapids Shared Time program: each provided classes on the premises of the religious schools, covering a wide range of subjects including some at the core of primary and secondary education, like reading and mathematics; while their services were termed "supplemental," the programs and their instructors necessarily assumed responsibility for teaching subjects that the religious schools would otherwise have been obligated to provide, cf. *Wolman v. Walter* (provision of diagnostic tests to religious schools provides only an incidental benefit). *** The obligation of primary and secondary schools to teach reading necessarily extends to teaching those who are having a hard time at it, and the same is true of math. Calling some classes remedial does not distinguish their subjects from the schools' basic subjects, however inadequately the schools may have been addressing them. ***

It may be objected that there is some subsidy in remedial education even when it takes place off the religious premises, some subsidy, that is, even in the way New York City has administered the Title I program after *Aguilar*. In these circumstances, too, what the State does, the religious school need not do; the schools save money and the program makes it easier for them to survive and concentrate their resources on their religious objectives. This argument may, of course, prove too much, but if it is not thought strong enough to bar even off-premises aid in teaching the basics to religious school pupils (an issue not before the Court in *Aguilar* or today), it does nothing to undermine the sense of drawing a line between remedial teaching on and off-premises. The off-premises teaching is arguably less likely to open the door to relieving religious schools of their responsibilities for secular subjects ***; if the aid is delivered outside of the schools, it is less likely to supplant some of what would otherwise go on inside them and to subsidize what remains. On top of that, the difference in the degree of reasonably perceptible endorsement is substantial. Sharing the teaching responsibilities within a school having religious objectives is far more likely to telegraph approval of the school's mission than keeping the State's distance would do. *** As the Court observed in *Ball*, "[t]he symbolism of a union between church and state [effected by placing the public school teachers into the religious schools] is most likely to influence children of tender years, whose experience is limited and whose beliefs consequently are the function of environment as much as of free and voluntary choice." ***

In sum, if a line is to be drawn short of barring all state aid to religious schools for teaching standard subjects, the *Aguilar-Ball* line was a sensible one capable of principled adherence. ***

II

Zobrest held that the Establishment Clause does not prevent a school district from providing a sign-language interpreter to a deaf student enrolled in a sectarian school. *** [T]he Court did indeed recognize that the Establishment Clause lays down no absolute bar to placing public employees in a sectarian school, but the rejection of such a per se rule was hinged expressly on the nature of the employee's job, sign- language interpretation (or signing) and the circumscribed role of the signer. *** The signer could thus be seen as more like a hearing aid than a teacher, and the signing could not be understood as an opportunity to inject religious content in what was supposed to be secular instruction. ***

The Court, however, ignores the careful distinction drawn in *Zobrest* and insists that a full-time public employee such as a Title I teacher is just like the signer, asserting that "there is no reason to presume that, simply because she enters a parochial school classroom, *** [this] teacher will depart from her assigned duties and instructions and embark on religious indoctrination ***." Whatever may be the merits of this position (and I find it short on merit), it does not enjoy the authority of *Zobrest*. *** *Zobrest* did not, implicitly or otherwise, repudiate the view that the involvement of public teachers in the instruction provided within sectarian schools looks like a partnership or union and implies approval of the sectarian aim. On the subject of symbolic unions and the strength of their implications, the lesson of *Zobrest* is merely that less is less. ***

Ball did not establish that "any and all" such aid to religious schools necessarily violates the Establishment Clause. It *** instead enquired whether the effect of the proffered aid was "direct and substantial" (and, so, unconstitutional) or merely "indirect and incidental," (and, so, permissible) emphasizing that the question "is one of degree." *Witters* and *Zobrest* did nothing to repudiate the principle, emphasizing rather the limited nature of the aid at issue in each case as well as the fact that religious institutions did not receive it directly from the State. ***

It is accordingly puzzling to find the Court insisting that the aid scheme administered under Title I and considered in *Aguilar* was comparable to the programs in *Witters* and *Zobrest*. Instead of aiding isolated individuals within a school system, New York City's Title I program before *Aguilar* served about 22,000 private school students, all but 52 of whom attended religious schools. Instead of serving individual blind or deaf students, as such, Title I as administered in New York City before *Aguilar* (and as now to be revived) funded instruction in core subjects (remedial reading, reading skills, remedial mathematics, English as a second language) and provided guidance services. Instead of providing a service the school would not otherwise furnish, the Title I services necessarily relieved a religious school of "an expense that it otherwise would have assumed," and freed its funds for other, and sectarian uses.

Finally, instead of aid that comes to the religious school indirectly in the sense that its distribution results from private decisionmaking, a public educational agency distributes Title I aid in the form of programs and services directly to the religious schools. *** In sum, nothing since *Ball* and *Aguilar* and before this case has eroded the distinction between "direct and substantial" and "indirect and incidental." That principled line is being breached only here and now. ***

JUSTICE GINSBURG, with whom JUSTICE STEVENS, JUSTICE SOUTER, and JUSTICE BREYER join, dissenting. [Omitted.]

————

GUY MITCHELL ET AL., v. MARY L. HELMS ET AL.
530 U.S. ____ [June 28, 2000]

Justice THOMAS announced the judgment of the Court and delivered an opinion, in which The Chief Justice, Justice SCALIA, and Justice KENNEDY join.

As part of a longstanding school aid program known as Chapter 2, the Federal Government distributes funds to state and local governmental agencies, which in turn lend educational materials and equipment to public and private schools, with the enrollment of each participating school determining the amount of aid that it receives. The question is whether Chapter 2, as applied in Jefferson Parish, Louisiana, is a law respecting an establishment of religion, because many of the private schools receiving

Chapter 2 aid in that parish are religiously affiliated. We hold that Chapter 2 is not such a law.

I
A

Chapter 2 of the Education Consolidation and Improvement Act of 1981,—is a close cousin of the provision of the ESEA that we recently considered in *Agostini* v. *Felton.* Like the provision at issue in *Agostini*, Chapter 2 channels federal funds to local educational agencies (LEAs), which are usually public school districts, via state educational agencies (SEAs), to implement programs to assist children in elementary and secondary schools. Among other things, Chapter 2 provides aid

> "for the acquisition and use of instructional and educational materials, including library services and materials (including media materials)', assessments, reference materials, computer software and hardware for instructional use, and other curricular materials."

LEAs and SEAs must offer assistance to both public and private schools (although any private school must be nonprofit). Participating private schools receive Chapter 2 aid based on the number of children enrolled in each school.***

Several restrictions apply to aid to private schools. Most significantly, the "services, materials, and equipment" provided to private schools must be "secular, neutral, and nonideological." In addition, private schools may not acquire control of Chapter 2 funds or title to Chapter 2 materials, equipment, or property.   A private school receives the materials and equipment by submitting to the LEA an application detailing which items the school seeks and how it will use them; the LEA, if it approves the application, purchases those items from the school's allocation of funds, and then lends them to that school.

***In the 1986–1987 fiscal year, 44% of the money budgeted for private schools in Jefferson Parish was spent by LEAs for acquiring library and media materials, and 48% for instructional equipment. Among the materials and equipment provided have been library books, computers, and computer software, and also slide and movie projectors, overhead projectors, television sets, tape recorders, VCR's, projection screens, laboratory equipment, maps, globes, filmstrips, slides, and cassette recordings.

***About 30% of Chapter 2 funds spent in Jefferson Parish are allocated for private schools. ***For 1987, 46 participated, and the participation level has remained relatively constant since then. Of these 46, 34 were Roman Catholic; 7 were otherwise religiously affiliated; and 5 were not religiously affiliated.

B

Respondents filed suit in December 1985, alleging, among other things, that Chapter 2, as applied in Jefferson Parish, violated the Establishment Clause of the First Amendment of the Federal Constitution.

***

The Fifth Circuit concluded that *Meek* and *Wolman* * controlled, and thus it held Chapter 2 unconstitutional.

II

The Establishment Clause of the First Amendment dictates that "Congress shall make no law respecting an establishment of religion." In the over 50 years since *Everso*n, we have consistently struggled to apply these simple words in the context of governmental aid to religious schools.***

In *Agostini*, we brought some clarity to our case law, by overruling two anomalous precedents (one in whole, the other in part) and by consolidating some of our previously disparate considerations under a revised test. Whereas in *Lemon* we had considered whether a statute (1) has a secular purpose, (2) has a primary effect of advancing or inhibiting religion, or (3) creates an excessive entanglement between government and religion, in *Agostini* we modified *Lemon* for purposes of evaluating aid to schools and examined only the first and second factors. *** We then set out revised criteria for determining the effect of a statute:

> "To summarize, New York City's Title I program does not run afoul of any of three primary criteria we currently use to evaluate whether government aid has the effect of advancing religion: It does not result in governmental indoctrination; define its recipients by reference to religion; or create an excessive entanglement."

In this case, our inquiry under *Agostini*'s purpose and effect test is a narrow one. Because respondents do not challenge the District Court's holding that Chapter 2 has a secular purpose, and because the Fifth Circuit also did not question that holding, we will consider only Chapter 2's effect. Further, in determining that effect, we will consider only the first two *Agostini* criteria, since neither respondents nor the Fifth Circuit has questioned the District Court's holding, that Chapter 2 does not create an excessive entanglement. Considering Chapter 2 in light of our more recent case law, we conclude that it neither results in religious indoctrination by the government nor defines its recipients by reference to religion. We therefore hold that Chapter 2 is not a "law respecting an establishment of religion." In so holding, we acknowledge — *Meek* and *Wolman* are anomalies in our case law. We therefore conclude that they are no longer good law.

---

* **[Ed. Note:** See casebook at p. 921 for this case.]

A

As we indicated in *Agostini*, and have indicated elsewhere, the question whether governmental aid to religious schools results in governmental indoctrination is ultimately a question whether any religious indoctrination that occurs in those schools could reasonably be attributed to governmental action. ***

In distinguishing between indoctrination that is attributable to the State and indoctrination that is not, we have consistently turned to the principle of neutrality, upholding aid that is offered to a broad range of groups or persons without regard to their religion. If the religious, irreligious, and areligious are all alike eligible for governmental aid, no one would conclude that any indoctrination that any particular recipient conducts has been done at the behest of the government. For attribution of indoctrination is a relative question. If the government is offering assistance to recipients who provide, so to speak, a broad range of indoctrination, the government itself is not thought responsible for any particular indoctrination. To put the point differently, if the government, seeking to further some legitimate secular purpose, offers aid on the same terms, without regard to religion, to all who adequately further that purpose, — then it is fair to say that any aid going to a religious recipient only has the effect of furthering that secular purpose.***

As a way of assuring neutrality, we have repeatedly considered whether any governmental aid that goes to a religious institution does so "only as a result of the genuinely independent and private choices of individuals." *Agostini, supra,* at 226. ***

The principles of neutrality and private choice, and their relationship to each other, were prominent not only in *Agostini*, but also in *Zobrest, Witters,* and *Mueller*. The heart of our reasoning in *Zobrest*, upholding governmental provision of a sign language interpreter to a deaf student at his Catholic high school, was as follows:

> ***[that] because the [statute] creates no financial incentive for parents to choose a sectarian school, an interpreter's presence there cannot be attributed to state decisionmaking."

As this passage indicates, the private choices helped to ensure neutrality, and neutrality and private choices together eliminated any possible attribution to the government even when the interpreter translated classes on Catholic doctrine.

***

Agostini's second primary criterion for determining the effect of governmental aid is closely related to the first. The second criterion requires a court to consider whether an aid program "define[s] its recipients by reference to religion." As we briefly explained in *Agostini*, this second criterion looks to the same set of facts as does our focus, under the first criterion, on neutrality, but the second criterion uses those facts to answer a somewhat different question—whether the criteria for allocating the aid "creat[e] a financial incentive to undertake religious indoctrination." In *Agostini* we set out the following rule for answering this question:

> "This incentive is not present, however, where the aid is allocated on the basis of neutral, secular criteria that neither favor nor disfavor religion, and is made available to both religious and secular beneficiaries on a nondiscriminatory basis.***

We hasten to add, what should be obvious from the rule itself, that simply because an aid program offers private schools, and thus religious schools, a benefit that they did not previously receive does not mean that the program, by reducing the cost of securing a religious education, creates, under *Agostini*'s second criterion, an "incentive" for parents to choose such an education for their children. For *any* aid will have some such effect.

B

Respondents inexplicably make no effort to address Chapter 2 under the *Agostini* test. Instead, dismissing *Agostini* as factually distinguishable, they offer two rules that they contend should govern our determination of whether Chapter 2 has the effect of advancing religion. They argue first, and chiefly, that "direct, nonincidental" aid to the primary educational mission of religious is always impermissible. Second, they argue that provision to religious schools of aid that is divertible to religious use is similarly impermissible. [7] Respondents' arguments are inconsistent with our more recent case law, in particular *Agostini* and *Zobrest*, and we therefore reject them.

1

Although some of our earlier cases, did emphasize the distinction between direct and indirect aid, the purpose of this distinction was merely to prevent "subsidization" of religion. As even the dissent all but admits, our more recent cases address this purpose not through the direct/indirect distinction but rather through the principle of private choice, as incorporated in the first *Agostini* criterion *(i.e.,* whether any indoctrination could be attributed to the government). If aid to schools, even "direct aid," is neutrally available and, before reaching or benefiting any religious school, first passes through the hands (literally or figuratively) of numerous private citizens who are free to direct the aid elsewhere, the government has not provided any "support of religion." Although the presence of private choice is easier to see when aid literally passes through the hands of

---

7. Respondents also contend that Chapter 2 aid supplants, rather than supplements, the core educational function of parochial schools and therefore has the effect of furthering religion. Our case law does provide some indication that this distinction may be relevant to determining whether aid results in governmental indoctrination, but we have never delineated the distinction's contours or held that it is constitutionally required.

individuals—which is why we have mentioned directness in the same breath with private choice,— there is no reason why the Establishment Clause requires such a form.

***It was undeniable in *Witters* that the aid (tuition) would ultimately go to the Inland Empire School of the Bible and would support religious education. We viewed this arrangement, however, as no different from a government issuing a paycheck to one of its employees knowing the employee would direct the funds to a religious institution. ***

As *Agostini* explained, the same reasoning was at work in *Zobrest*, where we allowed the government-funded interpreter to provide assistance at a Catholic school, "even though she would be a mouthpiece for religious instruction," because the interpreter was provided according to neutral eligibility criteria and private choice. *** (We saw no difference in *Zobrest* between the government hiring the interpreter directly and the government providing funds to the parents who then would hire the interpreter.*** Finally, in *Agostini* itself, we used the reasoning of *Witters* and *Zobrest* to conclude that remedial classes provided under Title I of the ESEA by public employees did not impermissibly finance religious indoctrination.***

To the extent that respondents intend their direct/indirect distinction to require that any aid be literally placed in the hands of schoolchildren rather than given directly to the school for teaching those same children, the very cases on which respondents most rely, *Meek* and *Wolman*, demonstrate the irrelevance of such formalism. In *Meek*, we justified our rejection of a program that loaned instructional materials and equipment by, among other things, pointing out that the aid was loaned to the schools, and thus was "direct aid." The materials-and-equipment program in *Wolman* was essentially identical, except that the State, in an effort to comply with *Meek*, loaned the aid to the students.***

That *Meek* and *Wolman* reached the same result, on programs that were indistinguishable but for the direct/ indirect distinction, shows that that distinction played no part in *Meek*.

Further, respondents' formalistic line breaks down in the application to real-world programs. In *Allen*, for example, although we did recognize that students themselves received and owned the textbooks, we also noted that the books provided were those that the private schools required for courses, that the schools could collect students' requests for books and submit them to the board of education, that the schools could store the textbooks, and that the textbooks were essential to the schools' teaching of secular subjects. Whether one chooses to label this program "direct" or "indirect" is a rather arbitrary choice, one that does not further the constitutional analysis.

Of course, we have seen "special Establishment Clause dangers," when *money* is given to religious schools or entities directly rather than, as in *Witters* and *Mueller*, indirectly.[8] *** But direct payments of money are not at issue in this case, and we refuse to allow a "special" case to create a rule for all cases.

2

Respondents also contend that the Establishment Clause requires that aid to religious schools not be impermissibly religious in nature or be divertible to religious use. We agree with the first part of this argument but not the second. Respondents' "no divertibility" rule is inconsistent with our more recent case law and is unworkable. So long as the governmental aid is not itself "unsuitable for use in the public schools because of religious content," and eligibility for aid is determined in a constitutionally permissible manner, any use of that aid to indoctrinate cannot be attributed to the government and is thus not of constitutional concern. And, of course, the use to which the aid is put does not affect the criteria governing the aid's allocation and thus does not create any impermissible incentive under *Agostini*'s second criterion.

***

The issue is not divertibility of aid but rather whether the aid itself has an impermissible content. Where the aid would be suitable for use in a public school, it is also suitable for use in any private school. Similarly, the prohibition against the government providing impermissible content resolves the Establishment Clause concerns that exist if aid is actually diverted to religious uses. In *Agostini*, we explained *Zobrest* by making just this distinction between the content of aid and the use of that aid: "Because the only *government* aid in *Zobrest* was the interpreter, who was *herself not inculcating* any religious messages, no *government* indoctrination took place." *** And just as a government interpreter does not herself inculcate a religious message—even when she is conveying one—so also a government computer or overhead projector does not itself inculcate a religious message, even when it is conveying one. In *Agostini* itself, we approved the provision of public employees to teach secular remedial classes in private schools partly because we concluded that there was no reason to suspect that indoctrinating content would be part of such governmental aid.

A concern for divertibility, as opposed to improper content, is misplaced not only because it fails to explain why the sort of aid that we have allowed is permissible, but also because it is boundless—enveloping all aid, no matter how trivial—and thus has only the most attenuated (if any) link to any realistic concern for preventing an

---

8. The reason for such concern is not that the form *per se* is bad, but that such a form creates special risks that governmental aid will have the effect of advancing religion (or, even more, a purpose of doing so). An indirect form of payment reduces these risks. It is arguable, however, at least after *Witters*, that the principles of neutrality and private choice would be adequate to address those special risks, for it is hard to see the basis for deciding *Witters* differently simply if the State had sent the tuition check directly to whichever school Witters chose to attend.

"establishment of religion." Presumably, for example, government- provided lecterns, chalk, crayons, pens, paper, and paintbrushes would have to be excluded from religious schools under respondents' proposed rule.***

C

The dissent serves up a smorgasbord of 11 factors that, depending on the facts of each case "in all its particularity," could be relevant to the constitutionality of a school-aid program. *** One of the dissent's factors deserves special mention: whether a school that receives aid (or whose students receive aid) is pervasively sectarian. The dissent is correct that there was a period when this factor mattered, particularly if the pervasively sectarian school was a primary or secondary school. But that period is one that the Court should regret, and it is thankfully long past.

There are numerous reasons to formally dispense with this factor. First, its relevance in our precedents is in sharp decline. Although our case law has consistently mentioned it even in recent years, we have not struck down an aid program in reliance on this factor since 1985.***

[I]n *Zobrest* and *Agostini*, we upheld aid programs to children who attended schools that were not only pervasively sectarian but also were primary and secondary. *Zobrest*, in turning away a challenge based on the pervasively sectarian nature of Salpointe Catholic High School, emphasized the presence of private choice and the absence of government provided sectarian content.***

Second, the religious nature of a recipient should not matter to the constitutional analysis, so long as the recipient adequately furthers the government's secular purpose. If a program offers permissible aid to the religious (including the pervasively sectarian), the areligious, and the irreligious, it is a mystery which view of religion the government has established, and thus a mystery what the constitutional violation would be. The pervasively sectarian recipient has not received any special favor, and it is most bizarre that the Court would, as the dissent seemingly does, reserve special hostility for those who take their religion seriously, who think that their religion should affect the whole of their lives, or who make the mistake of being effective in transmitting their views to children.

Third, the inquiry into the recipient's religious views   required by a focus on whether a school is pervasively sectarian is not only unnecessary but also offensive. It is well established, in numerous other contexts, that courts should refrain from trolling through a person's or institution's religious beliefs. ***

Hostility to aid to pervasively sectarian schools has a shameful pedigree that we do not hesitate to disavow. ***Opposition to aid to "sectarian" schools acquired prominence in the 1870' s with Congress's consideration (and near passage) of the Blaine Amendment, which would have amended the Constitution to bar any aid to sectarian institutions. Consideration of the amendment arose at a time of pervasive hostility to the

Catholic Church and to Catholics in general, and it was an open secret that "sectarian" was code for "Catholic."***

In short, nothing in the Establishment Clause requires the exclusion of pervasively sectarian schools from otherwise permissible aid programs, and other doctrines of this Court bar it. This doctrine, born of bigotry, should be buried now.

III

Applying the two relevant *Agostini* criteria, we see no basis for concluding that Jefferson Parish's Chapter 2 program "has the effect of advancing religion." Chapter 2 does not result in governmental indoctrination, because it determines eligibility for aid neutrally, allocates that aid based on the private choices of the parents of schoolchildren, and does not provide aid that has an impermissible content. Nor does Chapter 2 define its recipients by reference to religion.

***

Chapter 2 also satisfies the first *Agostini* criterion. The program makes a broad array of schools eligible for aid without regard to their religious affiliations or lack thereof. We therefore have no difficulty concluding that Chapter 2 is neutral with regard to religion. Chapter 2 aid also, like the aid in *Agostini*, *Zobrest*, and *Witters*, reaches participating schools only "as a consequence of private decisionmaking."***

Because Chapter 2 aid is provided pursuant to private choices, it is not problematic that one could fairly describe Chapter 2 as providing "direct" aid. *** The ultimate beneficiaries of Chapter 2 aid are the students who attend the schools that receive that aid, and this is so regardless of whether individual students lug computers to school each day or, as Jefferson Parish has more sensibly provided, the schools receive the computers.

Finally, Chapter 2 satisfies the first *Agostini* criterion because it does not provide to religious schools aid that has an impermissible content. The statute explicitly bars anything of the sort, providing that all Chapter 2 aid for the benefit of children in private schools shall be "secular, neutral, and nonideological."— The chief aid at issue is computers, computer software, and library books. The computers presumably have no pre-existing content, or at least none that would be impermissible for use in public schools. Respondents do not contend otherwise. Respondents also offer no evidence that religious schools have received software from the government that has an impermissible content.

There is evidence that equipment has been, or at least easily could be, diverted for use in religious classes. *** In addition, we agree with the dissent that there is evidence of actual diversion and that, were the safeguards anything other than anemic, there would almost certainly be more such evidence.

In any event, for reasons we discussed in Part II–B–2, *supra*, the evidence of actual diversion and the weakness of the safeguards against actual diversion are not relevant to the constitutional inquiry, whatever relevance they may have under the statute and regulations.

***

The District Court found that prescreening by the LEA coordinator of requested library books was sufficient to prevent statutory violations, see App. to Pet. for Cert. 107a, and the Fifth Circuit did not disagree. Further, as noted, the monitoring system appears adequate to catch those errors that do occur. We are unwilling to elevate scattered *de minimis* statutory violations, discovered and remedied by the relevant authorities themselves prior to any litigation, to such a level as to convert an otherwise unobjectionable parishwide program into a law that has the effect of advancing religion.

IV

In short, Chapter 2 satisfies both the first and second primary criteria of *Agostini*. It therefore does not have the effect of advancing religion. For the same reason, Chapter 2 also "cannot reasonably be viewed as an endorsement of religion." Accordingly, we hold that Chapter 2 is not a law respecting an establishment of religion. Jefferson Parish need not exclude religious schools from its Chapter 2 program.[19] To the extent that *Meek* and *Wolman* conflict with this holding, we overrule them.***

The judgment of the Fifth Circuit is reversed.

It is so ordered.

JUSTICE O' CONNOR, with whom JUSTICE BREYER joins, concurring in the judgment.

To the extent our decisions in *Meek* v. *Pittenger*, and *Wolman* v. *Walter*, are inconsistent with the Court's judgment today, I agree that those decisions should be overruled....

[T]wo specific aspects of the opinion compel me to write separately. First, the plurality's treatment of neutrality comes close to assigning that factor singular importance in the future adjudication of Establishment Clause challenges to government school-aid programs. Second, the plurality's approval of actual diversion of government aid to religious indoctrination is in tension with our precedents and, in any event, unnecessary to decide the instant case.***

I

---

19. Indeed, as petitioners observe, to require exclusion of religious schools from such a program would raise serious questions under the Free Exercise Clause.

[W]e have never held that a government-aid program passes constitutional muster *solely* because of the neutral criteria it employs as a basis for distributing aid. For example, in *Agostini*, neutrality was only one of several factors we considered in determining that New York City's Title I program did not have the impermissible effect of advancing religion. See *Agostini* at 226–228 (noting lack of evidence of inculcation of religion by Title I instructors, legal requirement that Title I services be supplemental to regular curricula, and that no Title I funds reached religious schools' coffers). ***

I also disagree with the plurality's conclusion that actual diversion of government aid to religious indoctrination is consistent with the Establishment Clause. *** In both *Agostini*, and *Allen*, we rested our approval of the relevant programs in part on the fact that the aid had not been used to advance the religious missions of the recipient schools.***

The plurality bases its holding that actual diversion is permissible on *Witters* and *Zobrest*. *Ante*, at 21–22. Those decisions, however, rested on a significant factual premise missing from this case, as well as from the majority of cases thus far considered by the Court involving Establishment Clause challenges to school-aid programs. Specifically, we decided *Witters* and *Zobrest* on the understanding that the aid was provided directly to the individual student who, in turn, made the choice of where to put that aid to use. ***Like JUSTICE SOUTER, I do not believe that we should treat a per-capita-aid program the same as the true private-choice programs considered in *Witters* and *Zobrest*.

First, when the government provides aid directly to the student beneficiary, that student can attend a religious school and yet retain control over whether the secular government aid will be applied toward the religious education. The fact that aid flows to the religious school and is used for the advancement of religion is therefore *wholly* dependent on the student's private decision. ***

Second, I believe the distinction between a per-capita school-aid program and a true private-choice program is significant for purposes of endorsement. ***Because the religious indoctrination is supported by government assistance, the reasonable observer would naturally perceive the aid program as *government* support for the advancement of religion. ***

Finally, the distinction between a per-capita-aid program and a true private-choice program is important when considering aid that consists of direct monetary subsidies. ***To be sure, the plurality does not actually hold that its theory extends to direct money payments.... That omission, however, is of little comfort. In its logic as well as its specific advisory language,...the plurality opinion foreshadows the approval of direct monetary subsidies to religious organizations, even when they use the money to advance their religious objectives. ***For these reasons, as well as my disagreement with the plurality's approach, I would decide today's case by applying the criteria set forth in *Agostini*.

II

Like the Title I program considered in *Agostini*, all Chapter 2 funds are controlled by public agencies—the SEAs and LEAs. The LEAs purchase instructional and educational materials and then lend those materials to public and private schools. [T]he statute provides that all Chapter 2 materials and equipment must be "secular, neutral, and nonideological." That restriction is reinforced by a further statutory prohibition on "the making of any payment...for religious worship or instruction." Although respondents claim that Chapter 2 aid has been diverted to religious instruction, that evidence is *de minimis*....

III

Respondents point to the distinct character of the aid program considered there. In *Agostini*, federal funds paid for public-school teachers to provide secular instruction to eligible children on the premises of their religious schools. Here, in contrast, federal funds pay for instructional materials and equipment that LEAs lend to religious schools for use by those schools' own teachers in their classes. [I]f the mere ability of a teacher to devise a religious lesson involving the secular aid in question suffices to hold the provision of that aid unconstitutional, it is difficult to discern any limiting principle to the divertibility rule. For example, even a publicly financed lunch would apparently be unconstitutional under a divertibility rationale because religious-school officials conceivably could use the lunch to lead the students in a blessing over the bread.***

IV

I would adhere to the rule that we have applied in the context of textbook lending programs: To establish a First Amendment violation, plaintiffs must prove that the aid in question actually is, or has been, used for religious purposes. *** Because I believe that the Court should abandon the presumption adopted in *Meek* and *Wolman* respecting the use of instructional materials and equipment by religious-school teachers, I see no constitutional need for *pervasive* monitoring under the Chapter 2 program.

[A]t the state level, the Louisiana Department of Education (the relevant SEA for Louisiana) requires all nonpublic schools to submit signed assurances that they will use Chapter 2 aid only to supplement and not to supplant non-Federal funds, and that the instructional materials and equipment "will only be used for secular, neutral and nonideological purposes."*** Regardless of whether these factors are constitutional requirements, they are surely sufficient to find that the program at issue here does not have the impermissible effect of advancing religion. For the same reasons, "this carefully constrained program also cannot reasonably be viewed as an endorsement of religion."

Accordingly, I concur in the judgment.

JUSTICE SOUTER, with whom JUSTICE STEVENS and JUSTICE GINSBURG join, dissenting. [1]

I

[Justice Souter begins the dissent by reasserting a bedrock principle to which, he says, all nine Justices subscribed, in *Everson v. Board of Education.*[2]   All agreed, in *Everson*, that the establishment clause forbids the state to use public funds to subsidize or to support religious establishments as such,[3] consistent with the principle putting every religion on an independent foundation of voluntarism (rather than "state support").

It follows, and so the Court had consistently held (and indeed could not hold otherwise), that insofar as a religious school is itself established by a church or congregation, and so established and conducted under religious auspices as a means of propagating the faith of its sponsoring religion, the state may no more use public funds to relieve it of depending upon the support of those who share its faith and mission, to advance its religious mission, any more than in respect to a church. The one is equally a breach of the establishment clause as is the other. And, he says, there has never been any departure from *this* understanding of basic establishment clause doctrine at any time during the half-century since the Court first addressed the meaning of the establishment clause, in 1947.

II

---

1. [**Ed. Note**: The dissent by Justice Souter, joined by Justice Stevens and Justice Ginsburg, is both elaborate and complex. It reviews virtually all of the Court's establishment clause doctrinal history and case law, and fills a full fifty pages in the U.S. Reports. The following edited summary is, unavoidably, a very severe abridgment. (So, for example, it entirely omits his elaborate review of previous cases–to explain, reconcile, defend, and account for the critical distinctions students have struggled to understand up to now, many of which are now abandoned in the opinion by Justice Thomas, writing for a plurality of the Court.) The reader may well want to see the full opinion; as it may likewise be helpful to see also the more complete opinion of Justice O'Connor (especially, as, for the moment, it may represent the critical "voice" on the Court).]

2. 330 U.S. 1 (1947) (casebook at p. 861).

3. (That is, *all* agreed that this was so, in *Everson*; and, rather, the only difference in the case was that five of the Justices simply did not see that there was any departure from, or inconsistency with, this understanding simply because parents of school-age children (not excluding those of parochial school students) were eligible to be reimbursed for ordinary bus fare, on ordinary public buses moving along their regular routes, in securing to their children a common means of safe travel (though, even then, four Justices disagreed and thought the mere bus-fare reimbursement plan as such was not permissible).

Coming, then, to this case, it is plain to Justice Souter that *that* line of separation was clearly crossed by the forms of religious assistance provided by the state in this case: (a) in the *nature* of the *direct* aid furnished *to* the religious schools themselves; (b) in the *manner* and *amount* of that aid; (c) in the *inextricability* of its use in the religious school setting in directly and substantially advancing the religious inculcative functions of the recipient religious schools; and (d) *in the actual uses* made of the materials supplied by state, even as the plurality opinion itself acknowledged had taken place. Under *all* previous precedent, he says, this would clearly require the court to sustain the original complaint--even as the lower court agreed--and require it to hold in favor of the complaining parties and enjoin the state's continuing disbursements of its various forms of substantial assistance. In short, the decision by the court of appeals was inevitable and correct.

III

Justice Souter then contrasts "the plurality's approach" (i.e., the opinion for four members of the Court by Justice Thomas *supra*). He declares it is "an utter departure" and "would break with the law." To be sure, he notes, because of the view taken of the case in the concurring opinion--by Justice O'Connor in which Justice Breyer joined--the plurality view is not yet the view of the Court.[4] Turning directly to the plurality opinion, however, he says (emphasis added): "[T]here is no mistaking the abandonment of doctrine that would occur if the plurality were to become a majority.***The plurality is candid in pointing out the extent of actual diversion of Chapter 2 aid to religious use in the case before us, and equally candid in saying it does not matter." But, he asks, why doesn't it matter, when heretofore (he says), it has always not merely mattered but been decisive?

--The reason it "does not matter" to the plurality of the four Justices, when previously it always had, Justice Souter notes, is evidently this: "To the plurality there is nothing wrong[5] with [using taxpayer public funds even in direct aid of] a [church-related] school's religious mission," when accomplished through a plan merely "also providing assistance to the public schools." This is the "doctrinal coup," he says, and, indeed, "it is a break with consistent doctrine...unequalled in the history of Establishment Clause interpretation."

How? In what way? In just this way: "***[I]n rejecting the principle of no [taxpayer funded] aid to a school's religious mission the plurality is attacking the most fundamental assumption underlying the Establishment Clause." "Religious missions" are not the business of government, either to subsidize or to subvert, under *Everson*,

---

4. (Thus, he says, this case does not itself "stage a doctrinal coup.")

5. (I.e., nothing inconsistent with the establishment clause.)

Souter says, but the view now taken by four members of the Court represent the clearest evidence yet that this understanding is increasingly fragile and at risk.

NOTE ON SCHOOL VOUCHERS

Increasingly in the last decade, states have enacted so-called "school voucher programs" which — although they vary in their precise features from state to state — at bottom provide state (taxpayer) funds to pay (at least a portion of) private and parochial school tuition for children in low income families. The Ohio program, for instance, which was recently sustained by the Ohio Supreme Court, *Simmons-Harris v. Goff*, 711 N.E.2d 203 (Ohio, May 27, 1999), requires the state superintendent to give scholarships to Cleveland students to attend a "registered" private school; scholarships are for 75 to 90 percent of actual tuition (depending on the family income) or up to $2500; and the tuition checks are made payable to the parents, but sent to the schools where the parents would then endorse the check over to the schools. *See also Kotterman v. Killian*, 972 P.2d 606 (Ariz. 1999) (sustaining voucher scheme); *Jackson v. Bensen*, 578 N.W.2d 602 (Wisc. 1998) (sustaining voucher scheme), *cert. denied*, 119 S. Ct. 466 (1999); *but see Chittenden Town School District v. Vermont Department of Education*, 738 A.2d 539 (Vt., June 11, 1999) (finding voucher program violates Compelled Support Clause of Vermont constitution).

The constitutionality of these schemes has been hotly debated, and although the Court denied certiorari in the Wisconsin case in 1999, it is expected one of these arrangements will wend its way to the Court in due time. Would these arrangements fail under *Everson* ("No tax in any amount, large or small, can be levied to support any religious activities or institutions . . .") or might it fall within some sort of "exception" carved by the cases in this section (*Mueller v. Allen* and *Agostini*, and *Mitchell v. Helms*)?

———

Casebook, p. 966
Add at beginning of NOTE following *McGowan v. Maryland*

1a. As noted in a recent student Note,[17a] "[E]ach year on a Friday in late March or early April — two days before Easter — Christians commemorate the crucifixion of their savior Jesus Christ. They call that day Good Friday. Many states have given Good Friday the status for a legal holiday, closing government offices and schools." The public employees (e.g., public school teachers, employees at closed state departments of motor vehicles offices, etc.) are paid their usual salaries, though no work is being done. Most of these state laws are of fairly recent origin. Several have

———

17a. *See* Justin Brookman, Note, *The Constitutionality of The Good Friday Holiday*, 73 *N.Y.U.L.* Rev. 193 (1998).

been challenged under the establishment clause, though none has reached the Supreme Court. Would the rationale of *McGowan* apply to sustain these laws? Would the rationale of the next principal case (*Marsh*)?

———

Casebook at 967
Add as footnote to end of Note 2

For additional discussion of these and similar practices, see Steven B. Epstein, *Rethinking the Constitutionality of Ceremonial Deism*, 96 Colum. L. Rev. 2083 (1996).

———

Casebook at 1011
Add as a new case following *Lee v. Weisman*

SANTA FE INDEPENDENT SCHOOL DISTRICT v. JANE DOE, ET AL.
530 U.S. ____ [June 19, 2000]

JUSTICE STEVENS delivered the opinion of the Court.

I

The Santa Fe Independent School District is responsible for the education of more than 4,000 students in a small community in the southern part of the State of Texas.***In their complaint the Does alleged that the District had engaged in several proselytizing practices, such as promoting attendance at a Baptist revival meeting, encouraging membership in religious clubs, chastising children who held minority religious beliefs, and distributing Gideon Bibles on school premises. They also alleged that the District allowed students to read Christian invocations and benedictions from the stage at graduation ceremonies, and to deliver overtly Christian prayers over the public address system at home football games.

On May 10, 1995, the District Court entered an interim order addressing a number of different issues. In response, the District adopted a series of policies over several months dealing with prayer at school functions. The policies enacted in May and July for graduation ceremonies provided the format for the August and October policies for football games. The August policy, which was titled "Prayer at Football Games," authorized two student elections, the first to determine whether "invocations" should be delivered, and the second to select the spokesperson to deliver them. The final policy (October policy) is essentially the same as the August policy, though it omits the word "prayer" from its title, and refers to "messages" and "statements" as well as "invocations." It is the validity of that policy that is before us.[6] We granted the

———

6. "STUDENT ACTIVITIES: PRE-GAME CEREMONIES AT FOOTBALL GAMES. The board has chosen to permit students to deliver a brief invocation and/or message to be delivered during

District's petition for certiorari, limited to th[is] question: "Whether petitioner's policy permitting student-led, student-initiated prayer at football games violates the Establishment Clause." We conclude, as did the Court of Appeals, that it does.

II

Although this case involves student prayer at a different type of school function, our analysis is properly guided by the principles that we endorsed in *Lee v. Weisman*: "It is beyond dispute that, at a minimum, the Constitution guarantees that government may not coerce anyone to support or participate in religion or its exercise, or otherwise act in a way which 'establishes a [state] religion or religious faith, or tends to do so.'"

[T]he District first argues that this principle is inapplicable to its October policy because the messages are private student speech, not public speech. It reminds us that "there is a crucial difference between government speech endorsing religion, which the Establishment Clause forbids, and private speech endorsing religion, which the Free Speech and Free Exercise Clauses protect." We certainly agree with that distinction, but we are not persuaded that the pregame invocations should be regarded as "private speech."

These invocations are authorized by a government policy and take place on government property at government-sponsored school-related events. Of course, not every message delivered under such circumstances is the government's own. We have held, for example, that an individual's contribution to a government-created forum was not government speech. See *Rosenberger v. Rector and Visitors of Univ. of Virginia* (1995). Although the District relies heavily on *Rosenberger* and similar cases involving such forums, it is clear that the pregame ceremony is not the type of forum discussed in those cases. The Santa Fe school officials simply do not evince either by policy or by practice, any intent to open the pregame ceremony to indiscriminate use by the student body generally. Rather, the school allows only one student, the same student for the entire season, to give the invocation. The statement or invocation, moreover, is subject to particular regulations that confine the content and topic of the student's message.***Granting only one student access to the stage at a time does not, of course, necessarily preclude a finding that a school has created a limited public forum. Here,

---

the pre-game ceremonies of home varsity football games to solemnize the event, to promote good sportsmanship and student safety, and to establish the appropriate environment for the competition.

Upon advice and direction of the high school principal, each spring, the high school student council shall conduct an election, by the high school student body, by secret ballot, to determine whether such a statement or invocation will be a part of the pre-game ceremonies and if so, shall elect a student, from a list of student volunteers, to deliver the statement or invocation. The student volunteer who is selected by his or her classmates may decide what message and/or invocation to deliver, consistent with the goals and purposes of this policy."

however, Santa Fe's student election system ensures that only those messages deemed "appropriate" under the District's policy may be delivered. That is, the majoritarian process implemented by the District guarantees, by definition, that minority candidates will never prevail and that their views will be effectively silenced.

Recently, in *Board of Regents of Univ. of Wis. System v. Southworth*, we explained why student elections that determine, by majority vote, which expressive activities shall receive or not receive school benefits are constitutionally problematic: "To the extent the referendum substitutes majority determinations for viewpoint neutrality it would undermine the constitutional protection the program requires." Like the student referendum for funding in *Southworth*, this student election does nothing to protect minority views but rather places the students who hold such views at the mercy of the majority.[15]

In *Lee*, the school district made the related argument that its policy of endorsing only "civic or nonsectarian" prayer was acceptable because it minimized the intrusion on the audience as a whole. We rejected that claim by explaining that such a majoritarian policy "does not lessen the offense or isolation to the objectors. At best it narrows their number, at worst increases their sense of isolation and affront." Similarly, while Santa Fe's majoritarian election might ensure that most of the students are represented, it does nothing to protect the minority; indeed, it likely serves to intensify their offense.

Moreover, the District has failed to divorce itself from the religious content in the invocations. It has not succeeded in doing so, either by claiming that its policy is "one of neutrality rather than endorsement"or by characterizing the individual student as the "circuit-breaker" in the process.***In addition to involving the school in the selection of the speaker, the policy, by its terms, invites and encourages religious messages. The policy itself states that the purpose of the message is "to solemnize the event." Moreover, the requirements that the message "promote good citizenship" and "establish the appropriate environment for competition" further narrow the types of message deemed appropriate, suggesting that a solemn, yet nonreligious, message, such as commentary on United States foreign policy, would be prohibited. Indeed, the only type of message that is expressly endorsed in the text is an "invocation"—a term that

---

15. If instead of a choice between an invocation and no pregame message, the first election determined whether a political speech should be made, and the second election determined whether the speaker should be a Democrat or a Republican, it would be rather clear that the public address system was being used to deliver a partisan message reflecting the viewpoint of the majority rather than a random statement by a private individual.

primarily describes an appeal for divine assistance. In fact, as used in the past at Santa Fe High School, an "invocation" has always entailed a focused religious message.[21]

The actual or perceived endorsement of the message, moreover, is established by factors beyond just the text of the policy. Once the student speaker is selected and the message composed, the invocation is then delivered to a large audience assembled as part of a regularly scheduled, school-sponsored function conducted on school property. The message is broadcast over the school's public address system, which remains subject to the control of school officials.

In this context the members of the listening audience must perceive the pregame message as a public expression of the views of the majority of the student body delivered with the approval of the school administration. In cases involving state participation in a religious activity, one of the relevant questions is "whether an objective observer, acquainted with the text, legislative history, and implementation of the statute, would perceive it as a state endorsement of prayer in public schools." *Wallace v Jaffree*, 472 U.S. at 76 (O'Connor, J., concurring in judgment) The text and history of this policy, moreover, reinforce our objective student's perception that the prayer is, in actuality, encouraged by the school.

Most striking to us is the evolution of the current policy from the long-sanctioned office of "Student Chaplain" to the candidly titled "Prayer at Football Games" regulation. This history indicates that the District intended to preserve the practice of prayer before football games. The conclusion that the District viewed the October policy simply as a continuation of the previous policies is dramatically illustrated by the fact that the school did not conduct a new election, pursuant to the current policy, to replace the results of the previous election, which occurred under the former policy.

School sponsorship of a religious message is impermissible because it sends the ancillary message to members of the audience who are nonadherants "that they are outsiders, not full members of the political community, and an accompanying message to adherants that they are insiders, favored members of the political community." *Lynch v. Donnelly*, 465 U.S. at 688 (1984) (O'Connor, J., concurring). The delivery of such a message—over the school's public address system, by a speaker representing the student body, under the supervision of school faculty, and pursuant to a school policy that explicitly and implicitly encourages public prayer—is not properly characterized as "private" speech.

III

---

21. Even if the plain language of the October policy were facially neutral, the Establishment Clause forbids a State to hide behind the application of formally neutral criteria and remain studiously oblivious to the effects of its actions.

The District next argues that its football policy is distinguishable from the graduation prayer in *Lee* because it does not coerce students to participate in religious observances. Its argument has two parts: first, that there is no impermissible government coercion because the pregame messages are the product of student choices; and second, that there is really no coercion at all because attendance at an extracurricular event, unlike a graduation ceremony, is voluntary.

One of the purposes served by the Establishment Clause is to remove debate over this kind of issue from governmental supervision or control. The two student elections authorized by the policy, coupled with the debates that presumably must precede each, impermissibly invade that private sphere. The election mechanism, when considered in light of the history in which the policy in question evolved, reflects a device the District put in place that determines whether religious messages will be delivered at home football games. The mechanism encourages divisiveness along religious lines in a public school setting, a result at odds with the Establishment Clause. Although it is true that the ultimate choice of student speaker is attributable to the students, the District's decision to hold the constitutionally problematic election is clearly a choice attributable to the State.

The District further argues that attendance at the commencement ceremonies at issue in *Lee* "differs dramatically" from attendance at high school football games. Attendance at a high school football game, unlike showing up for class, is certainly not required in order to receive a diploma. Moreover, we may assume that the District is correct in arguing that the informal pressure to attend an athletic event is not as strong as a senior's desire to attend her own graduation ceremony.

There are some students, however, such as cheerleaders, members of the band, and, of course, the team members themselves, for whom seasonal commitments mandate their attendance, sometimes for class credit. The District also minimizes the importance to many students of attending and participating in extracurricular activities as part of a complete educational experience. As we noted in *Lee*, "law reaches past formalism." To assert that high school students do not feel immense social pressure, or have a truly genuine desire, to be involved in the extracurricular event that is American high school football is formalistic in the extreme. Undoubtedly, the games are not important to some students, and they voluntarily choose not to attend. For many others, however, the choice between whether to attend these games or to risk facing a personally offensive religious ritual is in no practical sense an easy one. The Constitution, moreover, demands that the school may not force this difficult choice upon these students for it is a tenet of the First Amendment that the State cannot require one of its citizens to forfeit his or her rights and benefits as the price of resisting conformance to state-sponsored religious practice.

Even if we regard every high school student's decision to attend a home football game as purely voluntary, we are nevertheless persuaded that the delivery of a pregame prayer has the improper effect of coercing those present to participate in an act of religious worship. "[T]he government may no more use social pressure to enforce orthodoxy than it may use more direct means." *Lee* at 594. As in *Lee*, "what to most believers may seem nothing more than a reasonable request that the nonbeliever respect their religious practices, in a school context may appear to the nonbeliever or dissenter to be an attempt to employ the machinery of the State to enforce a religious orthodoxy." The constitutional command will not permit the District "to exact religious conformity from a student as the price" of joining her classmates at a varsity football game.

IV

Finally, the District argues repeatedly that the Does have made a premature facial challenge to the October policy that necessarily must fail. The District emphasizes that until a student actually delivers a solemnizing message under the latest version of the policy, there can be no certainty that any of the statements or invocations will be religious.

This argument, however, assumes that we are concerned only with the serious constitutional injury that occurs when a student is forced to participate in an act of religious worship because she chooses to attend a school event. But the Constitution also requires that we keep in mind "the myriad, subtle ways in which Establishment Clause values can be eroded," *Lynch* (O'Connor, J., concurring). One is the mere passage by the District of a policy that has the purpose and perception of government establishment of religion. Another is the implementation of a governmental electoral process that subjects the issue of prayer to a majoritarian vote. Under the *Lemon* standard, a court must invalidate a statute if it lacks "a secular legislative purpose." It is therefore proper, as part of this facial challenge, for us to examine the purpose of the October policy.

As [we have already noted], the text of the October policy alone reveals that it has an unconstitutional purpose. The plain language of the policy clearly spells out the extent of school involvement in both the election of the speaker and the content of the message. Additionally, the text of the October policy specifies only one, clearly preferred message—that of Santa Fe's traditional religious "invocation." Our examination, however, need not stop at an analysis of the text of the policy.

This case comes to us as the latest step in developing litigation brought as a challenge to institutional practices that unquestionably violated the Establishment Clause. One of those practices was the District's long-established tradition of sanctioning student-led prayer at varsity football games.***The District asks us to pretend that we do not recognize what every Santa Fe High School student understands clearly—that this policy is about prayer. The District further asks us to accept what is obviously untrue: that these messages are necessary to "solemnize" a football game and that this single-student, year-long position is essential to the protection of student speech. We refuse to turn a blind eye to the context in which this policy arose, and that context quells any doubt that this policy was implemented with the purpose of endorsing school prayer. Therefore, the simple enactment of this policy, with the purpose and perception of school endorsement of student prayer, was a constitutional violation.

This policy likewise does not survive a facial challenge because it impermissibly imposes upon the student body a majoritarian election on the issue of prayer. Through its election scheme, the District has established a governmental electoral mechanism that turns the school into a forum for religious debate. It further empowers the student body majority with the authority to subject students of minority views to constitutionally improper messages. The award of that power alone, regardless of the students' ultimate use of it, is not acceptable.[23] Such a system encourages divisiveness along religious lines and threatens the imposition of coercion upon those students not desiring to participate in a religious exercise. Simply by establishing this school-related procedure, which entrusts the inherently nongovernmental subject of religion to a majoritarian vote, a constitutional violation has occurred. No further injury is required for the policy to fail a facial challenge. The policy is invalid on its face because it establishes an improper majoritarian election on religion, and unquestionably has the purpose and creates the perception of encouraging the delivery of prayer at a series of important school events.

CHIEF JUSTICE REHNQUIST, with whom JUSTICE SCALIA and JUSTICE THOMAS join, dissenting.

The Court, venturing into the realm of prophesy, decides that it "need not wait for the inevitable" and invalidates the district's policy on its face. To do so, it applies the most rigid version of the oft-criticized test of *Lemon v. Kurtzman.* *Lemon* has had a checkered career in the decisional law of this Court.*** In two cases, the Court did not even apply the *Lemon* 'test.' Indeed, in *Lee v. Weisman,* an opinion upon which the Court relies heavily today, we mentioned but did not feel compelled to apply the *Lemon* test.***Even if it were appropriate to apply the *Lemon* test here, the district's student-message policy should not be invalidated on its face.

First, the Court misconstrues the nature of the "majoritarian election" permitted by the policy as being an election on "prayer" and "religion." To the contrary, the election permitted by the policy is a two-fold process whereby students vote first on whether to have a student speaker before football games at all, and second, if the students vote to

---

23. The Chief Justice accuses us of "essentially invalidating all student elections." This is obvious hyperbole. We have concluded that the resulting religious message under this policy would be attributable to the school, not just the student. For this reason, we now hold only that the District's decision to allow the student majority to control whether students of minority views are subjected to a school-sponsored prayer violates the Establishment Clause.

have such a speaker, on who that speaker will be. It is conceivable that the election could become one in which student candidates campaign on platforms that focus on whether or not they will pray if elected. It is also conceivable that the election could lead to a Christian prayer before 90 percent of the football games. If, upon implementation, the policy operated in this fashion, we would have a record before us to review whether the policy, as applied, violated the Establishment Clause or unduly suppressed minority viewpoints. But it is possible that the students might vote not to have a pregame speaker, in which case there would be no threat of a constitutional violation. It is also possible that the election would not focus on prayer, but on public speaking ability or social popularity.

But the Court ignores these possibilities by holding that merely granting the student body the power to elect a speaker that may choose to pray, regardless of the students ultimate use of it, is not acceptable. The Court so holds despite that any speech that may occur as a result of the election process here would be private, not government, speech. The elected student, not the government, would choose what to say. Support for the Court's holding cannot be found in any of our cases. And it essentially invalidates all student elections. A newly elected student body president, or even a newly elected prom king or queen, could use opportunities for public speaking to say prayers. Under the Court's view, the mere grant of power to the students to vote for such offices, in light of the fear that those elected might publicly pray, violates the Establishment Clause.

Second, with respect to the policy's purpose, the Court holds that "the simple enactment of this policy, with the purpose and perception of school endorsement of student prayer, was a constitutional violation." But the policy itself has plausible secular purposes: "To solemnize the event, to promote good sportsmanship and student safety, and to establish the appropriate environment for the competition." Where a governmental body expresses a plausible secular purpose for an enactment, courts should generally defer to that stated intent. The Court grants no deference to—and appears openly hostile toward—the policy's stated purposes, and wastes no time in concluding that they are a sham.

The Court bases its conclusion that the true purpose of the policy is to endorse student prayer on its view of the school district's history of Establishment Clause violations and the context in which the policy was written, that is, as "the latest step in developing litigation brought as a challenge to institutional practices that unquestionably violated the Establishment Clause." But the context—attempted compliance with a District Court order—actually demonstrates that the school district was acting diligently to come within the governing constitutional law.

The Court also relies on our decision in *Lee v. Weisman*, to support its conclusion. In *Lee*, we concluded that the content of the speech at issue, a graduation prayer given by a rabbi, was "directed and controlled" by a school official. In other words, at issue in *Lee* was government speech.   Here, by contrast, the potential speech at issue, if the policy had been allowed to proceed, would be a message or invocation selected or created by a student.***Had the policy been put into practice, the students may have chosen a speaker according to wholly secular criteria—like good public speaking skills or social popularity—and the student speaker may have chosen, on her own accord, to deliver a religious message. Such an application of the policy would likely pass constitutional muster. See *Lee* (Souter, J., concurring) ("If the State had chosen its graduation day speakers according to wholly secular criteria, and if one of those speakers (not a state actor) had individually chosen to deliver a religious message, it would be harder to attribute an endorsement of religion to the State"). The policy at issue here may be applied in an unconstitutional manner, but it will be time enough to invalidate it if that is found to be the case. I would reverse the judgment of the Court of Appeals.

———

Chapter 7

"*** OR PROHIBITING THE FREE EXERCISE THEREOF."

B. The General Test Refined and in Dispute

Casebook p. 1092
Add as new heading following Note

RECENT DEVELOPMENTS UNDER THE RFRA

As was to be expected, the Religious Freedom Restoration Act (RFRA) was at once invoked as an alternative to the free exercise clause or the fourteenth amendment. Indeed, as a practical matter, the RFRA quietly became virtually a congressionally-supplied "replacement" for the free exercise clause (i.e. a replacement for the clause as interpreted and as applied in *Employment Division v. Smith*).[24a] The effect of the RFRA was thus to make it of little consequence that a state law might, on its face and as applied, survive a fourteenth amendment free exercise clause challenge under the decision in *Smith*. For though that might be so, the law was still also examined under the more stringent "balancing" *Sherbert-Yoder* test, imposed by Congress under color of the RFRA.

As new cases continued to be filed, increasingly litigants no longer bothered to raise a free exercise claim as such, instead relying simply on the RFRA,[24b] and requesting that it be applied by the court as part of "the supreme Law of the Land," pursuant to Article VI of the Constitution. In this sense, therefore, it appeared to be irrelevant to try to understand what the Supreme Court may or may not regard as forbidden by the

---

24a. *See Douglas Laycock & Oliver Thomas, The Religious Freedom Restoration Act*, 73 Tex. L.Rev. 209, 219 (1994) (describing the RFRA as meant to be "a *replacement* for the Free Exercise Clause," and "as universal [in the scope of its coverage] as the Free Exercise Clause") (emphasis added). Some courts even became confused by the RFRA, suggesting that whether a state shall be held to have "violate[d] the free exercise clause of the First Amendment *** must be analyzed under the standard set forth in the recently enacted Religious Freedom Restoration Act." See, e.g., *Lucero v. Hensley*, 920 F. Supp. 1067, 1072 (C.D. Cal. 1996). Clearly this was incorrect, however, for whether a state shall be held to have violated the free exercise clause, as distinct from having violated the RFRA, is not a determination to be made by the RFRA, but by the precedents of the Supreme Court in respect to the free exercise clause itself. (Still, the court's error was instructive, in indicating how dominant the RFRA had already become even to the point of suggesting that the Act itself determined the standard of judgment in every first amendment free exercise case.)

24b. *See*, e.g., *Lewis v. Scott*, 910 F. Supp. 282 (E.D. Tex. 1995) (finding that state prison regulation requiring inmates to be clean shaven could not, consistent with the RFRA, be applied to Orthodox Muslim plaintiff — and containing no discussion of the first amendment, as interpreted by *Smith*), *reversed without opinion*, 127 F.3d 33 (5th Cir. 1997).

free exercise clause. Rather, it seemed important only to determine what was forbidden or not forbidden by the RFRA.[24c] Determining when and how the RFRA applied, however, did not prove to be an easy task. There have been substantial disagreements among the courts on what the RFRA requires.[24d]

Additionally, however, with ever increasing use being made of the RFRA, its constitutionality was increasingly called into question as well. The Supreme Court finally addressed that question in 1997.

24c. Of course, litigants might still invoke both the first amendment and the RFRA. And it was still more common than not that they did. In such cases, however, the lesson was pretty much the same: the treatment of the first amendment issue became of relatively little importance, since virtually anything it would reach was also reached by the RFRA, but not vice-versa. Recent case law vividly showed how this tended to be so. See, e.g., *Smith v. Fair Employment & Housing Comm'n.*, 51 Cal.Rptr.2d 700 (Cal. 1996) (religiously-anguished landlord sought relief on first amendment and separately, on RFRA, grounds from state anti-discrimination statute exposing her to damages for refusing to rent to unmarried cohabiting couples), *cert. denied*, 521 U.S. 1129 (1997). *Hamilton v. Schriro*, 74 F.3d 1545 (8th Cir. 1995) (rejecting both first amendment and RFRA challenges by state prisoner to a prison regulation that restricted hair length and to the prison's lack of a suitable "sweat lodge," one judge dissenting partly on the ground that the hair length regulation violated the RFRA — i.e. that although the hair length regulation would pass muster under the first amendment, it could not survive an RFRA challenge), *cert. denied*, 519 U.S. 874 (1996).

24d. The courts have not taken a uniform position with respect to the meaning of the requirement that persons invoking the RFRA must first show how compliance with the law would "*substantially*" burden them in respect to their religion. I.e. must it affect something "central" to their religion — and if so, just "how central"? Suppose the practice is not "mandated" by one's religion, but is part of an observant practice even close to the center of one's sense of a religiously-centered life? See *Lucero*, 920 F. Supp. at 1073 (noting that the Ninth and Tenth Circuits treat the matter differently, the Ninth Circuit having suggested that "the burdened practice [must] be [a practice] 'mandated' by one's religion" to meet the RFRA threshold, the Tenth Circuit having held it sufficient (to trigger the Act) that the regulation "significantly inhibit[s] or constrain[s] conduct or expression that manifest some central tenet" of an individual's religion, though it need not be conduct or expression actually mandated by his religion). The *Lucero* court observed that "[d]istrict courts in other circuits are split on whether to follow the religiously 'mandated' test or the religiously 'motivated' test."

Similarly, there is little agreement in respect to what suffices for a "compelling interest," and whether failure to force compliance with the law in a particular case would substantially (rather than only insubstantially) frustrate that compelling interest (such as it is). See, e.g., *Smith*, 51 Cal.Rptr.2d 700(court divided on the question whether, if only those landlords sincerely unable to reconcile their religious duty not to facilitate immoral acts by others (by renting them rooms) were exempt, such exemption would so undermine the state's anti-discrimination law (forbidding refusals to rent to unmarried cohabitants) as to work a serious frustration to the law).

Casebook p. 1092
Add as new case following Note

CITY OF BOERNE v. FLORES
521 U.S. 507 (1997)

JUSTICE KENNEDY delivered the opinion of the Court.

A decision by local zoning authorities to deny a church a building permit was challenged under the Religious Freedom Restoration Act of 1993 (RFRA). The case calls into question the authority of Congress to enact RFRA. We conclude the statute exceeds Congress' power.

[I-II]

Situated on a hill in the city of Boerne, Texas, some 28 miles northwest of San Antonio, is St. Peter Catholic Church. Built in 1923, the church's structure replicates the mission style of the region's earlier history. *** In order to meet the needs of the congregation the Archbishop of San Antonio gave permission to the parish to plan alterations to enlarge the building.

A few months later, the Boerne City Council passed an ordinance authorizing the city's Historic Landmark Commission to prepare a preservation plan with proposed historic landmarks and districts. Under the ordinance, the Commission must preapprove construction affecting historic landmarks or buildings in a historic district.

Soon afterwards, the Archbishop applied for a building permit so construction to enlarge the church could proceed. City authorities, relying on the ordinance and the designation of a historic district (which, they argued, included the church), denied the application. The Archbishop brought this suit challenging the permit denial in the United States District Court for the Western District of Texas.

*** The Archbishop relied upon RFRA as one basis for relief from the refusal to issue the permit. The District Court concluded that by enacting RFRA Congress exceeded the scope of its enforcement power under § 5 of the Fourteenth Amendment. The court certified its order for interlocutory appeal and the Fifth Circuit reversed, finding RFRA to be constitutional. We granted certiorari, and now reverse.

Congress enacted RFRA in direct response to the Court's decision in *Employment Div., Dept. of Human Resources of Ore. v. Smith*. *** In [*Smith*], we declined to apply the balancing test set forth in *Sherbert v. Verner*, under which we would have asked whether Oregon's prohibition substantially burdened a religious practice and, if it did, whether the burden was justified by a compelling government interest. *** The application of the *Sherbert* test, the *Smith* decision explained, would have produced an anomaly in the law, a constitutional right to ignore neutral laws of general applicability. The anomaly would have been accentuated, the Court reasoned, by the difficulty of determining whether a particular practice was central to an individual's religion. We explained, moreover, that it "is not within the judicial ken to question the centrality of particular beliefs or practices to a faith, or the validity of particular litigants' interpretations of those creeds." ***

These points of constitutional interpretation were debated by Members of Congress in hearings and floor debates. Many criticized the Court's reasoning, and this disagreement resulted in the passage of RFRA. *** The Act's stated purpose [is]:

> (1) to restore the compelling interest test as set forth in *Sherbert v. Verner* and *Wisconsin v. Yoder* and to guarantee its application in all cases where free exercise of religion is substantially burdened; and

> (2) to provide a claim or defense to persons whose religious exercise is substantially burdened by government. § 2000bb(b).

*** The Act's universal coverage is confirmed in § 2000bb-3(a), under which RFRA "applies to all Federal and State law, and the implementation of that law, whether statutory or otherwise, and whether adopted before or after [RFRA's enactment]." ***

III
A

Congress relied on its Fourteenth Amendment enforcement power in enacting the most far reaching and substantial of RFRA's provisions, those which impose its requirements on the States. *** In defense of the Act respondent contends, with support from the United States as amicus, that RFRA is permissible enforcement legislation. Congress, it is said, is only protecting by legislation one of the liberties guaranteed by the Fourteenth Amendment's Due Process Clause, the free exercise of religion, beyond what is necessary under *Smith*. It is said the congressional decision to dispense with proof of deliberate or overt discrimination and instead concentrate on a law's effects accords with the settled understanding that § 5 includes the power to enact legislation designed to prevent as well as remedy constitutional violations. It is further contended that Congress' § 5 power is not limited to remedial or preventive legislation. ***

Congress' power under § 5, however, extends only to "enforc[ing]" the provisions of the Fourteenth Amendment. *** The design of the Amendment and the text of § 5 are inconsistent with the suggestion that Congress has the power to decree the substance of the Fourteenth Amendment's restrictions on the States. ***

While the line between measures that remedy or prevent unconstitutional actions and measures that make a substantive change in the governing law is not easy to discern, and Congress must have wide latitude in determining where it lies, the distinction exists and must be observed. There must be a congruence and proportionality between the injury to be prevented or remedied and the means adopted to that end. Lacking such a connection, legislation may become substantive in operation and effect. History and our case law support drawing the distinction, one apparent from the text of the Amendment.

1

The Fourteenth Amendment's history confirms the remedial, rather than substantive, nature of the Enforcement Clause. The Joint Committee on Reconstruction of the 39th Congress began drafting what would become the Fourteenth Amendment in January 1866. *** In February, Republican Representative John Bingham of Ohio reported the following draft amendment to the House of Representatives on behalf of the Joint Committee:

The Congress shall have power to make all laws which shall be necessary and proper to secure to the citizens of each State all privileges and immunities of citizens in the several States, and to all persons in the several States equal protection in the rights of life, liberty, and property.

The proposal encountered immediate opposition, which continued through three days of debate. Members of Congress from across the political spectrum criticized the Amendment, and the criticisms had a common theme: The proposed Amendment gave Congress too much legislative power at the expense of the existing constitutional structure. ***

As a result of these objections having been expressed from so many different quarters, the House voted to table the proposal until April. *** The Amendment in its early form was not again considered. Instead, the Joint Committee began drafting a new article of Amendment, which it reported to Congress on April 30, 1866.

Section 1 of the new draft Amendment imposed self-executing limits on the States. Section 5 prescribed that "[t]he Congress shall have power to enforce, by appropriate legislation, the provisions of this article." Under the revised Amendment, Congress' power was no longer plenary but remedial. ***

The design of the Fourteenth Amendment has proved significant also in maintaining the traditional separation of powers between Congress and the Judiciary. As enacted, the Fourteenth Amendment confers substantive rights against the States which, like the provisions of the Bill of Rights, are self-executing. The power to interpret the Constitution in a case or controversy remains in the Judiciary.

2

The remedial and preventive nature of Congress' enforcement power, and the limitation inherent in the power, were confirmed in our earliest cases on the Fourteenth Amendment. *** Recent cases have continued to revolve around the question of whether § 5 legislation can be considered remedial. In *South Carolina v. Katzenbach*, we emphasized that "[t]he constitutional propriety of [legislation adopted under the Enforcement Clause] must be judged with reference to the historical experience *** it reflects." There we upheld various provisions of the Voting Rights Act of 1965, finding them to be "remedies aimed at areas where voting discrimination has been most flagrant," and necessary to "banish the blight of racial discrimination in voting, which has infected the electoral process in parts of our country for nearly a century." *** The new, unprecedented remedies were deemed necessary given the ineffectiveness of the existing voting rights laws, and the slow costly character of case-by-case litigation. ***

3

Any suggestion that Congress has a substantive, non-remedial power under the Fourteenth Amendment is not supported by our case law. In *Oregon v. Mitchell*, a majority of the Court concluded Congress had exceeded its enforcement powers by enacting legislation lowering the minimum age of voters from 21 to 18 in state and local elections. The five Members of the Court who reached this conclusion explained that the legislation intruded into an area reserved by the Constitution to the States. Four of these five were explicit in rejecting the position that § 5 endowed Congress with the power to establish the meaning of constitutional provisions. ***

There is language in our opinion in *Katzenbach v. Morgan*, which could be interpreted as acknowledging a power in Congress to enact legislation that expands the rights contained in § 1 of the Fourteenth Amendment. This is not a necessary interpretation, however, or even the best one. *** If Congress could define its own powers by altering the Fourteenth Amendment's meaning, no longer would the Constitution be "superior paramount law, unchangeable by ordinary means." It would be "on a level with ordinary legislative acts, and, like other acts, *** alterable when the legislature shall please to alter it." *Marbury v. Madison, 1 Cranch*, at 177. Under this approach, it is difficult to conceive of a principle that would limit congressional power. See Van Alstyne, The Failure of the Religious Freedom Restoration Act under Section 5 of the Fourteenth Amendment, 46 Duke L.J. 291, 292-303 (1996). ***

B

Respondent contends that RFRA is a proper exercise of Congress' remedial or preventive power. The Act, it is said, is a reasonable means of protecting the free exercise of religion as defined by *Smith*. It prevents and remedies laws which are enacted with the unconstitutional object of targeting religious beliefs and practices. ***

A comparison between RFRA and the Voting Rights Act is instructive. In contrast to the record which confronted Congress and the judiciary in the voting rights cases, RFRA's legislative record lacks examples of modern instances of generally applicable laws passed because of religious bigotry. *** Rather, the emphasis of the hearings was on laws of general applicability which place incidental burdens on religion. Much of the discussion centered upon anecdotal evidence of autopsies performed on Jewish individuals and Hmong immigrants in violation of their religious beliefs, and on zoning regulations and historic preservation laws (like the one at issue here), which as an incident of their normal operation, have adverse effects on churches and synagogues. It is difficult to maintain that they are examples of legislation enacted or enforced due to animus or hostility to the burdened religious practices or that they indicate some widespread pattern of religious discrimination in this country. Congress' concern was with the incidental burdens imposed, not the object or purpose of the legislation.

Regardless of the state of the legislative record, RFRA cannot be considered remedial, preventive legislation, if those terms are to have any meaning. RFRA is so out of proportion to a supposed remedial or preventive object that it cannot be understood as responsive to, or designed to prevent, unconstitutional behavior. It appears, instead, to attempt a substantive change in constitutional protections. Preventive measures prohibiting certain types of laws may be appropriate when there is reason to believe that many of the laws affected by the congressional enactment have a significant likelihood of being unconstitutional.

RFRA is not so confined. Sweeping coverage ensures its intrusion at every level of government, displacing laws and prohibiting official actions of almost every description and regardless of subject matter. RFRA's restrictions apply to every agency and official of the Federal, State, and local Governments. RFRA applies to all federal and state law, statutory or otherwise, whether adopted before or after its enactment. RFRA has no termination date or termination mechanism. Any law is subject to challenge at any time by any individual who alleges a substantial burden on his or her free exercise of religion. ***

*** Simply put, RFRA is not designed to identify and counteract state laws likely to be unconstitutional because of their treatment of religion. In most cases, the state laws to which RFRA applies are not ones which will have been motivated by religious bigotry. *** RFRA's substantial burden test, however, is not even a discriminatory effects or disparate impact test. *** It is a reality of the modern regulatory state that numerous state laws, such as the zoning regulations at issue here, impose a substantial burden on a large class of individuals. When the exercise of religion has been burdened in an incidental way by a law of general application, it does not follow that the persons affected have been burdened any more than other citizens, let alone burdened because of their religious beliefs. In addition, the Act imposes in every case a least restrictive means requirement — a requirement that was not used in the pre-*Smith* jurisprudence RFRA purported to codify — which also indicates that the legislation is broader than is appropriate if the goal is to prevent and remedy constitutional violations. ***

*** When the Court has interpreted the Constitution, it has acted within the province of the Judicial Branch, which embraces the duty to say what the law is. *Marbury v. Madison*. When the political branches of the Government act against the background of a judicial interpretation of the Constitution already issued, it must be understood that in later cases and controversies the Court will treat its precedents with the respect due them under settled principles, including *stare decisis*, and contrary expectations must be disappointed. RFRA was designed to control cases and controversies, such as the one before us; but as the provisions of the federal statute here invoked are beyond congressional authority, it is this Court's precedent, not RFRA, which must control.

It is for Congress in the first instance to "determin[e] whether and what legislation is needed to secure the guarantees of the Fourteenth Amendment," and its conclusions are entitled to much deference. *Katzenbach v. Morgan*. Congress' discretion is not unlimited, however, and the courts retain the power, as they have since *Marbury v. Madison*, to determine if Congress has exceeded its authority under the Constitution. Broad as the power of Congress is under the Enforcement Clause of the Fourteenth Amendment, RFRA contradicts vital principles necessary to maintain separation of powers and the federal balance. The judgment of the Court of Appeals sustaining the Act's constitutionality is reversed.

It is so ordered.

JUSTICE STEVENS, concurring.

In my opinion, the Religious Freedom Restoration Act of 1993 (RFRA) is a "law respecting an establishment of religion" that violates the First Amendment to the Constitution.

If the historic landmark on the hill in Boerne happened to be a museum or an art gallery owned by an atheist, it would not be eligible for an exemption from the city ordinances that forbid an enlargement of the structure. Because the landmark is owned by the Catholic Church, it is claimed that RFRA gives its owner a federal statutory entitlement to an exemption from a generally applicable, neutral civil law. Whether the Church would actually prevail under the statute or not, the statute has provided the Church with a legal weapon that no atheist or agnostic can obtain. This governmental preference for religion, as opposed to irreligion, is forbidden by the First Amendment. *Wallace v. Jaffree*.

JUSTICE SCALIA, with whom JUSTICE STEVENS joins, concurring in part. [Omitted.]

JUSTICE O'CONNOR, with whom JUSTICE BREYER joins except as to a portion of Part I, dissenting.

I dissent from the Court's disposition of this case. I remain of the view that *Smith* was wrongly decided, and I would use this case to reexamine the Court's holding there.
***

[I]f I agreed with the Court's standard in *Smith*, I would join the opinion. As the Court's careful and thorough historical analysis shows, Congress lacks the "power to decree the substance of the Fourteenth Amendment's restrictions on the States." Rather, its power under § 5 of the Fourteenth Amendment extends only to enforcing 7the Amendment's provisions. In short, Congress lacks the ability independently to define or expand the scope of constitutional rights by statute. Accordingly, whether Congress has exceeded its § 5 powers turns on whether there is a "congruence and proportionality between the injury to be prevented or remedied and the means adopted to that end." This recognition does not, of course, in any way diminish Congress' obligation to draw its own conclusions regarding the Constitution's meaning. Congress, no less than this Court, is called upon to consider the requirements of the Constitution and to act in accordance with its dictates. But when it enacts legislation in furtherance of its delegated powers, Congress must make its judgments consistent with this Court's exposition of the Constitution and with the limits placed on its legislative authority by provisions such as the Fourteenth Amendment. ***

[But] *stare decisis* concerns should not prevent us from revisiting our holding in *Smith*. *** I believe that, in light of both our precedent and our Nation's tradition of religious liberty, *Smith* is demonstrably wrong. Moreover, it is a recent decision. As such, it has not engendered the kind of reliance on its continued application that would militate against overruling it. *** Accordingly, I believe that it is essential for the Court to reconsider its holding in *Smith* — and to do so in this very case. I would therefore direct the parties to brief this issue and set the case for reargument.

I respectfully dissent from the Court's disposition of this case.

JUSTICE SOUTER, dissenting.

*** I have serious doubts about the precedential value of the *Smith* rule and its entitlement to adherence. *** I am not now prepared to join JUSTICE O'CONNOR in rejecting it or the majority in assuming it to be correct. In order to provide full adversarial consideration, this case should be set down for reargument permitting plenary reexamination of the issue. ***

JUSTICE BREYER, dissenting. [Omitted.]

———

NOTE

Five Justices (Rehnquist, C.J., Stevens, Thomas, Scalia, and Ginsburg, JJ.) express-ly joined "the opinion of the Court" by Justice Kennedy, in holding that the RFRA exceeded Congress's power under § 5 of the fourteenth amendment (and may have overstepped the separation of powers). A seventh Justice, O'Connor, while dissenting on the disposition of the case (see her Opinion *supra* in text), declared that she, too, would "join the opinion," holding RFRA unconstitutional but for her disagreement with *Smith* (which she, Souter, and Breyer, JJ., merely declared should be reconsidered in this very case or in an appropriate case newly challenging the Court's decision in *Smith* itself).

It thus appears to be very clear that the RFRA is "unconstitutional," in exceeding Congress's authority, a minimum of six Justices of the Supreme Court having so con-cluded in this case. Accordingly, it appears to be equally clear that the RFRA therefore cannot now be successfully pleaded in lieu of, or additional to, a free exercise claim.

Query, however, whether this is necessarily true. Note that the RFRA applies to all "*Federal*" as well as to all "State" (and local) laws — and applies also to the "imple-mentation" of all Federal laws "whether adopted before or after the enactment of this Act." Note, further, that the very next subsection of the Act (headed "Rule of Con-struction"), provides that "*Federal statutory law adopted after the date of the enactment of this Act is subject to this Act unless such law explicitly excludes such application by reference to this Act.*" (Emphasis added.) What is the status of these provisions today? Consider the following simple case.

Suppose a federal prisoner requests exemption from a federal prison rule of general application on one's length of hair (e.g., a Sikh claiming a religious requirement of longer hair or a Rastafarian with a similar claim). There is no suggestion the rule was instituted from religious animus or partiality. May the prisoner invoke the RFRA to assert a claim against the Warden of the federal prison (though clearly his counterpart, one held in a state prison, could not do so)? Is the power of Congress to provide the RFRA "accommodation" in respect to federal statutes derived from § 5 of the fourteenth amendment, or may it be derived from some other enumerated source of power, e.g, the "necessary and proper"clause in Article I? Is the RFRA a severable statute, such that its provisions in respect to federal statutes, past and future, are still applicable?"[25]

---

25. *See Young v. Crystal Evangelical Free Church* ,141 F.3d 854 (8th Cir. 1998); for a discussion of the application of RFRA to federal laws after *Boerne*, see Edward J.W. Blatkik, Note, *No RFRAF Allowed: The Status of the Religious Freedom Restoration Act's Federal Application in the Wake of City of Boerne v. Flores*, 98 Colum. L. Rev. 1410.

Chapter 8

DEFINING "RELIGION"

Casebook, p. 1104
Add as additional reference to footnote 8

Eduardo Penalver, Note, *The Concept of Religion*, 107 Yale L.J. 791 (1997).

Casebook, p. 1133
Add as an additional reference to footnote 30

See also Combs v. Central Texas Annual Conference of the United Methodist Church, 173 F.3d 343 (5th Cir. 1999).